Greetings to Mike —

my favorite
postal carrier

Best,
Doris O'Donnell
Sept 2007

Front-Page Girl

DORIS O'DONNELL

Front-Page Girl

THE KENT STATE UNIVERSITY PRESS
Kent, Ohio

Library of Congress Catalog Card Number 2005036455

ISBN-10: 0-87338-846-1

ISBN-13: 978-0-87338-846-7

Manufactured in the United States of America

10 09 08 07 06   5 4 3 2 1

Library of Congress Cataloging-in-Publication Data

O'Donnell, Doris, 1921–

Front-page girl. / Doris O'Donnell.

p.   cm.

ISBN-13: 978-0-87338-846-7 (pbk. : alk. paper) ∞

ISBN-10: 0-87338-846-1 (pbk. : alk paper) ∞

1. O'Donnell, Doris, 1921–

2. Journalists—United States—Biography.

I. Title.

PN4874.O46A3 2006

070.92—dc22   2005036455

British Library Cataloging-in-Publication data are available.

In memory of two great newspapermen and editors,
Howard Beaufait and Nat Howard,
and my newspaper colleagues—
smart, funny, tough, compassionate men and women.
We had it all.

-30-

Contents

Foreword

$\mathcal{T}$o people who know about journalism from *Superman* or *The Front Page,* Doris O'Donnell's book will come as a real surprise. Here's young Doris, straight out of parochial school, wearing heels and stockings with seams, suddenly in a world without women. No, she does not become a "sob sister" like Lois Lane; she turns into an ace reporter.

She had to earn her spurs to become one of Cleveland's top reporters with such stints as being a cab driver and working in the county jail. You don't win a story like the Dr. Sam Sheppard case because you happened to be in the newsroom when the story broke. You win it because you have become known as a top police reporter.

And her reporting counted. When Cleveland was hit by the Glenville race riots in 1968, managing editor Ted Princiotto refused to clear his front page the following Sunday for a story written by Jim Naughton, Joe Eszterhas, and Bill Barnard. "I've got a big Doris O'Donnell story about a big murder in Michigan," he said. Hearing this, the three men quit (two later retracted their resignations). Such was the power of Doris's byline. And over the years, the big stories fell to her: Cyrus Eaton, Anastas Mikoyan, and Mayor Carl Stokes.

Yet she still had to grind out her share of shorts that really were nothing but short paragraphs for ethnic events or stories being planted by advertisers or stories the city desk got from the promotion department, plugging the publisher or members of his family. Those, too, are what reporters have to do, even when they are stars.

Through the telling of all this, Doris serves up a taste of what life is like in that unnatural universe called a newsroom, where everything you thought you knew about life on a newspaper turns out to be myth.

STEPHEN C. ESRATI

Copy Editor of the *Cleveland Plain Dealer*

Prologue

O n the morning of September 11, 2001, eyeing the television from the kitchen, I saw a black oily fire engulf the upper walls of one of the World Trade Center towers in New York City. I gasped, amazed that a wild movie was on so early in the day. Then a plane swung low and smashed into the south tower, and I realized it was no movie. This was reality, and suddenly my old reportorial self snapped into action. I stripped off my gown, stuffed arms and legs into pants and jacket, cut the stove heat, raced to the bank, withdrew $500, filled the gasoline tank, and then sat there in the gas station. Where did I think I was going? To cover a story, naturally. Then reality jolted me—I was retired. Slowly I drove home, where, like every other American, I breathed in the television drama for hours, numbing myself in the process.

After that terrible day I saw an Associated Press story that quoted retired CBS anchorman Walter Cronkite: "When a big story is breaking, you want to be there. Not being on the air, that's not important. But I'd like to be in the newsroom."

My first fledgling publication was a handwritten neighborhood newsletter of events happening on Stickney Avenue, stories about the Kuntz twins, and the bootlegging operation of the Irwins. Dinner table conversation invariably focused on city politics, because my mother was entrenched in Democratic Party candidates and elections. I was a staffer on my high school newspaper in my freshman year and editor in my sophomore year, and I wrote editorials for daily newspapers on school bond issues. In the summer I worked on a suburban newspaper. Later I took night classes at college and worked on the college paper. Without the means to attend college full time, I went to work at a bank and later a war plant before I landed my first genuine newspaper job on a daily paper.

My dream has always been aimed at the newsroom, the heart of newspapers. This is a story of my dream, which began more than six decades ago when I became madly, insanely obsessed with becoming a newspaper reporter, influenced strongly by newspapers my father brought home from the firehouse, papers from Los Angeles, New York, Chicago, Dublin, London. I read everything I could about the women behind the bylines—Annie Laurie, Ishbel Ross, Nellie Bly, Imogene Stanley, Irene Kuhn, Lorena Hickok, Dorothy Dix. Their journalist lives, as mine would be, were shaped not by gender but by personal and economic needs and what freedom editors gave inside the city room. I saw a woman's byline and fantasized that one day mine would be in newsprint. "By Doris O'Donnell"; I knew this was my destiny.

I am telling this story not as an ego trip but as a look back at the great life of newspapering. While it is a woman's story, it is not sexist or antimale. In fact, without the encouragement of many men I would never have made it. But male competition did force me to work two, no three times as hard. (One day I had sixteen bylines in the paper; the managing editor blew a gasket.)

My generation of female reporters had the best of the profession, warts and all. Take it from a survivor—the past years in the newsroom were glamorous, frivolous, and deadly serious. The idea of being at the apex, the nerve center of everything happening in town, was enough to make your head spin. We loved the pace, deadlines, risks, challenges. We were in love with a dream, sometimes to the detriment of our personal lives. It was a career then tailor-made for those who wanted it all, who wrote about life served up daily in courts, city hall, schools, the street, the debutante's ritzy ball. I was there every minute, totally consumed by getting and writing the story. When I fantasized as a child about what would someday happen to me, I never foresaw me in the presence of world leaders, talking with them, taking notes, and covering historical events.

For fifty-eight years I worked as a reporter for the *Cleveland News* and *Cleveland Plain Dealer* as well as the suburban *Heights Sun-Press, News-Herald,* and the *Tribune-Review* in Greensburg, Pennsylvania. I hung up my hat at the *Plain Dealer* on February 20, 1996. Today, as I write these stories of the past, my memories, my history, lie in a configuration of boxes and cartons full of newspaper pages, carbon copies of stories, and steno books filled with miles of shorthand and longhand and half-finished sentences smashed down on paper with thick black copy pencils. My journalistic journey took me from the police beat to the Soviet Union, to courthouses and city halls, to murder scenes, to assassination sites. I was lucky. I got great assignments even though I worked with many men and women I knew were more talented than I was. But my special talent was working hard, producing copy on deadlines. I was like a whirling dervish when it came to pursuing a story, always conscious that being a reporter did not mean I was a one-man band. When I was on the bottom of the news chain—on the street where the action was—I was also on the top, because without the street reporter, the editors had nothing to work with and circulation had nothing to peddle.

I was lucky to work in the ferocious climate of circulation battles between three Cleveland dailies, where scooping the other paper was a daily challenge. Lucky, too, that we women who came into newsrooms during World War II weren't fired when the men came marching home. Instead we were folded into the news business with the men and found our niches covering, among other things, food, kids, music, theater, sports jocks, business entrepreneurs, citizens of all economic and cultural status—from the homeless to millionaires. Although I handled my share of obituary writing and soft stories on octogenarians, I somehow carved out a niche from the police beat to investigative reporting.

Looking back at this rich tapestry of reporting, I recall most vividly my fellow reporters, editors, circulation guys, and the fantastic variety of people I met on the beats, from the top executives of Cleveland's big steel plants and industries to the hustlers and hoods that hung around Short Vincent (a short street between East 9th and East 6th streets in Cleveland, where flashy restaurants were the mecca for the town's racy crowd) and the flotsam and jetsam of life I saw at the old Central Police Station.

I had a wild, passionate affair with my job. I could barely wait to get to work. In our black patent leather opera pumps, nylons with seams, snappy white gloves, smart little hats with veils, and svelte Chanel-type woolen suits, we had the best of the century. I even met and spoke to Princess Elizabeth before she was queen. But I would never have swapped my job for hers.

-30-

- 1 -

Zigzagging into Journalism

On the cool, silvery, misty dawn of March 7, 1936, two battalions of German soldiers, beating drums and flying flags, marched into the Rhineland, a buffer zone between Germany and France that had been demilitarized by the Treaty of Versailles after World War I. I was fifteen at the time, in the eighth grade at Our Lady of Good Counsel elementary school. My memory of that day is understandably fuzzy.

In the ensuing days, family members spoke of uncles and brothers who had been gassed in Germany in the First World War, and others who, after they returned home, were "never the same." Fear struck many households, as the peacetime treaty had clearly been broken. World War I was propagandized as the "war to end all wars." Could another war lie ahead?

In January 1939, at seventeen, I graduated from James Ford Rhodes High School, having been editor of the school paper. I enrolled nights at Cleveland College and, thanks to an uncle's help, was hired as a bookkeeper at the Morris Plan Bank. My brother and cousins, older by two, three, or four years, talked of

Author and brother Jack, 1929, on the day of his First Communion. Author's collection.

the military draft or of enlisting. Adults watched grainy black and white newsreels of German chancellor Adolph Hitler shouting slogans in arenas jammed with thousands of uniformed Hitler Youth. American newspapers reported on Hitler's contempt for democracies. He assailed America, defining it as a materialistic society that had lost its way. "What is America but millionaires, beauty queens, stupid phonograph records and Hollywood?" Hitler shouted to his slavish followers.

The big news in Cleveland at the time was of Jesse Owens, a graduate of Central High School (a popular and academically high-rated public school on Cleveland's Near East Side that had a racial mix of blacks and whites), who won an Olympic Gold Medal in 1936 at the Berlin Games. Owens, who was black, hastily left the Olympic stadium because of the tensions created by the now imminent war. A tree in his memory still graces the grounds of Rhodes High.

Watching the militancy of Germany chilled the minds of everyone, affecting what we thought, what we did. In the two years from September 1939 to September 1941, the world was jolted by the German army's butchering all before it, which allowed it to gain control of Europe from Biarritz, France, to Smolensk, Russia. In August 1941 no one expected the Russians to last the winter. Hitler's mad military venture hopped, skipped, and jumped from victory to victory. On September 3, 1939, the Brits announced war against Germany. Tabloid headlines on London streets shouted: "Special Late News—War Official."

War news from London was brought to American airwaves by thirty-two-year-old Edward R. Murrow, American chief of CBS news in London. With sirens blaring raid warnings, Murrow began broadcasts with "This . . . is London." Writer Archibald MacLeish said Murrow "laid the dead of London at our doors, and we knew that the dead were our dead." Murrow's grim report of October 10, 1940, dramatized his gritty style: "This . . . is London, ten minutes after five in the morning. Here was peace and quiet inside the shelter for twenty minutes. Then a shower of incendiaries came down far in the distance. Half an hour later a string of firebombs fell right beside the Thames. Their white glare was reflected in the black, lazy water near the banks and faded out in mainstream where the moon cut a golden swatch. We could see little men shoveling those firebombs into the river. Finally, those white flames all went out." We heard Murrow day after day bring the war over the airwaves.

Little did I know my future part in America's war effort. In 1939 our industry was slowly creeping along, with 9.4 million men and women unemployed due to the Great Depression. It's incredible to envision the worldwide bulge in manufacturing production that took place after the war began. Germany and Russia led the pack between 1940 and 1943, but when industry went to war, America

"Tomboy" Doris with brother Jack (right) and Stickney Avenue neighbors. Author's collection.

outproduced these countries, and Japan, by 25 percent. From 1889 to 1939 American production had been a mere 2 percent of total international production. But when twenty million Americans (and I was one of them) punched time clocks in war plants, the Depression was over for America. At no time since has there been anything to rival that industrial expansion, the outrageous vitality of men and women undergirding a stupendous job.

On Sunday, December 7, 1941, I was tucked in on a studio couch, recovering from an emergency appendectomy. Our family had been glued to the radio all day, and my brother Jack, two years my senior, talked to his buddies of what the Japanese attack on our Pacific fleet at Pearl Harbor meant. Some of his pals were already serving in the 37th Division of the Ohio National Guard. During my December recuperation, all I thought of was my return to the newly hatched Fawick Airflex plant, where I worked for the personnel manager. I tried to focus on preparing for Christmas, but it was scary. Sure, we decorated a tree. But with the radio blaring and newspaper headlines bold and black with war news, it was difficult to focus on holiday joy. We learned of a rumored invasion of Seattle, within bombing distance to Kiska and Attu Islands. New York mayor Fiorello LaGuardia said his city would be attacked first. "The war will come right to our cities and industrial districts. Never underestimate the strength and cruelty of the enemy."

Getting the job at Fawick was a fluke. Having left the Morris Plan Bank, I was a bookkeeper at the Union Bank of Commerce when I frequently ran into Mike Scanlon on Euclid Avenue and lunched with him. Mike, part of the Friday night parties that a handful of former friends and I held, worked for the U.S. Office of War Production, recruiting workers. Cleveland's mighty industrial machine was gearing for an extended war. New plants opened for specific military hardware; old ones retooled overnight. Mike said Fawick, a subsidiary of General Motors Corporation, was completing construction of a new plant. At Rhodes I had taken precollege courses, but I was also proficient in typing and shorthand, winning awards for speed. Mike provided proper credentials and in no time I was the twenty-fifth employee at Fawick, a huge, airy, two-story plant that smelled of damp concrete and fresh paint. Within weeks of starting I became personnel manager after my boss, Virgil Cutts, failed to return from lunch. Junius R. Clark, vice president, told me: "Keep hiring."

Author (second from left) with Patsy Nolan (third from right), Junius R. Clark (second from right), then vice president of Fawick Airflex, and naval officers as they attend a holiday party. Author's collection.

At twenty-one years of age, I found myself setting up an office adjacent to the shop, running daily ads for workers, handling applications, working with shop foremen to conduct interviews for specific jobs, and arranging medical tests. In the first few months I hired more than three hundred men and women, from toolmakers to drill-press operators to secretaries to sweepers, and all without ever having seen a Johansen Block or a radial drill press. We worked three shifts around the clock. I worked days and some nights when I was called back to a shift for food deliveries, since the plant was in the "boonies." On occasion, company founder and president Thomas L. Fawick, an inventive mechanical genius and violinist who also built violins, brought in international musicians for a concert. He thought nothing of shutting down the plant for these musical events. No one was docked in pay.

I never knew exactly what our end product was destined for. I did know that our plant was making reverse gears for diesel engines. We were not told that the gears were for top-secret landing craft. We should have guessed it was a big-time operation when navy brass was flown in from Washington, D.C., and eventually naval officers were stationed at the plant. What a time. Gad! Were those naval engineers handsome! They bunked at a nearby naval barrack, and Patsy Nolan, our industrial nurse, and I had an infrequent beer with them after work.

Patsy and I pretty much ran the back office. When a worker lost a finger or suffered an injury, she acted quickly, getting the injured to a nearby hospital or handling first-aid on the spot. We were on a first-name basis with not only the guys in the shop but also the office staff on the second floor. General Motors executives frequently inspected the plant, impressing us with the urgency of our jobs. The bosses even sent our top engineer, Willard Reese, to Long Beach, California, to coordinate production with the navy.

One day Lil Reese, Willard's wife, said her husband wanted her to drive west, and she asked if I would go with her. I jumped at the chance, clearing the trip with Mr. Clark, and Lil and I took off in her station wagon with a pocketful of precious gas rations stamps, which had been mandated by the government to limit the use of gas to designated "needed," such as defense and emergency workers, and a carefully packed set of gear components in oiled paper and burlap in a wooden box. Lil and I were excited at the cross-country venture. We drove until we couldn't drive anymore, making only a few stops, where we'd sack out a few hours in a fleabag motel. Four days after leaving Cleveland we were at the Long Beach naval harbor, dirty, disheveled, exhausted, and exhilarated. Willard and the navy guys greeted us and treated us to a dinner of delicious spaghetti and Chianti served in a straw-covered bottle. The previous days' meals of hot dogs and cokes just couldn't compare.

I soon faced a tough decision: return to Fawick or stay on the West Coast. In the back of my mind, I had planned to apply for a job at the *Los Angeles Herald-Examiner*. The only thing I ever wanted in my life was a newspaper job, and I figured this was my big chance. I called Mr. Clark and severed my services, knowing he'd have no trouble replacing me with a shop supervisor who

Author at Laguna Beach, California, during her trip west with Lil Reese in 1944. Author's collection.

The author takes some time out with marines from the El Toro Marine Air Base in Santa Barbara during a trip to California. 1944; author's collection.

Clowning around with Lauretta McCarthy in Chinatown, Los Angeles. 1944; author's collection.

wanted my job. In Los Angeles I stayed with former neighbors from Denison Avenue, Lauretta and Florence McCarthy. The sisters had worked at the New York Central base in the Terminal Tower concourse before going west, easily finding work at the Southern Pacific Railroad transporting soldiers, sailors, and marines up and down the West Coast. We had a grand time there, going to United Service Organizations dances and parties (once at the home of the singing Andrews sisters) and attending picnics and baseball games in Laguna Beach and Santa Barbara, near the El Toro marine base. We met our Cleveland servicemen who were waiting to ship out or were at the base for R & R, the rest and recreation breaks the servicemen were granted from their bases for short spells before returning to duty. We had laughs and fun and farewells. There were more goodbyes than hellos. I look at snapshots from the summer of 1944 and know that many of those handsome, strong young men never came home. I was briefly engaged to a Marine in the First Marine Air Wing, a boy from home, but when he completed his tour safely, we parted ways. I was by then a reporter for *The Cleveland News* and no longer interested in marriage.

I did apply at the *Los Angeles Herald-Examiner*; that was my dream, my goal. My widowed mother could not afford college for me and my brother, so we settled for paychecks and night school. But I would never deviate from my goal. Sadly, I lacked a wartime certificate of availability, and the *Herald-Examiner* could not hire me. My choice was a job at Boeing or Douglas—more war work. So without employment, I got on the next train for Cleveland.

At seventeen, fresh from high school, I had luckily gotten an appointment with the famous editor of the *Cleveland Plain Dealer*, Paul Bellamy. How this gracious man decided to talk to this teen-ager, I have no clue. After a nice chat, his advice was: get a job on a small Ohio weekly and then come back. Now home, in October 1944, when it came time to look for that job at a small Ohio weekly, I sought the advice of Eugene A. Kelly at the *Cleveland News*. He was the journalism adviser for the Cleveland public school system when I was editor of the *Rhodes Review*. Now back at the *News* as labor editor, he introduced me to Hugh Kane, managing editor, who hired me. I was in seventh heaven; I could have exploded with joy. For years I'd read bylines of women working for wire services or the New York papers, and now I was in their sisterhood. Incredible! Just as the war had ended the Great Depression, it opened the newsroom doors for women.

The *Cleveland News* city room was housed on the second floor of an impressive building at E. 18th and Superior Avenue that was built in 1921 by Daniel Rhodes Hanna, of the famous political Marcus Alonzo Hanna family of Ohio, and Dan Hanna's father-in-law, Charles Otis. Dan, a worldly and sophisticated man, was a good publisher. He was at home in the newsroom, knew reporters by name, and passed along significant news tips. On election nights, with returns coming in late, he mingled with the staff, eating from trays of food he'd ordered in. Dan and his wife Queenie Otis Hanna were a remarkable couple who used salty language and had keen perceptions of Cleveland's hotshots and politicians. Their son, a flier in the war, was lost in the European theater of operations. This motivated Dan to order extensive coverage of lost, injured, and heroic military men and women. Dan's editor, Nat Howard, on leave with the War Censorship Board in Washington when I was hired, also wanted the spotlight on area servicemen. In fact, there was much competition between the *News,* the *Press,* and the *Plain Dealer* for military coverage. I joined six other young women on the military desk, an "island of desks" with phones, typewriters, tons of copy paper, carbon paper, black lead pencils. We pulled long tails of Associated Press wire copy from clattering teletype machines. The copy was a never-ending list from the War Department of wounded, killed, or those lucky to get battlefield promotions. With phone directories and the Haines Criss+Cross (a directory of residents by address, first and last name, and phone number) we located families or neighbors of service people. We needed confirmation of name, family, service records, and a photograph. We begged for the photos and many times took a hired Hertz car back to the home, returning the cherished photo the same day. Sadly, sometimes we were the first to notify a mother or wife of the bad news.

My Fawick connection followed me into the newsroom in late 1944 when our labor writers, Gene Kelly and Bob Kehoe, went out to Clinton Road to cover a bloody strike at the Fawick plant. Mounted police were taunted and stoned by striking members of the United Electrical Workers' Union, attempting to organize the plant and stop production. The union organizer was a welder, Morris Stamm, whom I had hired months before. Within hours following his hiring, the FBI was at my office, warning that Stamm fought with the Abraham Lincoln Brigade in Spain. President Franklin D. Roosevelt refused to repatriate these Americans who fought with the Communists against Gen. Francisco Franco. I told Clark the FBI was in my office with the warning, and Clark responded: "Do we need a welder?" I said, "Yes." Clark said the FBI could "get lost." I did not cover the strike, which resulted in arrests and court cases, but I knew the names of all the employees, and I gave them to Kelly and Kehoe.

After work on May 8, 1945, VE ("Victory in Europe") day, a bunch of us reporters joined the downtown crowds in celebration. There was dancing in the streets, and all the bars overflowed with happy people. Then when the Japanese officially surrendered, nearly a month after the United States dropped the atomic bomb on Hiroshima, there was another victory parade. The cost in American dead was 292,131 out of 16,353,659 armed forces. We young women journalists thought we'd be fired when the men came home. Not so. At the *News* Nat Howard, Hugh Kane, and *City* editor Howard Beaufait concurred that the paper would not have been published each day "without the girls" (six at first, then eight): Janice Fleming, Doris Millavec, Doris Cunneen, Margaret Rose, Margaret Campbell, Jane Artale, Marjorie Blossom, and Albina Molek. All of us were blended into the staff along with the much-decorated men from the navy, air force, army, and marines. Journalistically, it was historic.

-30-

-2-

New Girl on the Block

$\mathcal{W}$hen the war was officially over in September 1945, Peter Bellamy, our drama and film critic, sashayed into the *Cleveland News* newsroom, sporting a floor-length raccoon coat, a bit ratty after a mothball-bag entombment, concealing, except for the ankles, his white-bright navy uniform. The *Harold Teen*–era coat was a remnant of his Harvard college days. Other guys on the staff made equally flamboyant entrances, flaunting rows of battle ribbons on military uniforms soon to be replaced with "civvies" (civilian clothes). They were home safely, noticeably more mature, from their service in the army, air force, marines, and navy. After handshakes and hugs, tears and kisses, the guys said they could hardly wait to get back to typewriters.

We girls—their wartime replacements—were in awe of these men who saw the Burma-Chinese road, the South Pacific, Paris, Berlin, prisoner-of-war camps, Nazi death camps. It would take days and months before they spoke of these experiences. To a man, each felt he was a better reporter for those months as a warrior.

Among our female clique who wrote of war casualties, we owed deep gratitude to Nathaniel R. (Nat) Howard, the *News* editor who also served in Washington D.C., on the national censorship board, because he kept us on the payroll and ordered us blended in with the staff. Janice Fleming married handsome George Ghetia, returned from the air force to the *News* staff. Jane Artale welcomed home her husband, Mike Artale. Marjorie van Horn Blossom wanted desperately to move out of a girls' residence club to create a real home for husband, Steve Blossom, a reporter at the *Cleveland Plain Dealer.* My brother Jack was home after four years of stateside army duty, having missed combat due to blindness in one eye from a childhood accident. Two of my favorite cousins died tragically after their overseas service—one committed suicide, jumping from the Harvard-Denison Bridge into the Cuyahoga Valley, and the other drank himself to death, leaving a large family in Cleveland and dying alone in Chicago. There were many silences within families. No one wanted to talk about the missing, the dead, the tragedies. This was a sobering time of adjustment. The unspoken motto was "Get on with it." Most did, relocating in tracts of hastily constructed housing and using the GI Bill to enroll in colleges and universities. I had broken my engagement and was not dating. My eye was on the sparrow—my job—the only thing I wanted.

Each day as we checked into the newsroom at 8 A.M. for the first deadline of 9 A.M., we were timorously unprepared for what was on tap. We took assignments from the city editor, who had spikes on his desk with memos for a wide variety of possible stories. Mostly, the distaff side handled feature assignments, ranging from covering a Rotary or Kiwanis club speaker to interviewing couples marking golden wedding anniversaries. Perennial features highlighted individuals honored by their schools, factories, or government for long years of service. Newspapers were reader-friendly, striving to print as many names as possible. The *News* and the *Press* were in keen competition for the afternoon market, and both papers battled to scoop the morning *Plain Dealer.*

I got a good feature assignment called "Made in Cleveland," a weekly text-photo layout about Cleveland industries retooling

Reporter O'Donnell in the *News*'s city room, February 2, 1946. Photograph by Bill Nehez, *Cleveland News.*

from wartime to peacetime production. This took me into many factories. At Lincoln Electric, I was outfitted in safety clothes and a mask and learned how to weld. It was great fun. In these shops I honed a skill of asking questions about a lot of detailed engineering operations I never knew existed. My factory guides were more than helpful. I also wrote dozens of "shorts," those two or three paragraph pieces, about Red Cross meetings and future events. Once I filled in for the vacationing society editor, a job I didn't warm to.

A regular Friday night buffet at the *Cleveland Press* Club above the Gay Nineties Nightclub in downtown Cleveland, where *News, Press,* and *Plain Dealer* staffers gathered. Ca. 1950; author's collection.

I knew more people on the police vice squad than in the social register. That turned out easier than I imagined. I simply called people listed in the Blue Book, a register of the town's elite. One incident sticks out. Miss Johanna Grasselli, a grande dame of society, advised me, when I asked what she was doing, that "We don't entertain during the wah," even though the war had wound down. I was learning the craft soaking it up. Nothing was too small working the clock for the nine, noon, and three P.M. deadlines.

The innovative *Cleveland Press* soon sent Leah Jacoby to the all-male police beat, breaking tradition. Leah—lithe and attractive—was an energetic reporter, scooping the men at her paper. They had never faced a hustler like Leah. The *News,* not to be outdone, sent me to the police beat. Some of the guys on our staff knew I had family connections in the safety departments through uncles and cousins. Leah and I were tough competitors.

I spent many hours at the old Central Police Station at E. 21st and Payne Avenue. The building smelled of caustic cleaning fluid and cigarette smoke. On Monday mornings, when the weekend parade of drunks and gamblers, who had been locked up since Friday, Saturday, or Sunday nights, were hauled before municipal court judges, the place had a strong stench of urine, stale alcohol, and body odors. Hallways were jammed with families of the jailed and a retinue of up-and-coming young attorneys who later went on to fame and fortune as top defense counsel or judges. Families hired these guys in the halls to defend their kin in trouble. The judicial system began in this smelly old Central Station. It was nothing like the sanitized cop-and-law television shows. Justices on the bench worked a production-line variety. A municipal prosecutor told the judge the charge—public drunkenness, numbers' gambling, assault and battery. The judges placed cases by what the prosecutor said: a first offence yielded probation; repeated offences landed the defendant at the Warrensville Work House. Gambling was usually a fine, and assault, depending on severity, usually gave the perpetrator a second chance. Watching this daily grind, I marveled at the stamina of judges and lawyers in their thirties and early forties putting in time until another election boosted them into a more refined courthouse with a "higher" class of criminal.

For the first few weeks I felt lost. Cops were not especially helpful. Testifying in court took them from their regular beats, away from patrol duty. It wasn't their job to break in reporters. Reporters from competing papers were not giving an inch either. It was sink or swim. The starting point for a rookie like me was the booking office, matching prisoner names to the municipal codes denoting the crimes—vagrancy, prostitution, traffic, etc. The address of the prisoner was a clue to a possible story. Matching the municipal code violation to the prisoner was tedious but that's how reporters ferreted news. For instance if ten males were arrested for a particular code violation, say gambling, that meant a big police raid on a policy or numbers house. Arrests for women on prostitution were a clue to a brothel, for instance, perhaps in a downtown hotel. There were policewomen, but they were only visible in Juvenile Court blocks away from Central.

At first, I never told a soul how tough this job was. There was pressure to produce three solid stories a day. Most times, I simply made just one, because I spent too much time on one individual, chasing false or unproductive leads. Or the prisoner's case I focused on was continued, leaving me without a court decision to report. And there were the statutory crimes. Would you believe I didn't know what sodomy was? Municipal Court judge Julius Kovachy, a tubby Santa Claus of a man, sat me down with the crime code one lunch hour to read up on that biblical crime. So much for my religious education. I kept plugging away, wearing the same black patent leather opera pumps, nylons, suits and sweaters or plaid skirts, jackets, and white blouses. At the newsroom, I reported in with veiled hat and white gloves. No white gloves here. The newsroom at Central was the pits. Cracked plaster, walls covered with phone numbers and porn cartoons. Male reporters jumped into the room through an open window from the roof of the underground garage. Picture me flying in like Peter Pan in heels and skirts! I came through the front doors.

Nearly sixty years later I learned what a spectacle Leah and I were—she in her slim black gowns, jet black hair, and high heels. "Reporters, the guys on the beat, were panting. Well, not quite, but taking a lot of notice," recalled Pete Shimrak, onetime *Press* police reporter who worked the beat then. I don't know about Leah, but I was unaware of the attention. There were no hoots, whistles, or pats on the fannies from either fellow reporters or cops, even if anyone was "panting." My focus was the job: deadlines; filling folded pages of rough copy paper with notes, knowing there were only precious minutes to translate written words into a typewritten story. I don't recall how many "leads" I rewrote until one clicked.

Central Station, not unlike other institutional places, didn't accommodate females. We used the same small, tawdry washrooms and toilets as the public. The "boys' club" of male reporters didn't share much with Leah and me, aside from an occasional pornographic cartoon or picture for shock value. The male reporters secretly joined cops in a private viewing room for the "hot" confiscated porno films. When a big homicide came along, the male reporters got the assignments, because they were more experienced, and because they got first tips from pals of theirs in homicide. The men went to extremes to make friends of key officers for advance tips on breaking news. On one occasion, hungry for a follow-up on a homicide that was denied us by detectives, Paul Sciria, a television reporter, and I removed a metal plate from the floor air duct into the homicide office. We bellied in far enough to hear the detectives talk things over. We learned about a major suspect and were ahead of the story when he was arrested. Once I was physically shoved off the sidewalk of the home of a murder victim by two strapping detectives, Carl Delau and Del O'Hara. It wasn't vicious. These guys, ex-military tough guys, weren't accustomed to pushy girl reporters. Later we became close friends. Leah worked closely with her male counterpart, Hilbert Black, an African American who had great rapport with cops. I was truly lucky to have as my mentor Sanford (Soggy) Sobul, the "king" of police reporters. He came from Doan's Corners—old E. 105 and Euclid—where he grew up with Bob Hope, later the famous actor-comedian, and Alex "Shondor" Birns, one of the city's most notorious hoodlums.

Sobul was a wise, street-smart, Damon Runyon Rat Pack character with tons of friends among beat cops, high-ranking officers, and politicians. He helped greenhorn cops and reporters, and I was lucky that he chose to befriend me and Marjorie Blossom on big police stories, such as missing children and families of female murder victims. It could be as simple as telling the cop on the homicide detail that Margie and I "were okay to talk to." Sobul had a unique knack of communicating with officers at crime scenes. Not a flashy dresser, Sobul's identifying mark was a smashed-in gray fedora hat. He ran, not walked, and my vision of him remains of a whirling dervish through the halls of old Central Station. He never knocked at the chief's door; he barged in with bulletlike questions. With his front-page arrogance Sobul always expected the chiefs to give him answers—straight. They usually did, sometimes in confidence.

Often, we learned the best news after hours at one of several dingy bars that lined Payne Avenue, across from Central where cops and reporters hung out. Jim Byers, a six-foot-four ex-G.I. reporter for the *News,* invited me along on occasion. He was an impish guy, and I suspected he brought me along as a kind of "trophy" and to test my mettle. Jim's favorite barkeep was Maxie Lischt, who warned male patrons when Leah or I came in to "Be civil. Lady in house." Jim picked up lots of tips from Maxie and his patrons. One of them was Louie-the-Bear, an ironworker, brawny and built like a fire hydrant, who claimed he could rip a telephone directory in half (and he could, I soon learned after I challenged him). He and I developed a working friendship that helped later with stories about certain members of the Ironworkers' Union. Some of these men were arrested and convicted of major crimes.

Several of these tough union guys were investigated in the death of an old friend of mine. Eddie Holden supposedly fell to his death from a building construction job. Eddie, I suspect, was cooperating with police on illegal union activities before his untimely accident. About this time I got to know Danny Greene, another hoodlum and longshoreman, who eventually was blown apart in the parking lot of a suburban mall by vengeful gang members on October 4, 1977. Experts in organized crime believe that his death haunted Cleveland's mafia, and ensuing federal investigations eventually crippled the Mafia families in Cleveland, Los Angeles, Kansas City, and Milwaukee, because high-ranking racketeers turned states' evidence in exchange for light sentences. Danny and I had many breakfasts at the old Carter Hotel in downtown Cleveland, where he clued me in on activities of various "crime families." Later I learned he was an FBI informant, although he was up to his eyeballs in criminal activities himself. So proud of his Irish roots, he sent his pregnant girlfriend to Ireland to give birth to their child on Irish soil. Reportedly, he wore green shorts and had green toilet paper in his bathroom. Danny was a real savvy guy during the era when Cleveland was a "small town," and criminal factions were easily identified in ethnic and neighborhood enclaves.

My days on the police beat, in the courts, and on the street, put me in contact with a motley assortment of people. From Sobul I learned to operate as a horse-trader, you give me something, I give you something. No favors for a slanted story, but small things like a short piece about a Boy Scout event or a story on someone's grandparents' fiftieth wedding anniversary, an obituary, or merely looking up an old clipping for a date or a name. Like every other reporter, I kept small black notebooks with names and phone numbers. Every contact went in there. Frequently returning to the newsroom with half a story, I got "on the pipe" and called officers at homes, bars, or wherever and "milked the phone" until I had enough to write a story.

Along my desk at home are six of these old notebooks. Leafing through I see names and numbers of police, firemen, lawyers, judges, FBI and CIA agents, social workers, labor leaders, heads of steel companies, priests, managers of all the best hotels. Most are dead; a few are still around. My old phone records came in handy when Cuyahoga County prosecutor Bill Mason was retrying a civil phase of the old Sam Sheppard murder case in 2003. The prosecutor's office hired a San Francisco private eye to locate Susan Hayes, the woman Sam was shacking up with in California before his wife's death in Bay Village on July 4, 1954. Her married name, old phone number, and address were in the book. The private investigator called me—how he got my name I don't know—and he located Hayes in 2003. And when in 1961 the FBI arrested Cleveland hoods in Las Vegas who were skimming money from casinos, the wires—Associated Press, United Press International—carried parts of the story. Using my list of police contacts, I was able to identify the Cleveland culprits and their associates.

It was rewarding working with the big boys on crime stories. Especially at the *News,* where there was no sex barrier when it came to getting facts for stories on demanding deadlines. The *News* staff was smaller than the other dailies, and we were family. There were home and family parties and picnics. On a deadline story, if one of the guys asked the girls to make phone calls, we did it pronto. We were not prima donnas. The gals blended in well, and I was not aware of envy or jealousy about stories. There was always another day coming up with unknown assignments. Perhaps when Nat Howard sent me to the Soviet Union in 1956, there was some male grumbling. I don't know. It didn't bother me. The city editors knew on any assignment I would come back with the story. There were times when males went out four or five times and came back empty. On the sixth try, I got it. Who can argue with success?

-30-

-3-

Hare-brained Assignments

*E*ditors tore their hair out developing headline-catching editorial projects—criminal investigations, City Hall escapades, lurid court cases, hatchet murders, dazzling sports pages, Wall Street machinations, comics, give-away cash puzzle prizes. They lived by reports of circulation figures from the Audit Bureau of Circulations (ABC), posted twice annually in the monthly publication *Editor & Publisher.* And so it was in the summer of 1951 that *News* editor Nat Howard posed a "stunt" assignment.

No doubt, Howard had in mind duplicating—on a minor scale—the exploits of the intrepid Nellie Bly. Nellie, born Elizabeth Jane Cochran in Cochran Mills, Pennsylvania, in 1885, was hired by the *Pittsburg* [sic] *Dispatch.* She took the Nellie Bly name from a popular Stephen Foster song, "Nelly (cq) Bly." In 1887 she was hired as a reporter by Joseph Pulitzer's *The World* in New York City. For a spectacular story, she feigned insanity to gain admittance to the Women's Lunatic Asylum on Blackwells Island, New York. Her exposure of inmates' treatment was shocking news. Her next dangerous assignment was traveling around the world in eighty days to beat the record set by Jules Verne's fictional character, Phineas Fogg. In seventy-two days, Nellie traveled by train, rickshaw, donkey, and boat to achieve her goal. Nellie stands as the first girl reporter on the sensational road to capture readers' attentions—and sell papers. Oh how I envied her when, as a star-struck wannabe reporter, I read about her. I even figured out how I could replicate her trip, even pay my own way. What a goofy dream!

What did Nat have in mind for me? He suggested I "job sample." "Get out, get hired to drive a cab, hire as a char lady, cigarette girl. You get the idea," he said. My guess was that he wanted a "summer feature" gimmick, since newspaper circulation dipped during vacation months when readers tripped around the country. I had been perfectly happy on the police beat, comfortable in the routine, better acquainted with cops and judges and lawyers as the weeks wore on. I did a stint at Juvenile Court where Juvenile Court judge Harry L. Eastman "vetted" me before allowing me in the courtroom. None of my stories identified the juveniles or their families. All articles were accurate but anonymous. Perhaps they read like social work fiction, but they were real stories of real people. The facts were sordid and sickening but not as graphic as today's tabloid crime reports. The court faced child abuse, incest, criminal neglect of minors, young thieves, and many truants. Leaving the court some days I was sick with revulsion and pity. How the social workers kept sane, I don't know. And worse yet, I recognized several men who were charged with incest. I never talked about that to anyone.

There were no text books for stunt stories or old hands for guidance. I made a list of jobs with some drama to them that I could reasonably handle. I set out to be a cab driver, and with the help of the Yellow Cab's management, I enrolled in a three-day training period, naturally on newspaper time and pay. Upon graduation day as a cabette, my head was filled with heavy rules and safety regulations of the road and the company's mission. I had been driving since I was sixteen, as my mother insisted I take driving lessons with my brother, who had vision in only one eye. On my first day on city streets as Badge 2621, with state and city chauffeur's licenses, I hauled twenty-five passengers—from mothers with babies in arms to an aged woman and a blind man—over eighty-four miles of Cleveland pavement during an eight-hour stretch. My meter tallied $12.05 for Yellow. I earned $3.35 in tips. My pay was 42.5 percent of the day's returns.

On the job I learned my fellow cabettes were hard workers. Helen Edwards said her factory job was easy compared to this. So was my writing job! Drivers moved rapidly from cab trips to phone stations and back on the road. It was a seven-day-a-week job, with one Sunday off a month. Fellow cabettes worked other jobs too, earning extra money for new houses they bought with their husbands, catching up with new lives after the war. William C. Conley, manager of Yellow, hired more than two hundred women during World War II. Only one woman he hired smashed a cab, near the Hollenden Hotel on Superior Avenue, while making a wrong turn. I confessed to Conley one night I broke a company rule and bought six bottles of beer in a saloon for a male passenger who was blind. I even carried the bottles into his rooming house. It took a few weeks for our readers to catch on to this series. Finding stunts was like keeping balls in the air. I had to plan ahead to keep the series going.

I upped my driving skills by talking the manager of the Cadillac Tank Plant, southwest of Cleveland Hopkins Airport, into putting me into an enormous 260 Walker Bulldog Tank being tested for the U.S. Army. My trainer, chief tank tester Ralph Sterns, told me, "Driving? It's simple. As easy as pedaling a bicycle." He gave me three minutes of instructions—"That button there, one there, and low, high, reverse"—and outfitted me in white overalls, a crash helmet, and I was ready to go. Heart thumping! For the first few yards my bravado almost froze in low gear, and it took grunts and groans from me and the tank to make top speed. The rat-a-tat-tat of the motor was unnerving. This was not my old comfortable Ford. This was a ten-ton baby that cost about $100,000, waddling at six miles an hour on four cylinders. Snuggled in the driver's hatch, a cozy well on the left side of the tank, I felt like I was in a giant corn popper. I had started it by turning on the magneto, generating a spark for the ignition, squeezing two levers, shifting gears, and stepping on the accelerator. Ten miles an hour seemed like forty. Moving

Driving a 260 Walker Bulldog Tank as part of an assignment on the Cadillac Tank Plant, July 9, 1951. Photograph by Perry Cragg, *Cleveland News.*

along, I rose off the seat frantically tugging on the T-shaped steering bar. "The faster you go, the easier to steer," Sterns had said. With growing confidence, I zoomed ahead on the marked course. Testers before me who tested the tank's transmissions cleared the roadway. I dipped along high, wide, and handsome, crisscrossing the white line in the road. There was no rearview mirror to view any possible damage in my wake. I didn't turn Brook Park or Berea into a private battlefield. Just in case, I was told about an emergency exit mechanism—a lever on the tank floor—that dropped my seat through a trap door. That story brought letters and phone calls to the effect that I was a bit "looney" to drive a tank. To this day I pay attention to military tanks in real service pictured on television from Afghanistan to Iraq.

Another assignment was with the Visiting Nurse Association (VNA), the angels of the street. During a week's time, I accompanied Mrs. Henrietta Bull on daily visits, traveling by streetcar, to some of the city's poorest and roughest neighborhoods. Lugging a sturdy black medical bag with pills and bandages and lots of compassion and tenderness, Mrs. Bull nursed many indigent people. After only a very short time visiting and tending to dying children and sick and crippled elderly people, I was struck by the enormity of the job and the stamina it took for nurses like Mrs. Bull on her routine, day after day. This assignment was not a lark, and the stories touched a nerve among some readers. The VNA had responses from readers to assist in volunteer work and contributions. That was a good feeling, making readers care.

Rough, gruff Cuyahoga County sheriff Joseph M. Sweeny lifted his bushy eyebrows when I asked to work with his matrons in County Jail. He studied me quite a while, then: "If I say yes, you have to stay on the job three days." He didn't think I could handle the job on the seventh floor where women were incarcerated. Those rows of cells were a catch-all of women, some irretrievably lost to society, others in legal troubles for the first time. They ranged from young women to grandmothers and were confined for drunkenness in combination with criminal acts, prostitution, vagrancy, robbery, drug use, or drug peddling. After three days, I came away feeling as gray and cold as the jail walls, with a painful memory of unfortunate women. There was a nurse who craved drugs and an armed bandit and a "thrill-seeking-stickup girl." Miss Helen Quilty, a jail matron since 1937, broke me in on the 7:30 A.M. shift with her hard-boiled philosophy. "I used to think woman prisoners were all right. But everyone's a faker, especially ones who've been in trouble before. I don't trust them, and I don't tell them a thing."

As Deputy O'Donnell I rolled out a food cart at noon with macaroni and two slices of white bread. We counted spoons before meals and after. Spoons could be pounded into knives. "The sheriff's running a jail, not a hotel," a deputy told me. Patients with psychiatric problems were noted by Miss Quilty, who recommended to the

Up the stairs to a suspected abortion mill over an East Side saloon. 1954; Photograph by Perry Cragg, *Cleveland News.*

sheriff they be given priority court hearings. These problem cases were on the jail's eight psycho wards where I was stationed in a glass cubicle. I was as caged as the women behind their shatter-proof glass. Matron Stella Willkon described these prisoners as unpredictable, screaming, abusive, and irrational. I was afraid to smile back at them. Willkon said a few weeks before, "We had several who tore clothes, sheets, pillow cases, everything in shreds. They tossed shoes out the windows. They put on a dance." Their

On the construction site of Erieview in downtown Cleveland while ironworkers complete the project, 1958. Photograph by Perry Cragg, *Cleveland News.*

futures rested with tests and recommended treatment at Cleveland State Receiving Hospital, Cleveland State Hospital, Hawthornden State Hospital, or Lima State Hospital for the Criminally Insane. I stayed three days. That was my Nellie Bly moment, and I was deeply depressed. What happens to these women? Their futures were so bleak. I nearly gave up on the assignment, but Nat thought the stories were great. "Keep going," he said. I did. I was curious about the next job. That was as an attendant for two days at a state mental hospital. It was time spent in a half-world where reality is an intruder. Events I witnessed and lived through shook me up, and I went back to the newsroom with deep sympathy for the workers and families who kept their loved ones at home until they couldn't face another minute with them. Talking to staff, I learned it was easier to get out than in. I actually met a fellow reporter there who escaped before he could be treated. A clinical director said: "We don't fool ourselves. We know many people go home who are still ill. But we believe we have taken them to a stage where they have a grasp on reality again and can care for themselves." From what I saw, I hoped he was right.

This heavy-duty emotional stuff made working as a charlady in the fifty-two-story Terminal Tower like a vacation at Club Med. My fellow chars and janitors there dusted 3,017 desks, 6,135 chairs, and 1,428 tables nightly for the skyscraper's 3,350 tenants. High up in the Tower built by the entrepreneurial Van Sweringen brothers on Public Square, I dusted the table and desk of famous Cleveland railroad and ore magnate Cyrus S. Eaton, whose desk drawers were locked (I tried them), and I dusted around a big chunk of iron ore, the sole object on his desk. Later Eaton told me the piece of ore reminded him of several failed business deals. It always gave him hope that new business would surface Phoenix-like from ashes of old ones. In his luxurious Van Sweringen suite I pressed my nose against the window, looking down on the city. Lights on main arteries stretched out like rows of simulated diamonds. Red neon signs, garish at close range, took on a rubylike charm, and smoke from the blast furnaces tinted the night's navy blue sky. My companion chars had no time for my nonsense. These women, European immigrants, lived within the shadows of downtown buildings. They were mothers and grandmothers, wives of rugged steel mill workers. Romance was not found in scrubbing sinks and toilets of the rich and powerful. Their rewards were sending children to high school and if dreams came true, to college. This job, for me, was a lesson in humility.

Before summer ended, I took a walk-on role at the Chagrin Falls Straw-Hat Theater, worked as cigarette girl at Herman Pirch-

Riding an elephant in the Mills Brothers Circus in Circleville, Ohio, 1950, for a stunt story. Photograph by Perry Cragg, *Cleveland News*.

ner's Alpine Village, put my foot on the pedal and hand on the throttle of a New York Central diesel engine on a run from Cleveland, Ohio, to Bellefontaine, Ohio. There were stunts as a disc jockey, an airline stewardess on Capital Airlines, a model at the Higbee Company, a carhop, a coremaker at a foundry, a welder at Lincoln Electric, an elephant rider in the Mills Brothers Circus in Circleville, Ohio. I flew in a military glider over Cleveland

Hopkins airport, worked with Cleveland policewomen, collected money as a Salvation Army "Sallic" in front of the downtown May Company, played Santa Claus to children at the Sterling-Lindner Davis Coy. In the circus, my girl companions on elephants, high wires, acrobats, and clowns were Chinese, German, Slavs. Few spoke English. I watched them between breaks wash their undies out in shallow basins of water and hang them on make-do clothes lines around motor homes. No glamour here.

Readers had a variety of comments and suggestions, ranging from school teacher to parachutist. One woman dropped a note: "When you tire of interviewing yourself, interview some interesting people." She had a point. But the stunts had benefits. I did not suddenly become Lois Lane or a star reporter, but on later assignments a lot of people recognized me or at least the stories. And that gave me a bridge of friendship into their lives as I interviewed them.

Nat never said whether circulation had shot up. I had my Nellie Bly moments. The adventures brought me closer to my city and its people. I loved it.

-30-

-4-

Gals in the Newsroom

The Way We Were

*T*oday, whenever I attend journalism awards events and seminars, young women invariably ask me, "Did the male journalists harass you and other women in the newsroom?" They seem almost disappointed when I answer, "No."

I can say in all truthfulness that I never experienced sexual harassment, if what is meant by that overt remarks or sexual physical passes. I learned many years later from male police beat reporters about whistles and male locker-room humor that bubbled up when newspapers hired fresh young women reporters. My experience was really quite the opposite; in fact I remember the older male reporters from my early days with the *Cleveland News* as courteous and accepting. Keep in mind that all the young eligible males were in military uniform, fighting World War II in faraway places. We were their temporary replacements.

Since I was already an inveterate newspaper reader when I began working in the newsroom, I recognized my new colleagues by their bylines, and I admired tremendously these men who gave advice freely and filled me in on the nuts and bolts of the city room, as it was called. They showed me and the other new reporters, mostly female, how to take and make police calls and write police briefs, how to rewrite piles of mail from advertising agencies, public relations firms, and club and church notices. This small band of aspiring girl reporters had worked on high school newspapers and came with basic journalistic skills, but city newspapers are essentially just big bulletin boards. Notice today how major newspapers list television, radio, and movie schedules, and weekend tabloids are devoted to the major culture of eating and entertainment. But it still has the small-town weekly flavor where one finds hometown news—scouts, churches, bazaars, and parent-teacher and zoning meetings, and this is where our focus was to be.

I was hired along with other young female writers for the military desk, where our daily assignment was using the Associated Press lists of military news to create features on battlefield promotions, heroism, and, sadly, death. There was no shortage of daily stories on young men killed in Europe and later in the Pacific. During these long months we were an isolated island, working away from the city desk, dominated by experienced male city editors and assistant editors. We worked on tight deadlines three times a day, leaving very little time for socializing. But later we became full-time reporters and were seated among the men, not quite their equal in knowledge or in the paycheck, but at least among them. What a glorious triumph, because now we were "reporters," and we fraternized with the old hands. Bill Dinwoodie, the dignified religion editor and my desk companion, recommended we read Ernest Hemingway for his concise use of language. He even loaned us his Hemingway books. Arthur Spaeth and Peter Bellamy, the theater and film reviewers, tutored us on plays and novels to read to expand our worldview and hone our aesthetic sensibilities. I was Art's fill-in at Karamu Theater, the city's black experimental drama group, when he had conflicting assignments. Bellamy taught Shakespeare at evening college classes and loaned his notes to supplement our reading of the Bard in addition to attending the Play House's presentations of Shakespeare. We gals loved getting free passes to downtown theaters. Remember our

The ladies of the *News* attend a baby shower for Margie Blossom (seated front, far left). Ca. late 1940s; author's collection.

salaries were under $100 a month until we were upgraded to Newspaper Guild salaries on par with the men.

As pretty much a tomboy growing up with an older brother and his friends, I loved playing baseball with them, hiking and ice skating alongside them. So I really never thought about harassment, but several other gals had different experiences. A man from the copy desk had a quirky habit of rubbing up against girl reporters when they researched clippings in the newspaper morgue (now in the library). I recall one gal laughing about it, and then several others chimed in with tidbits about this guy. One of the gals mentioned it to librarian Louise Runyan. Louise, a tough, no-nonsense lady, watched him in action, shuffling close to a young reporter at a file cabinet, and she soon filed a harassment grievance with the

Newspaper Guild. Management suspended him. But this was the exception to the rule in the newsroom. We did hear expletives from the guys working fast and furiously on deadlines. Bob Kehoe, labor reporter, usually had a few choice words after he hung up on a call when he failed to extract answers he needed during the phone conversation. I can't recall ever hearing a four-letter expletive, but there were plenty of "bastards." In fact, I thought "bastard" was an affectionate term, like "you lucky bastard." The city room wasn't pristine, but compared to the police beat it was a seminary. I thought then and do now that it was because the police beat turned up life's most sordid things, and police reporters and cops painted the horror stories over with crude jokes and raucous laughter. There's a lot of muck in the underbelly of a big city.

A few incidents in particular reside in my memory. Once, a policewoman who was working vice with women and children, gave me a book of graphic sexual acts to take home. She had confiscated this pornographic stuff when working a case, and the material was to be used in a court case against this man. I wondered if she wanted to shock me or introduce me to her role as a cop. Nonetheless, I left the cartoons in my bedroom, and when I looked again my mother had taken the book and burned it in the basement furnace. Fortunately, the lady cop had a similar book for her case. Another time, one of Cleveland's most notorious hoodlums, Alex "Shondor" Birns, invited me and Peggy Wisner—one of our first female photographers—to his lakeside home for a party. Well, I chickened out, but Peggy reported later that Mr. Birns had a closet full of costumes—from waitress to ballet dancer—for his female guests to wear to entertain his male guests. Another time, we were invited by a fellow-reporter and his house guest, a prominent governor of a Southern state, to a showing of a pornographic film. We knew better by this time to say we were busy.

Fred Mollenkopf and I, who partnered in lots of investigative stuff not because of gender but because of good investigations, attempted to investigate Reuben Sturman, who was under federal indictment for publishing a book called *The Sex Life of a Cop*. We could have been chewed to death by police dogs guarding his publishing warehouse when we tried to walk in for an interview with the "porn king." He ran a worldwide network of porn, amassing a fortune, and was eventually arrested by the feds and died in prison. Fred and I also, on a tip, saw the blueprints for one of Sturman's suburban mansions that had speakeasy glass on bedroom and bathroom walls for the benefit of prurient "customers." At times Fred sort of apologized about the sordid stuff we turned up. He was very proper.

There were a few romances in the newsrooms of the dailies. Janice Fleming married George Ghetia when he returned from service. Margaret Campbell married Norman Vail in circulation at *The News*. Doris Millavec married Harry Linge, another newspaperman. Jospehine Robertson of the *Plain Dealer* was married to fellow newsman Carl Robertson. And Nancy Gallagher of the *Press* married John Depke of the *News*. The staffs of the three papers socialized at the Press Club of Cleveland, a downtown landmark, and at regular meetings of the Cleveland Newspaper Guild. *News* and *Press* reporters were the most active Guildsmen, concentrating on pension plans from both the Forest City Publishing Company, publisher of the *News* and *Plain Dealer,* and Scripps-Howard, publisher of the *Press.* We struck the newspapers four or five times to improve wages but mostly to obtain pensions. Many walked on picket lines; others worked at strike newspapers for better wages and pensions. Thank God we did—we got pensions.

Looking over old pictures taken in the newsrooms, I see slender, lovely young women. We thought of ourselves as "young ladies," and we presented ourselves in such a manner. We copied clothes worn by slender models in *Vogue* and *Glamour.* Society editors at the three daily newspapers were fashion plates, as were the women who covered the beauty and cosmetic fields. We envied their trips to New York City fashion shows and to the houses of Revlon and Coty. The fashion editors were the doyennes in their category. The *Plain Dealer*'s Winifred Goodsell took her own silk sheets and pillow cases and even personal light bulbs to New York hotels when she covered the runway shows and cosmetic houses. Those were the days. The fashion gals even shared sample cosmetics with us (we could never afford the real thing). Our male counterparts came to work in suits, ties, and shirts with button-down collars. Some males were the tweedy type, with leather patches on elbows; others wore the standard navy blue jacket with twill trousers. Pretty formal stuff.

All of us, no matter the beat—from fashion to general assignment to police—sometimes worked long hours because of early morning or late evening assignments. Someone had to cover a 9 A.M. breakfast or an 8 P.M. meeting. We gradually learned to dress to accommodate the hours, meaning we stuck to basic suits but had plain or fussy blouses to dress up or down our "uniforms." The society editors got small stipends to get their hair done or to buy an evening gown. A lot of us slipped away on lunch hours for shampoos and sets at downtown beauty parlors. Our hair style was more June Allyson than Carmen Miranda. I recall in Bonn, Germany, in the 1990s on a NATO-sponsored trip, when German premier Helmut Kohl refused to meet with several male reporters who wore blue jeans and sports shirts. Kohl held up the meeting until the men returned in shirt, tie, jacket, and khaki trousers. We neophytes learned from older hands that neat, clean clothes and appearances were vital when interviewing public officials and visiting celebrities. And in knocking on doors of families caught by tragedies, a good appearance and politeness was the difference in getting an interview or having a door slammed in your face.

As with other aspects of the newsroom, gender also played a role in beats—the men had their beats and the women theirs. I never met a man on the fashion beat or a woman in sports. One exception was Oscar Bergman, who wrote a male fashion column for the *Plain Dealer.* But usually the men did features on aviation, since Cleveland was home to the famous Cleveland Air Races, and they wrote on labor, factory and automotive production, government agencies, city hall, and civil, criminal, and federal courts. The girls were assigned to features on children, schools, welfare, Red Cross, community fund drives, the elderly, births of baby zoo animals, golden wedding anniversaries, and "fluffy features." I don't recall rebelling against the barrier between gender and beats. We were happy to have jobs. Jane Artale was the most persistent in demanding a sports job, and eventually she did women's sports. I got the police beat, not because I demanded it but because the com-

FOREST CITY LOG

Vol. III, No. 2   For the Members of the Forest City Family   March 15, 1956

New E. 18 Center to Cost $4,640,120

DORIS O'DONNELL

Photo by Jerry Horton

Doris Does a Man's Job, Yet Puts 'Oomph' in Her Commas

By BILL SILVERMAN SR.
News Editorial

When a certain young woman walks past the Snake Pit—a term of polite endearment used by some News reporters to describe the copy desk—nine sighs rise in unison, and 18 eyeballs pop with a singleness of purpose. At the telegraph desk all work actually comes to an instantaneous stop.

The cause of all this is a young woman reporter whose first by-lines came out "by Doris O'Donnell," simply because linotype operators couldn't read the city editor's handwriting. It has taken a little doing, but the "Doris" has finally emerged into its proper gender. All hands now have learned that when the city editor writes what looks like an "N," he is merely slurring his R's and I's.

One of the Snake Pit's less venomous denizens who learned how to sigh in the limestone caverns of Kentucky, explains the phenomenon at 18th and Superior thus:

"Doris O'Donnell is the only reporter I ever knew who could put oomph into a little old comma."

Elephant-riding, cab-driving, tank-jockeying and debunker of phonies O'Donnell—she's all of that—conceals an inquisitive mind and a somewhat ruthless persistence beneath a smiling manner.

She's won more honors and accomplished more things than any other woman on the company's payroll. Her work has

(See DORIS, Page 9)

Confidence in Future Is Shown by Huge Expenditure, Graham Says

The Forest City Publishing Co. is investing $4,640,120 in the development of the E. 18th Street publishing center, President Sterling E. Graham has announced.

Confidence in the future of Greater Cleveland and the newspaper industry is reflected by the huge expenditure, he pointed out.

Forest City's original contract for construction of the modern center was for $2,250,000.

Since then several additional expenditures have been approved. Construction in the fourth floor light court area added some $100,000 to the building contract. Engineering changes, the mail room addition and other modifications in the original plans have added to the cost, Graham added.

Mechanical Equipment

Second largest item in the development budget is approximately $1,500,000 for mechanical equipment.

This figure includes $925,000 being spent for the new seven-unit color convertible printing press and additional color equipment for existing presses.

Other mechanical equipment purchases included in the budget will be typesetting machines, stereotype equipment and the mailroom stuffing machines. A story about the stuffing machines which will cost approximately $70,000 installed, may be found elsewhere in this issue of the LOG.

Included in the cost are such major items as $35,000 for the cafeteria equipment and $25,000 for the new photo lab equipment.

P.D. Mails Reprints of Humphrey Editorial

The Plain Dealer's timely editorial suggesting that Treasury Secretary George M. Humphrey be nominated as the Republican vice presidential candidate is being sent to more than 2,000 persons in the United States.

The editorial was written by Ralph Donaldson and ran the morning after President Eisenhower's address to the nation on his state of health and his intention to run again.

Forest City Buys Stuffing Machines

Purchase of two Sheridan stuffing machines for use in the Forest City mail room is announced by Leon A. Link, production manager.

The machine is a circular device developed to automatically stuff or insert newspaper sections into a jacket or wraparound section.

Cost of the machines, installed, is approximately $70,000, Link added.

The machines will be used primarily for stuffing American Weekly, This Week, Pictorial

See Photo on Page 9

Magazine and special sections into the Plain Dealer's Sunday comic section. This operation is now done by hand.

Newspaper sections to be stuffed by the Sheridan machine are manually stacked in the hoppers of their respective feeding sections. From there, they are automatically fed into V-shaped pockets which rotate below the feeding stations in a horizontal orbit.

Each feeding station is equipped with a detecting device which insures accurately assembled papers. If any feeding station misses feeding a section into a pocket, or if more than one section is delivered, the error is detected and the machine stops.

APRIL COPY DEADLINE

Copy for the April edition of the Log must be in by Friday, March 30. Photos should be submitted as early as possible. Copy should be typed, double or triple spaced.

Article from the *Forest City Log,* March 15, 1956, showcasing the newness of women in the newsroom.

peting *Press* sent Leah Jacoby there first. Like in a movie, where producers see "types" in actors and actresses, every reporter had a type. Somehow, I was not the PTA or society editor type. Through family I knew politics and politicians. I was intrigued with police news and stories, read mysteries and Westerns. Zane Grey was one of my favorite authors, along with Sherlock Holmes. My bosses guessed, and they were right, that I'd take on any assignment. My adrenaline flowed with a challenge. Pack journalism was not for me. Many times I waited for my competition to leave and then doubled back to the source and convinced the reluctant person to give me their side of the story. I felt no need to share my interviews with my competition.

Women reporters today have much more than we did. Cell phones. Tape recorders. Their own cars. Better salaries. Better working conditions. Bigger staffs on metropolitan newspapers. More equality, although few women ever rise to the position of hiring and firing. More women are editors and columnists. But I doubt they are as close to the community as we were, being on the street day in and day out. More women columnists today write tirelessly of their personal lives. We had to write features about our readers. We could not use "anonymous sources." Television and radio have opened new vistas for women, but news is so compressed and packaged between commercials that viewers and listeners are forced to concentrate to get news. Entertainment has swamped news columns, and investigative journalism has slipped. Today's focus is more on social and cultural issues when ours was on crime and corruption in public office, plus lots of civic and community stuff. Computer-generated stories are apt to overwhelm readers with facts and stats. We wrote thoughtful daily copy that was more reader-friendly. When gals in Theta Sigma Phi meet annually, we report on our past careers in daily and international journalism, public relations, advertising, and as information officials in medical and government fields. We conclude: we had the best of the century. We loved our jobs, our colleagues—well most of them—moaned over pathetic salaries that increased over the years. I didn't hear complaints of harassment. In fact, the dazzling former *Press* society editor once quipped: "Occasionally, I liked a pat on the ass."

-30-

-5-

The "Cabbie" Assignment

Breaking through the Racial Divide

*N*athaniel "Nat" Howard was a great editor. He was a reporter's editor with a collegial management style, sensitive copy editing skills, and keen insights and comments. He didn't slaughter copy—he enhanced it with suggestions written in tiny, tight, handwritten notes in margins. He had an open-door policy and was in touch with his newspaper audience. Every working day he lunched at the Union Club, the hub of the town's leaders, not least of all the men who ran the big downtown department stores, or, our big advertisers. He walked from the *News* office at E. 18th and Superior to the Club at E. 12th and Euclid but always took a Yellow Cab back, explaining to rookie reporters that cabbies had the pulse of the town. He regularly asked what they wanted in the paper. Cabbies must have been creative creatures because Nat overwhelmed the newsroom with their ideas.

One such "cabbie" idea turned out to be me living with a black family in the fall of 1948. Today it would be called embedded, with the focus of bringing issues of community diversity into the *News* readers' homes. That's not how I saw it then. It was an exploration, taking me into an unknown world. As it developed, however, I found it closer to my own world than I ever imagined. It was not a story about "whitey versus blackie," race or superiority. It was about the humanity that happened to live off of Cedar Avenue.

Nat and I worked with black community leaders to find a family willing to participate in the venture. I was eventually assigned to write sixteen stories, which would appear daily after two months of close contact with an East Side family that included a mother, father, grandmother, and five children who lived in their own home off Cedar Avenue. My stories were more mundane than sensational, but they took readers directly and intimately into the lives of Jesse and Pearl Jackson (we called them the Watsons in the stories) in their gray fame home on E. 86th Street. The best times I had during the assignment were after school when Pearl sat at the living room piano. The children lost their inhibitions in front of me, dancing and singing pop and spiritual songs.

Growing up in Cleveland's West Side in the 1930s, I never knew any black people. Never saw them, either. No one at my Catholic grade school or public high school was black. In fact, I only knew one Jewish kid at high school, Benny Madow. There were no blacks at the Morris Plan Bank, my first real paying job, or later at the Union Bank of Commerce, and not even at Fawick Airflex. Hard to believe that the Cuyahoga River was such a territorial divide between East and West! Despite my youthful environment in an all-white neighborhood, I don't recall ever being personally touched by racial thoughts such as hatred. Our neighbors were German, Irish, Polish, Italian, and one was French-Canadian. I was, however, appalled as the civil rights movement spread throughout the country. I guess if I searched my soul when I watched the turmoil on television, I would have wondered out loud: What took them so long? But I was a reporter, a spectator, an observer, not an activist. I guessed that Nat sensed this in me and trusted my naïveté and honesty to report to whites the lives of blacks. I really wanted this story. Newspapers around the country were becoming conscious of social change. A Pittsburgh newspaper sent a white male reporter, with cosmetically shaded skin, down South to report on what it was like to be a black in white America. He won the Pulitzer Prize for the series.

Each work day, and some Sundays, I rode a city bus from downtown to the Jackson home. Pearl Jackson was a tall, energetic, fun-loving woman, undaunted by her five children (four girls and one boy) and an aging, frail mother-in-law. Jesse, born in the South, was, like his wife, a gentle, almost shy man. He washed trucks and cars for a living, at first using a hose and a bucket, but later, with the financial help of a white truck owner, he ran his own business. The kids, ranging in age from six to nineteen, attended city schools, and the oldest girl was headed for the University of Hawaii upon graduation from Central High. While the parents tried to prepare their family for my reporter's eye, they were still shy at first. But gradually they warmed up as I blended into the family routine of shopping, sewing, and cooking. Leaving their home one evening, Merle, age six, told her neighbor girlfriends I was "a cousin from Mississippi." I loved that! Unfortunately my white bus drivers were not as kind to me as they tried to figure out what a white passenger was doing riding public transportation in an all-black neighborhood.

Pearl set the daily agenda, and I was a willing and supportive companion. She drove us to thrift shops, Goodwill and Salvation Army stores, and public markets in wholesale food terminals. She watched her dollars like a hawk, which reminded me of my mother, who also shopped at public market stalls for bargains. Pearl bought lots of greens, carrots, onions, potatoes, and cheap cuts of meat for soup and stews. Pots of these items were forever bubbling over gas burners on the kitchen range. Old coats from the thrift shops were torn apart and brushed to free them of extra threads and lint. Pearl gave me patterns, made of newspapers, and I cut dozens of mittens from the plaid and checkered material, while nearby she pumped away at a treadle sewing machine, turning out dozens of mittens for her kids and her neighbors'. We talked, talked, talked. Southern style cooking was new to me, and I learned to crumble bacon on lettuce and potatoes. She introduced me to boiled beet tops, decorated with mashed, hard-boiled eggs. We fixed kale, squash, cabbage—things bought cheaply at farmers' markets, especially if they were losing freshness. I still use Pearl's recipes.

I loved Sundays with the entire family. In suits and frocks, hats and gloves, we attended their Baptist church. One Sunday Larry Doby, an outstanding black Cleveland Indians outfielder, was a guest. Throughout the service, distracting smells of rich barbecue sauce simmering in the church basement kitchen wafted upstairs. A special party was on tap for Doby, who joined the crowd of jovial churchgoers who were eager to meet him. Churches, I quickly learned, were the social heart and soul of the black community. How different from my home Catholic Church, which seemed somewhat sterile in comparison. After Sunday mass we simply went home.

A few sour notes underscored this assignment. My mother, a suffragette, Democrat ward leader, and someone I considered progressive, thought the paper should have given the assignment to a man. She objected to my daily solo trips by bus to E. 86th and Cedar. Mother once ran a confectionary store at E. 79th and Hough, which in her day was in an upper-middle-class white neighborhood. White flight began in the late 1930s, and in the 1940s much of the inner East Side housed blacks, many brought from the South during World War II, to work in Cleveland war plants. The migration from Southern states in those years was voluminous.

Another sour note involved a woman who worked at the paper and who also worked at her father's greengrocer stand in the open market. When I once stopped there with Pearl, my coworker pretended she didn't know me. Several fellow reporters called me a "nigger lover," mixed letters landed at the paper after the stories appeared. But by far public response was positive.

Jock Williams, a columnist for *Call & Post,* weekly newspaper whose readers were principally black, praised the series as a "factual account of one family living on our own East Side. In our opinion, Miss O'Donnell has given a very vivid word picture of the family's social background, daily experiences, mode of living, community interests and racial attitudes." He said the series portrayed "the family's way of life which is typical of thousands of struggling families throughout Greater Cleveland." I proudly received state and national awards, one from the Newspaper Women's Association of Ohio, another from the Cleveland Newspaper Guild, and a third from Lincoln University in Springfield, Missouri, a college that was populated by mostly black students. Perhaps the greatest reward was that the Jacksons and I remained friends after the series ended. I often thought there could (and should) have been similar series about life in Cleveland neighborhoods that were homes to other ethnic populations whose cultures were frequently ignored.

I was a different person after living with the Jacksons. The stories marked a turning point in my life and my career. It frustrated me that there was a rich cultural life so close and yet so ignored. One prominent black woman friend said later: "We have been invisible too long." Yet when she invited me to her charming home for lunch, she drew the blinds. She meant "invisible" in white metro newspapers. She was right. Crimes involving blacks made news. Or conversely, if blacks were involved in minor crime, nothing was reported. Could things change? Nat Howard and Tom Vail, publisher of the *News,* talked about my experiences with black churches, the black Karamu Theater, and in private homes. Vail ordered Society editor Mary Strassmyer to cover the annual dinner dance of Links, the national black women's organization, a parallel to the white society's Junior League. Mary and a photographer covered this landmark event, and a series of photos made the society page for the first time. Links had arrived—so too had our ability as reporters to look beyond race for quality stories.

Through the Jacksons and Municipal Court judge Perry B. Jackson (no relation of Jesse and Pearl), my contacts in the black community grew. Some people called me with stories, and I called them back for explanations, the other side of the story, and a two-way communication opened. Other assignments into the community came, and I never hesitated going into the homes of blacks, to their civic clubs, churches, political rallies. I covered tons of city council races among black candidates. On night assignments in questionable parts of town with high crime rates, sometimes I drove home, put my big black Newfoundland dog in the back seat for comfort and security, and then covered the meeting. I didn't worry about my safety then.

These were historic years for newspaper reporters. True, I wasn't in the land of Bull Connor and his police dogs in the South, but I was in my hometown during our own social upheavals. I went on with my career with a strong identification in the black community, and I was proud that the *News* editor and publisher were part of a new policy that embraced the former "invisible ones."

-30-

-6-

"Bad Boys"

The Mafia and Crime in Cleveland

People often ask, "What column did you write?" Actually, I didn't write a column. I was a general assignment reporter, but through a fluke (or a chance) I found a niche—organized crime. I simply slipped into it by immersing myself in histories of crime figures thanks to conversations within my family and reading local newspapers while growing up. My parents took me to political rallies in veterans' and nationality halls and outdoor political campaign fundraisers in country groves. My father was a city fireman whose brothers and sisters were active in labor unions and politics. My mother, a Democrat ward leader, tuned into local politics by lining up immigrants and assisting them in obtaining federal green cards. They could be future Democrats. Dinner table conversions swirled around politics and baseball. Save for less than a year in an East Side apartment where my mother was recuperating from major surgery, I grew up and went to school on the West Side. My ninth grade was at Miles Junior High School in the fall of 1936.

My father died after he had a stroke when I was eleven, a pupil at Our Lady of Good Counsel parochial school. His death came shortly after my parents were divorced, on the heels of losing our Stickney Avenue home through foreclosure. My brother and I saw Dad weekly, and we were devastated by his unexpected death. After our short life on the East Side, my brother and I urged my mother to return to the West Side. We eventually rented a home on Denison Avenue, near Brookside Park, where we were reunited with old classmates and spent winters skiing and ice skating at the park and summers at the pool. There were few girls my age nearby, and during grade school I was a tomboy, joining my brother's friends in building tents and forts. Our friends were from Counsel and St. Mark's Lutheran School, James Ford Rhodes, St. Ignatius, Lourdes, Cathedral Latin. At Counsel my friends were Rosemary Heidkamp, Mary Corrigan, Ann Welgan, Agnes Webster, and Margaret Spellacy. We worked closely with the Precious Blood order of nuns on school projects, plays, and Christmas pageants. At Rhodes my entire free time was given to the *Rhodes Review* and the creative writing class. As a child of the Great Depression, I learned early on that to get a new dress, I had to make it. Mother gave me two or three dollars and streetcar fare to shop Saturday morning at the downtown May Company. A simple cotton dress could be finished by evening. My mother, a good seamstress, though not as good as her sisters, made her own clothes and my father's uniform shirts. Today I can hardly pass up a Vogue pattern book.

During my high school days my ice-skating pal was Sam Scaravelli, a student at Cathedral Latin who drove a shiny black Cadillac, a spectacular eye-catcher for the time. We dated only on Sunday nights, when we saw a movie and had a chocolate milk shake at Harvey's in the Terminal Tower concourse. Then we drove around collecting his late father's share of money owed the family from downtown saloons. Sam's father was shot and killed during the Prohibition "sugar wars" in Cleveland. Sugar kept the attic booze stills running, and competitive bootleg gang wars led to vengeful murders. After Prohibition, many bootleggers transferred their skills to legitimate tavern business. The family etiquette of the gangster syndicate granted Sam's mother her widow's "due." Sam drove to shady sections of town, shut off the engine, locked me in, and went about the family business. We made four or five stops in one evening. I was all eyes and ears, though Sam was mysterious. Once Sam's best friend, Chuckie Miller, saw packages of cash fall from the back of a stand up radio in Sam's home when Sam's mother cleaned behind it. This intrigued me.

More intriguing "crime" could be found at bootleg joints, the poor man's social clubs, where my dad hung out with his firemen friends. Our next-door neighbors, the Irwins, were bootleggers, and there were rumors others on the street made "bathtub gin." Laws were broken, and a lot of people made bootleg money. At political picnics, I watched political candidates and political figures—judges and lawyers and mayors—guzzle whiskey from brown-tinted whiskey bottles. During these school years I became a good spectator, watcher, listener. Jack and I confided in each other about what we saw. Our parents' families never concealed things that were in our face. Perhaps I was more of a loner than I realized because I buried myself in books and newspapers. The library was a second home. With classmates, I went to dances and weddings, mostly ethnic ones in church halls.

My first big-paying job at the Morris Plan Bank (I had worked for a fifty-cent-a-week school streetcar pass at the *Heights Sun-Press* while in school) introduced me to a new world of bright attractive young women who wore perfume, pancake makeup, eye shadow, and dressed exquisitely. A few took me under their wings into the sisterhood of makeup and clothes. Try to imagine these early career girls, who were bookkeepers, concealing their engagement and wedding bands—to disclose a marriage meant dismissal from a job. Even their wedding showers were kept secret from the bosses. We've come a long way, baby.

Later at Fawick Airflex, Patsy Nolan, the registered nurse who worked with me in the personnel office, became a close friend. We palled around with her older brothers' friends, who for various reasons were draft-exempt. As regulars at Sunday night parties, we were surrounded by a group of wild, humorous storytellers. Among the best was a handsome blonde, Bob Mulgrew. A close second was the rugged Hank Erhardt. Beer was on tap, but it was up to the gals to furnish platters of sandwiches and potato salad. These mostly Irish young men were street guys with Catholic school educations. Summers they worked construction jobs as their father and grandfathers had. They were in the trades: bricklayers, ironworkers, carpenters, electricians, and they were part of the trade unions controlled by the Irish bosses. Their summer salaries paid tuition to the newly opened John Carroll University, run by the Jesuits from St. Ignatius. Mulgrew and his buddies moonlighted as croupiers at Tommy McGinty's Harvard and Thomas gambling clubs. I knew where these places were in the suburbs but never was inside. Mulgrew's stories covered the characters who jammed the joints on weekends and the money he saw "dropped" at the tables.

Dad and his brothers knew about these clubs run by Tommy McGinty and Shimmy Patton. During the heyday of these clubs, my dad's brother, Cuyahoga County sheriff Martin L. O'Donnell, believed in "home rule." His philosophy was: If the mayors of these suburbs wanted the clubs, it was okay. However, *Cleveland Press* editor Louis B. Seltzer issued an edict: No gambling in Cuyahoga County. And with the power of his newspaper, he forced police to raid the joints with axes and battering bars. It didn't take a building to fall on me to discern strong political and criminal threads in our communities and the battle between the rogues and the reformers. Raids made big, bold newspaper headlines, too, showcasing the good versus the bad. The depressed citizens who gambled away their paychecks argued they needed recreation from economic plights. Their bosses had plush suburban country clubs. The gambling raids and high jinks among the newspapers, the police, and the crooks made titillating reading.

The city was an exciting place, and I became a larger part of it when I was hired by the *Cleveland News* in October 1944. One of my assignments sticks in my memory as a turning point in my reporting career. A tall, frail, well-dressed woman, who simply walked into the newsroom "with a story," was assigned to me. From her hometown of Ashtabula, she was in Cleveland visiting former dancing colleagues. She brought a large photo album of pictures of herself and her friends as willowy dancers in Broadway's *Ziegfeld Follies*. In my mind's eye, I could picture the old black and white song-and-dance movies with those tall regal dancers in skimpy erotic gowns, tottering with glittering headdresses of sparkling faux stones and feathers, swanning across the boards of a famous stage. This hometown gal was one of them, faded but still attractive with large almond eyes. Describing herself as a "country girl," she said she found fame and love of sorts on the Great White Way. I took copious notes, borrowed her photos, and wrote a colorful feature piece. Several days later she returned for the album, praised the story, and said she wanted to return the favor. "An old boyfriend, a stage-door-Johnnie, was very nice to me then, and we have kept in touch. He lives in Chicago and calls me with tips on horses. He's more right than wrong. I live on what I make on horses."

Surprise. An O. Henry ending to my story. She left me a slip of paper with racetrack names, horse names, cities, times of races. It was Greek to me, but our Associated Press telegrapher, in a back office at the *News,* was "one of the boys" in the Saturday night poker games. The AP carried race results, a growing feature of sports pages everywhere. Guys in the newsroom talked about "rooms downtown" with banks of phones, handling wire traffic from a growing number of racetracks in Ohio, Kentucky, and around the country. I gave Izzy Kolitsky, a handsome, gray-haired smiley guy, the slip of paper and forgot about it. Two days later he snagged me in the corridor. "Hey, call your friend. They were winners." Ah, her Chicago connection was for real. It was a tempting thought. I gave Izzy her home address. Then I realized the tremendous linkage via the new telephone-telegraph wires between legitimate news— which came over the wires—and racing news that underwrote a burgeoning gambling industry. The wires carried race results and the newspapers printed the results. A happy marriage! And my interest in organized gambling only blossomed from there. After the end of Prohibition gambling on racehorses became a new national pastime and new for organized crime riches.

When I landed on the *News*'s police beat, I was lucky to be mentored by Sanford (Soggy) Sobul, chief police reporter. During lulls, I picked his brain about the hoodlums he had grown up with and the nefarious connections between the Irish-Italian-Jewish mobs that ran the city's underworld. He filled in the chinks in my growing background of the major players, whose names made headlines in all Cleveland papers and in Las Vegas, Los Angeles, Miami, Chicago, and New York. He gave me true crime books and magazines and told me about big-time newspaper reporters, the experts on organized crime. I came to know one of the very best, Hank Messick of the *Miami Herald.* I ate it up. I started a library of organized crime, and my collection became a backup resource on days when we needed fast bios on deadlines. These deadline stories came from wire news of FBI raids, major court decisions, and murders. Recently I gave my horde of boxes to a young author, Rick Porello, another specialist on organized crime.

In the 1940s and 1950s Cleveland was down the line from New York and Chicago for ethnic communities, with the runoff of immigration from Europe following our Civil War. Today there are sad, almost ghettoized remnants of ethnic enclaves. Once the streets were defined by nationality: Buckeye Road was Hungarian, Murray Hill Road, Italian. The population in the Flats, in downtown Cleveland on the banks of the Cuyahoga, was Irish. Clark Avenue belonged to the Germans, and E. 105th and Euclid were predominately Jewish. More Italians lived in Collinwood. Slovenes and Slovaks in Euclid. The black neighborhoods were in Cedar, Central, and Woodland. Greeks settled on Boliver Road. It seemed the Jewish groups had the brains; the Irish and Italian the muscle. Other groups had money and support. But the lawbreakers hung together, eventually merging into the mega gambling capital of Las Vegas. They were also eventually targeted by the FBI, the IRS, and state and local cops.

From the Murray Hill-Mayfield Road district emerged a group of lawbreaking characters, including Louis "Babe" Triscaro. We knew him at the paper as the big-shot head of the Teamsters Union who had close ties to the big Teamsters boss, Jimmy Hoffa. Our political reporter, Jack Kennon, bragged that his friend, Babe Triscaro, also ran a landscaping business. One night Jack got home to find his Forest Hills property "landscaped by the Babe" for free. This was hardly ethical, but it illustrates the cozy overlap of the various elements—reporter and Teamster. There were in-house discussions about such friendships. A few editors took a "so what?" approach. One editor wouldn't comment, but he liked it when his reporters could call a Teamster or a hood and get good quotes or background on a story. Who do reporters call on crime stories? This editor was known to say: "You can't call a PTA lady. She wouldn't know what you were talking about."

-30-

-7-

Confession Time

Collecting clips and data on local and national mobsters was like eating popcorn. I was addicted. These guys and some gals were newsmakers, and in pre-tabloid journalism, the era of green-sheet or pink-sheet journalism, their flamboyant and illegal escapades captured headlines. These special sections were targeted at a certain core of readers such as book readers or theatergoers. I loved reading these feature stories, and now I was writing them for the *News* and later for other papers. I loved even more the investigations of these crooks on the police beat and working with cops and FBI agents. My coterie of reporters and editors shared this sleuthing nature, largely because they had covered criminal trials in both county and federal courts. Editors teamed me with reporters such as Fred Mollenkopf and Harry Stainer, experts in this genre. Together Fred and I tracked contractors who cheated the city of Cleveland on sidewalk deals. And Harry and I followed the trail of one of Ohio's biggest drug dealers who won a presidential commutation. In writing these chapters, I relive the hours, days, and weeks spent zeroing in on paper trails of miscreants;

hours of searching public records, making dozens of phone calls, having personal interviews in bars, hotels, and private homes. Our notebooks bulged with dates, financial contracts, quotes—a lot of the stuff today's investigative reporters might find on an Internet search engine. It was disciplined work, and when it came to writing our stories, the facts were nailed down. They had to be, otherwise the stories weren't printed. And we always copied court and public records in longhand, which was a real chore.

At the former *Cleveland News,* my mentor in the field of crime, Sanford "Soggy" Sobul, chief police reporter, knew every hood in the county along with the names of their grandparents, where they were born, and where they went to school. He was a human vacuum cleaner when it came to scooping up vital information. He told me to "pick the brains" of certain trial lawyers who defended gamblers, shady characters, or felons. And he taught me what books on the mob to read and which cops were walking encyclopedias. There were books on Cleveland's organized crime guys by Ovid Demaris and Hank Messick. Ovid was an expert on the figures behind Las Vegas gambling casinos, and Hank, who won foundation grants to write books on organized crime, was a crime historian. Hank and I became telephone pals, and his book *Silent Syndicate* is still a bible of the city's racy past. Hank was a reporter for the *Miami Herald* when I knew him and was a big help when I vacationed in Miami with my mother in 1951. Neither my mother nor I had ever visited an Atlantic Ocean beach before, and we were elated about the seaside vacation until I read in the *Miami Herald* that the Kefauver hearings were under way in a downtown federal courthouse. I skipped the beach entirely and instead spent days in the crowded courtroom. Hank described our hotel, the Wofford, as "the mob's joint." I didn't file copy from Miami; the *News* used wire copy, but I kept copious notes to use later on Clevelanders "outed" by testimony. I was on vacation and not authorized by my editor to file or send stories by Western Union.

Tennessee senator Estes Kefauver was chairman of the Special Committee on Organized Crime in Interstate Commerce. The hearings (some of which were televised) began in May 1950 and lasted fifteen months and covered fourteen cities. Eight hundred witnesses were questioned. Witnesses described high-ranking members of the crime syndicate in America, and the hearings enforced the legend of a tightly held crime family called the Mafia, which had been imported from Sicily. The hearings showed that, rather than just Italian, all ethnic groups found crime to be the magic stairway to upward social and financial mobility. But the Cosa Nostra Italian syndicate traced its American roots to bootleggers and racketeers in the 1920s to longshoremen, fish markets, and labor unions in the 1930s, and gambling casinos and real estate in the 1940s. Significant results were state crime commissions and bans on legalized gambling in many states. The U.S. Senate followed with a Permanent Subcommittee on Investigations that held hearings under Sen. John McClellan from 1957 to 1963. Robert Kennedy was special counsel responsible for sending Teamster bosses Dave Beck and Jimmy Hoffa to federal prisons. When Bobby Kennedy became U.S. Prosecutor under his brother, President John F. Kennedy, Fred Mollenkopf and I were confidentially tipped to wire taps Kennedy ordered on phones of questionable crime figures in Youngstown with ties to characters in Cleveland and Pittsburgh. We could not use this off-the-record stuff until arrests became public in the courtroom. We would have jeopardized our federal source, but the *Plain Dealer* editors always demanded proof, verification from federal people who refused.

At the *News* I knew Louis "Babe" Triscaro was our Teamster official, whose union covered the circulation drivers. This union had a hammer on newspaper publishers. At the Miami hearings, I learned Babe was the liaison between Jimmy Hoffa, head of the Teamsters International, and the Cleveland Mafia. The hearings developed interlocking connections and revealed that the headquarters of the Cleveland group was the Italian-American Brotherhood (IAB) on Mayfield Road in Little Italy, run by Tony Milano, reputed underboss who worked under the real boss, "Big Al" Polizzi. In this clique were Johnny DeMarco and "Johnny King" Angersola, with his brothers Fred and George. The Jewish mob, known as the Cleveland Syndicate, included Louis "Lou Rhody" Rothkopf, Morris Kleinman, and Moe Dalitz. Dalitz operated gambling joints in Cleveland and in Newport and Covington, Kentucky, with the blessings of Big Al's Mayfield Road gang. Others in the Syndicate were Sam Tucker, Ruby Kolod, and in later years, Lou Rhody's nephew, Bernard "Bernie" Rothkopf. He later became president of the MGM Grand Hotel in Las Vegas. The hearings disclosed ties to Buckeye Enterprises, which controlled various other gambling concessions and was the hidden link between the Mayfield Road gang and the Cleveland Syndicate.

As I sat in the hot, crowded Florida courtroom, I recalled our U.S. Customs director, Mrs. Bernice Pyke, telling me during long interviews about Prohibition days in Cleveland when the Cleveland Syndicate ran armor-plated, rum-running craft on Lake Erie, bringing booze from Canada into spots along Cleveland's lakefront. She opened a closet in her federal office to point to a cache of unopened liquor bottles seized in one of many raids. She said from rum-running the gangsters went on to illegal distilleries and bootlegging. Based on Mrs. Pyke's memories of her pioneering political life in the Democratic Party, I later wrote a series of stories on her life for the *News*. In the bloody, internecine warfare of the 1930s, families fought each other, and in 1934 a truce was called, not just locally but nationally. The Kefauver hearings laid out the "crime" territories granted families of mobsters as a result of the truce. Meyer Lansky got Florida. Bugsy Siegal got the far west and Nevada. Frank Costello got the Eastern Syndicate and the Atlantic Coast, along with slots. Legs Lepke got the garment industry. Lucky Luciano got narcotics and prostitution. "Trigger Mike" Coppola got numbers. The Cleveland Syndicate got Arizona, and Al Capone's heirs got Chicago.

The Associated Press carried the daily stories, but my copious Miami notes were the start of a voluminous file I kept for decades. When the Kefauver hearings came to the Cleveland Federal Courthouse in 1952, a group of reporters got the assignment. I covered the interrogation of the major bookkeeper for the wire services. Webb Seeley and Howard Beaufait, veteran *News* reporters, handled the main witness testimony and wrote daily stories. These hearings gave the public a behind-the-scenes look at gambling as it related to racetracks and sports pages of daily newspapers and sporting news publications. The public read of the glitter of casinos, show girls, slots, and the fabulous wire services that reported daily racetrack results. This wasn't Wall Street or what you'd read in the business pages, but it sure was Big Business Bucks.

Kefauver and Company focused on this underbelly of nationwide gambling, but I also got a snapshot of Cleveland's newspaper history. A handful of the men destined for the criminal syndicates worked for newspapers during the bloody circulation wars of the early 1900s. Marcus Alonzo Hanna, who installed William McKinley into the White House in 1896, eventually fought Cleveland reform mayor, Thomas L. Johnson, for the control of the city streetcar system. Hanna decided he needed a newspaper for his voice and so bought the morning *Leader* and the afternoon *News*. Incidentally, the daughter of Daniel P. Rhodes, a big coal and iron merchant, married Mark Hanna. When Hanna died, his son, Daniel Rhodes Hanna, became editor. Dan was editor of the *News* when I joined the staff in 1944. Cleveland's bloody, head-crushing newspaper wars were history when I started, but old clippings revealed how Mark Hanna's *Leader* and *News* hawkers fought in the streets against vendors of the *Plain Dealer* and the *Press*.

Dan Hanna brought Arthur B. "Mickey" McBride, a twenty-seven-year-old scrappy redhead from Chicago, to Cleveland in 1913 to run the *News*'s circulation department. Mickey recruited a bunch of tough Italian guys from Mayfield Road and the Old Angle, an Irish conclave, to beat up the competitors' street vendors. Eventually these toughies from Mayfield Road became the Mafia Brotherhood of the Cleveland Syndicate. The files of the Kefauver committee concluded that the Cleveland Syndicate—Kefauver called them the "Cleveland Boys"—were Maurice "Mo" Dalitz, Morris Kleinman, Sam Tucker, and Lou Rothkopf. And the files also found that the boys in Cleveland ran the stills that turned out illegal booze to a headquarters in the old Hollenden Hotel, to the wire service of Mickey McBride (who left the paper for an independent wire service), and to a string of casinos in Kentucky and later the Desert Inn in Nevada, the Stardust in Tucson, and operations in Miami Beach. The files named principal lieutenants in the Syndicate such as Irishman Thomas J. McGinty of the old Harvard and Thomas gambling clubs in Cleveland and Charles A.

"Chuck" Polizzi. Messick told me the Jewish Syndicate "hid behind the shadow of the Mayfield Road mob for years." McBride had long loyal friendships with his former Italian toughies in circulation at the *News,* and he eventually built much of Coral Gables, Florida, with their help. In Cleveland he owned the Yellow Cab Company and the Rams professional football team, later the Cleveland Browns.

And McBride influenced the Cleveland community in other ways as well. One of his old newsboys, "Mushy" Wexler, later graduated to circulation truck driver before various turns in his life led him to running the most famous bar and grille in the city, Theatrical Grill on Short Vincent. A handful of girl reporters were only too happy to lunch with Sobul at this bar and grille, where he introduced us to the town's racy characters, including Shondor "Shon" Birns, the club bouncer, and Mushy himself. I found Mushy's record in the Kefauver files. When he left the *News,* he went into the wire service business with his brother-in-law, Sam "Gameboy" Miller. Miller developed *Empire News,* a track-wire service. It was pretty obvious that McBride, Wexler, Miller, and others observed how the legitimate wire services, Associated Press (AP), United Press International (UPI), and International News Service (INS), worked in the legitimate news field. And in essence these guys, in their daring gambling ventures, were "graduates" of the newspaper business, quickly adapting it to race results. *Empire* was an Ohio division of the Cleveland-based *Continental Press,* cofounded by Mickey when he left the *News.*

Kefauver described *Continental Press* as "a vast organization which took over the job of supplying race information to the nation's bookies, when Moses 'Mo' Annenberg of Philadelphia went to prison for income tax evasion in 1940." Mo Annenberg was circulation manager of the *Hearst Journal American* in Philadelphia. After prison he built an empire of newspapers, magazines, and racing publications. Mo Annenberg's son, Walter H. Annenberg, took over *Triangle Publications* and the *Daily Racing Form* when his dad was jailed. Walter founded *TV Digest* and later *TV Guide,* and he was U.S. ambassador to Greater Britain and Ireland from 1968 through 1974. He also founded the Annenberg School of

News city room with city editor John R. Rees (center) giving the author an assignment. January 1955; *Cleveland News* photograph.

Communications at the University of Pennsylvania and a similar school at the University of Southern California in Los Angeles.

As with the other boys, there was a Cleveland connection to the Annenbergs. When Mo went to jail, the general manager of his Nationwide News Service, supplying handbooks to thousands of operators with data on races run and coming up, was James Ragen. Ragen was Mickey McBride's brother-in-law. Ragen had been circulation manager of Hanna's *Leader* in 1913, and, in 1946, he was murdered in a Chicago hospital room during the "Wire Service Wars" there. The Pioneer News Service, owned in Chicago by Annenberg and Ragen, wound up in the hands of the Al Capone Syndicate in the later 1940s. While Ragen and McBride worked for the Hannas and their papers, Thomas "Tommy" Jefferson McGinty, an Irish tough guy, was the strong-armed man for the *Plain Dealer.* From there McGinty ran the town's two big gambling clubs,

Harvard and Thomas, and cops told Kefauver that McGinty was the force of the Irish underground who became the highest ranking non-Jewish member of the Cleveland Syndicate. I daresay not many of today's reporters know this, and it strikes me as humorous our former lady mayor, Jane Campbell, a bit on the sanctimonious side, wanted to reestablish gambling joints . . . err . . . casinos . . . in downtown Cleveland. I wonder if she knows of the city's gambling history and the reformers who tried to shut it down.

In the forties, when my reporting career started, most of the old-timer newsmen knew McBride, McGinty, Birns, Wexler, Triscaro, and that ilk, and polished off a few beers in their company at downtown bars after football and baseball games. These old-timers never had trouble getting them to talk, mostly off the record, on big crime stories. Actually, my husband, Howard Beaufait, was an old friend of Mickey's from the *News* circulation days. We saw him frequently at daily mass at St. John's Cathedral on E. 9th, from where we walked down Superior with him. His office was around E. 16th, and the newsroom where we worked was at E. 18th. My husband received great football tickets from Mickey when he owned the Rams, and yes, we attended his funeral where FBI agents copied numbers of license plates. Incidentally, my aunt Nellie O'Donnell Smart was a dispatcher for Yellow Cab, Mickey's company, and another aunt, Annie O'Donnell Meehan, was a secretary to city safety director Eliot Ness. Ness, the "gangbuster," was brought from Chicago to Cleveland by *Press* editor Louis B. Seltzer and other civic reformers to smash the McGinty Harvard and Thomas Clubs. Small world, eh?

While some editors and civic leaders took hypocritical views of gambling, the afternoon *Press* and *News* papers were fighting over whose circulation drivers would get the Stox or Final editions into the hands of the numbers runners the speediest. The Stox or Final editions, which were the last of the three daily editions printed, at 3 P.M. every day, showed the U.S. Treasury numbers, used by the illegal numbers' kings to pay off betters. Once an intern at the *News,* on his last day at work, switched the treasury numbers, and since our paper beat the *Press* to the numbers' guys, payoffs were made on wrong numbers. City police had a time figuring out what caused a bunch of knifings overnight until they learned the true numbers were printed in the *Press,* whose drivers delivered the paper after the *News.*

One afternoon when I was subbing for Peter Bellamy, our theater beat reporter, I interviewed Peter Lind Hays and his gorgeous wife Mary Healy at the paper. They were scheduled to perform at Lake County's swankiest gambling joint, the infamous Mounds Club. My feature story appeared the next day after the opening night of Peter and Mary's sophisticated show. As the Broadway couple opened their act and as applause filled the club, masked hoods swarmed in, holding up the moneyed crowd. Women were hustled into restrooms and stripped of their diamonds and rubies. Men lost their trousers and bankrolls. It was a clean sweep. The heist was big time but never solved. Peter Hays later called to thank me with sardonic humor for the great publicity, adding that management had cancelled their next week's engagement thanks to the hooded goons.

Lots of times I was assigned to crime news because I knew the players and had lots of files on them. When asked what my beat was, I'd say "organized crime." That usually caught some attention. And in Cleveland, because of the stretch of organized crime in many neighborhoods, people who questioned me usually added a personal memory of a local "hood." Cleveland was small town, and its citizens were "hip" to numbers' joints, cheat spots, and the private clubs that had pornographic shows. There was also culture, of course—the museums, theaters, churches—but the action was with the subculture.

-30-

-8-

Sam Sheppard Murder Case

Summer, Sex, Suburbia

I tire easily of the name Sam Sheppard. The story of the man convicted of killing his pregnant wife consumed more than ten years of my reportorial life, mainly because I became a sort of expert on the subject. For years after the crime, when unexpected news stories about Sam, his love life after prison, and his legal forays would arise, I'd usually get the assignment because I was on the story from the beginning, when it all started.

On July 4, 1954, Marilyn Reese Sheppard was murdered in her Bay Village home, savagely beaten and stabbed in her bedroom. Marilyn's husband, Sam, an osteopathic physician-surgeon, was convicted the same year of second-degree murder. But on everyone's lips that holiday weekend was "Who was the killer?" That was the question of the hour in this small lakeside community. In days immediately following the tragedy all sorts of stories floated among Sheppard neighbors on Lake Road—rumors about burglars and intruders and furtive vagrants and sexual infidelities. But in domestic homicides the investigative focus is usually on the spouse, and this was certainly the case here. Sam was the focus from day one. The suspicion was reinforced as rumors of Sam's illicit peccadilloes started to become public and as his and his family's intimate lives came under the scrutiny of official eyes. Bay Village officials, at a disadvantage in handling major homicide, immediately called on the services of Cuyahoga County officials, including County Coroner Dr. Samuel R. Gerber, and experienced City of Cleveland police homicide officers. The investigation into Marilyn's death thus began within the hours of her death with the coroner and city detectives on the scene with two Bay Village policemen. Thus the task was before these men of gathering every scrap of visible crime evidence at the scene and then conferring with ranking Cleveland officers, preparing material for an eventual prosecution of a suspect.

Cleveland police sergeant Harold C. Lockwood was assigned to the case and charged with piecing together the puzzle based on written reports and interviews with the cops first on the scene. He prepared a scenario of the crime based on the physical condition of the murder scene inside the Sheppard home and the surrounding area. Lockwood and Detective John Doyle worked on this report under the direction of Cleveland deputy inspector James McArthur, who, in turn, would help the prosecutor's office prepare an indictment, a prelude to the trial. The Lockwood-Doyle report of July 25, 1954, that landed on McArthur's desk stated that the evidence tended "to prove a strong case against the victim's husband."

The first red flag raised was Sam's intimacies with Susan Hayes, a former Bay View Hospital medical technician, and Sam's denial of the long-standing affair. The report stated that "it was no fly-by-night romance." The second item in the report was Sam's purchase of two large, eight-inch knives at the May Company department store prior to the murder. Sam was positively identified as the buyer, though later a cousin of mine, an assistant treasurer of May Company, had proof that Sam returned the knives to the store for a refund.

While Marilyn's dead body was found in her bed, detectives found Marilyn's watch on the floor of the downstairs den with blood on the face and band, and Lockwood speculated that Marilyn had prepared for bed, dressed in pajamas, and then became involved in an argument with Sam downstairs, in either the kitchen or the den. The report claimed that "Sam was known to have a terrific temper, having knocked Marilyn down the stairs about four years before the murder, and as a result she had a miscarriage. They were known to have argued over Sue [Sam's mistress], as well as the fact that Sam was very friendly to Dr. [Lester] Hoversten, an old friend of Sam's and a houseguest of the Sheppards' over the holiday weekend, and insisted on having him as a guest despite Marilyn's dislike of him."

Lockwood theorized that the Sheppards started fighting downstairs, where Sam took off his corduroy coat and threw his undershirt in with dirty clothes lying nearby. He conjectured that Sam chased Marilyn into the den, the farthest room from where their son, Chip, slept upstairs, and physically assaulted her, causing blood to be drawn and her watch to be ripped from her arm, leaving blood flecks on the watch. Indicating the struggle were two statuettes found lying broken on the den floor. The detectives believed that two different weapons could have been used on Marilyn and that one of the statuettes could have caused the smaller wounds on Marilyn's face. The report said blood was on Sam's leather chair in the den. This report, which later guided the preparatory trial work for prosecutors, said that Marilyn, bleeding, either ran or was carried upstairs, where the most serious assault was made. It was unclear whether she climbed into bed or was thrown into bed unconscious. Sam proceeded to finish her off, the report said, with repeated blows to the left side of her head. Lockwood conjectured that then Sam, wearing only brown trousers and shoes, checked first on their sleeping son before setting about cleaning up the gruesome scene, first wiping the railing and his shoes clean with toilet paper.

Sam's injuries to his face and neck could have resulted from Sam missing the top of the stairs at the back of his house leading to Lake Erie, as he surely would have been in a highly emotional state, going in darkness to wash blood off himself in the lake. (Sam, taken to Bay View Hospital, was x-rayed for swelling on the right side of his face, loose teeth in the upper jaw, and three-inch bruises at the base of his skull. In public, Sam wore a large orthopedic neck collar.) The fact that Sam put his watch, key chain, and fraternity ring in a green cloth bag and tossed it into underbrush at the bottom of a path, Lockwood contended, lent credence to a theory that he was on his way to clean up in the lake. The bag had been used to store motor boat tools before he replaced them with his personal items.

The Lockwood report continued: After Sam's emotions cooled, he returned to the den and ransacked the drawers and contents of the desk to make it look as though a burglary had taken place. The hour and fifty minutes between Marilyn's death (which had been established in an autopsy) and the time Sam called neighbor Spencer Houk, Bay Village mayor, Sam washed himself, straightened up signs of a downstairs struggle, secreted the murder weapon, cleaned blood off the upstairs steps, rearranged the desk drawers, composed himself, and called for help.

The Lockwood report was not made public but was the backbone of the prosecution case, as we reporters in the courtroom learned. Prosecutors developed the points in the report to obtain firsthand testimony from various witnesses, such as the Boy Scouts who found the green bag on the hillside; Bay Village officer Fred Drenkhan, the first policeman on the scene; Mayor Houk, whom Sam called for help; and, ultimately, the femme fatale in the case, Sam's mistress, Susan Hayes. These various factors built a prosecutorial circumstantial murder case, and while the charge of first-degree murder was considered, the prosecutor rejected premeditation, instead substituting a crime of passion and second-degree murder.

There was a drumbeat of stories. Cleveland's three competing daily newspapers and a young television presence were focused on sex in suburbia—including couple swapping—that summer. It became a contest among reporters—who would get the best story each day? But every available reporter got an assignment to go to Bay Village, and we talked to everyone no matter how peripheral. Sam Sheppard's brother Dr. Steve Sheppard became a one-man PR agency for his brother and the medical dynasty family of three brothers and a father running Bay View. Steve gave personal letters from Marilyn's aunt to Severino P. Severino of

Forest City Newshawks Swarm Scene

Doris O'Donnell

Eugene Segal

Karl Rauschkolb

Bill Levy

Doris O'Donnell

Todd Simon

Prosecutor
Thomas J. Parrino

Pat Garling

John G. Blair

Dr. Samuel R. Gerber

Robert J. Drake

Forest City Log spread of pictures featuring reporters and photographers investigating the Marilyn Sheppard murder. Ca. 1954.

the *News,* which were published. Steve wildly pointed accusing fingers at his suspects. He urged William J. (Bill) Corrigan, the tenacious criminal attorney the family had hired, to investigate every hitchhiker, fisherman, and bum that had passed through Bay Village that summer.

At that time, during the buildup to the first criminal trial, little light shone on Dick Eberling, a local window washer who cut his finger on a kitchen screen when he washed windows at the Sheppard home. Dick told me Marilyn gave him a Band-Aid for the cut. Police did investigate Eberling, who was later accused of burglarizing about three hundred homes in the West Shore neighborhoods where he washed windows. Years later, in 2000, Eberling became the Sheppard family's prime suspect in a civil suit brought against the State of Ohio for financial reimbursement in the alleged wrongful imprisonment of Dr. Sam Sheppard. The family lost the case when the jury reaffirmed Sam's guilt.

But in the summer of 1954, we reporters were sleuthing and reporting. And the law was trying desperately to interview Sam, who was kept under wraps at the family's Bay View Hospital by brother Steve and Bill Corrigan. Sam finally consented to a downtown interview by two Cuyahoga County detectives, but the real heat on Sam came from editorial demands of *Press* editor Louie (as he was known by staff and friends) Seltzer *and* his hotshot city editor, Louie Clifford. Front-page headlines shouted: "Who Speaks for Marilyn?" "Why Isn't Someone in Jail?" They inferred a double standard of justice for a doctor from a wealthy suburb. The headlines and stories were incendiary and put pressure on both law enforcement and the Sheppards.

During the two summer months before the September trial of Sam Sheppard, I had a few headlines. When Assistant County Prosecutor Thomas J. Parrino brought Susan Hayes back from her home in California, he placed her under police guard in the Hotel Carter. I virtually lived in the corridor outside her room until policewomen finally ejected me. Later, when I learned she was living in her parents' Rocky River apartment, I staked out the apartment house, hoping someone would come out. With the top down on my convertible, I settled in to read and watch. To my great surprise, one day Susan ran across the lawn to my car and jumped in, saying she had to get away from her family. "Just let's ride around."

Susan was a slender, auburn-haired young woman with large brown eyes, a young Katherine Hepburn type. For several hours we drove in, out, and around several western suburbs. She said Parrino had prepared her for the witness chair, so she could not tell me about their conversations, but she did give me some background on her job at Bay View Hospital, described the hospital parties and dances where she and Sam became an item, and said that she decided to leave Ohio for California where other former Bay View Hospital medical technicians had found higher-paying jobs. Yes, she told me, she had seen Sam there earlier in the spring, and she definitely believed his family, his parents, would never consent to his divorce from Marilyn. She said repeatedly that she didn't believe Sam capable of murder.

While I missed an afternoon deadline that day, I had enough copy for several days' stories. I was pretty sympathetic to her. Of course, on the stand she had more to say about the affair, about Sam's gifts to her, and about her sharing a bedroom with Sam at the home of mutual doctor friends in California while Marilyn was staying in another city.

I also wrote the story of the suicide-death of Sam's mother, Ethel. I had been parked outside the Rocky River home of Steve Sheppard, where she was staying, when an ambulance pulled up for her body.

The Sheppard doctors were not strangers to the public prior to Marilyn's murder. They were self-promoters of their hospital and its services. As osteopaths, they were held to a lower standard of Ohio state medical regulations regarding publicity than were registered medical doctors. After Dr. Richard Sheppard Sr. moved his small Euclid Avenue clinic from downtown Cleveland to the old Leisy beer-baron estate in Bay Village and gave it the "hospital" name, he looked for publicity opportunities. Thanks to its east-west highway location, the hospital handled numerous traffic accidents and had direct contact with many police officers in the Shore communities. It was well known to us reporters that the three brothers would take turns calling the daily papers with stories of their life-saving medical skills.

Once the *News*'s city editor turned Sam over to me after our noontime edition had gone to press. He told me how he'd saved the life of a Fairview Park woman who had suffered multiple injuries in an auto accident. He described setting her legs in casts and inserting hundreds of stitches on her face and body that put her back together. We ran a front-page story in the final stock edition.

The woman was Julie Lossman of Lakewood, the wife of a foreign-car dealer who later raced cars with Sam on Put-in-Bay Island. Sam Giamo, a *Press* reporter, and I heard more about her while we haunted Bay View after the murder and decided to call on her together. We'd all had doors slammed in our faces before, and we were game for another rejection. To our great surprise, Julie invited us in with something like, "Well, everybody else knows about it so come on in." She told us that after her accident she and Sam had numerous trysts in secluded places in the Rocky River reservation as well as in the Sheppard Clinic in Fairview Park. Sam and I had a scoop, or so we thought. Our editors nixed the story, preferring to wait for her official testimony from the witness stand. She wasn't called once the county prosecutors decided Susan Hayes was the "motive" gal, their case being that the errant doctor eliminated his pregnant wife for his marital freedom.

But the big story was the trial. When it finally began in September, our *News* staff was assigned in relays to provide up-to-the-minute reports on the testimony from the witness stand. The local press had chairs inside the railing, and Cuyahoga County Common Pleas Court judge Edward J. Blythin relegated out-of-town reporters to back benches, leaving only two rear benches for the families and the public, and even that on a first-come, first-serve basis. Our knees were our desks. With three daily deadlines, we kept our eyes on the clock. One reporter would run out with notes to the phone as another reporter quietly slipped into her place. This system worked fine until hotshot television star Dorothy Kilgallen waltzed into town. She was known nationally for being a regular on "What's My Line?" but to New Yorkers she was a King Features columnist who wrote "The Voice of Broadway" column. She was a star reporter, and *Newsweek* described her as "a kitten-faced columnist with a catty tongue." She had a personalized style of reporting, and she used it unsparingly in the Sheppard case.

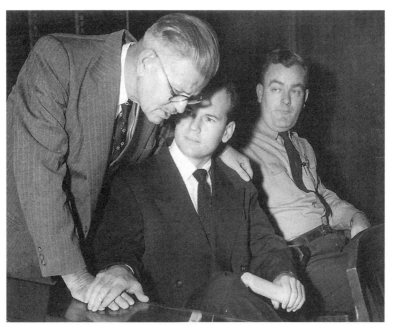

Dr. Richard Sheppard (left) confers with son Sam during the first trial for the murder of Sam's wife, Marilyn. Deputy James Kilroy looks on. 1954; Photograph by Perry Cragg, *Cleveland News.*

Kilgallen and her husband, Dick Kollmar, a producer and former actor, had a live, early-morning daily radio broadcast from their New York apartment. Commuting to Cleveland on early flights for the Sheppard trial was tricky for her. At first she arrived on time—but frazzled. A tiny hat was pinned to her flyaway hair, seams were split on her cotton blouses, and her lipstick was awry. This was a woman in a terrific hurry, one trying to cover all the bases. Yet she was a big hit with the locals, especially the male reporters who interviewed her. I, too, was impressed, knowing and admiring the reputation of her father, Jimmy Kilgallen, a flamboyant Hearst police reporter.

Everything was fine in the courtroom as long as Kilgallen was on time for the prompt 9:00 A.M. trial. Judge Blythin, known for his thick Welsh burr, was a stickler for process, and when he said 9:00 A.M., that did not mean 9:05 A.M. Everyone had to be in place. On one day of the trial, Kilgallen made a late entrance, causing a disturbance to the entire courtroom, from judge to jury, defendant to spectator. After that the trial courtroom doors were locked sharply at 9:00 A.M. and guarded by a deputy. If she was late, Dorothy couldn't get in—and we couldn't get out for our relays of spot news. This, of course, made us *all* angry—our editors at us, we at her, and her at the judge.

Since the *News* carried her column, at noon recesses a locked-out Dorothy would grab the *News* people for a summary of the morning's testimony. The guys would fill her in, and as fast as a bat she knocked out a column on her portable typewriter. Once, spotting me, she called, "Boy," and handed me her copy for our city room. I refused to run her copy. I told her to take it herself to the *News,* just two blocks from the courthouse. Needless to say, she found a willing male reporter to run it over. Despite her manner, I was really impressed with how quickly she knocked out a story based on other reporters' notes. But things got uncomfortable when Dorothy's personal style of reporting included poking fun at the names of Chief Eaton and Patrolman Drenkhan of Bay Village, calling them "eating 'n drinking" and "Boy Scouts," and when she wrote that adultery was not murder. Eventually Nat Howard killed her column, never running it again during the trial.

Years later, when the Sheppard appeals went through the appellate courts, Kilgallen surprised a New York Press Club audience with the news that Judge Blythin—before the strict media rules were in place—had told her in a closed meeting that "Sam was guilty as hell." What a bombshell. Asked why it took her more than ten years to expose the judge, she came up with a weak excuse. This revelation found its way into Sam's pleadings for a new trial before the U.S. Supreme Court, which remanded it back to the Ohio Common Pleas Court for a new trial. For those of us who knew Judge Blythin, Kilgallen's remarks were shocking. The man never said so much as "God darn it." His family, including a son who was a detective and son-in-law Bob Dvorak, a *Plain Dealer* reporter, came to his rescue. But the damage was done; the judge's integrity was shot. (Incidentally, on November 8, 1965, Dorothy Kilgallen was found dead in her twenty-two-room, five-story townhouse in New York City. She was fifty-two. The cause of death was a combination of alcohol and pills.)

As I walked into Judge Blythin's courtroom in September 1954, like the rest of my colleagues I waited for a shoe to drop or some unexpected drama. We remained neutral on Sam's guilt or innocence. It was a circumstantial case. Prosecutors John Mahon, an aging legal eagle; Tom Parrino, a bright, aggressive lawyer; and Saul Danaceau, an experienced prosecutor, were low-key yet vigorous. Defense attorney Bill Corrigan, thatched white hair askew, had a ferocious reputation to live up to, although the years hung on him like a heavy jacket. Cases are built brick by brick, and the trial proceeded in a classic style—like building a pyramid. The courtroom was small, and we all eyeballed each other as the trial droned on.

There were long hours of testimony, full days of court. The Sheppards' Lake Road neighbor Spencer Houk recounted the call from Sam and his rush over to the house with his wife. Marilyn's close friend and neighbor, Nancy Ahern (who had encouraged Marilyn to play golf and join a country club, even though Sam objected) told of Marilyn ordering a dishwasher, which was installed while Sam was away, and of the argument that ensued when Sam came home and found it. A big moment was the dramatic unveiling of a wax model of Marilyn Sheppard's head, sans hair, showing some thirty-five individual wounds. The jurors gasped when Dr. Lester Adelson lifted a white covering from the bald head. Sam buried his head in his arms on the trial table. And the courtroom was hushed when Susan Hayes, in a demure white-collared dress, admitted on the stand to her illicit liaison with Sam. Less dramatic, but no less memorable, was Sam, who in his squeaky voice droned "I don't know" over and over again in response to cross-examination by the prosecution.

We all tried reading the jurors' reactions, and I especially had my eye on one juror who worked with close friends of mine. He never made eye contact with me, and his face gave away nothing. And we kept our eyes on Sam, as well. He sat motionless, expressionless next to his legal co-counsel, Corrigan and Fred Garmone. Photographers were banned from the courtroom, although at recess a few were allowed to take interior shots of the empty room. My wily veteran photographer Perry Cragg got permission from Dr. Richard Sheppard to photograph him with Sam during a recess at the trial table. As the senior doctor was set to pose, Perry—using a trick as old as the world—said he had specks on his glasses. The good doctor removed them, wiped them with a handkerchief, and Perry snapped the photo of father and son. Of course in print it appeared as though the elder man was crying. Later, in January 1955, when Bill Corrigan filed an appeal based on trial errors he cited the photo as an example of the breach of the judge's rules.

I watched the trial as though I was on the jury. In my heart I believed Sam killed his wife in rage, over a buildup of many things—his infidelities, his wife's pregnancy, the new dishwasher, Marilyn's attempt to forge a wider social life outside of the hospital crowd, to break out on her own socially. There were so many signs of Sam's frustration and fury. He wanted a divorce. He wanted out of this marriage. He was trapped. Sam's body language in court disturbed me too. It said: "Steve always got me out of trouble. He will now." Sam sat there like a guy in another world. "This bad dream will fade, and I'll be back in California with Sue." I wrote him a note asking for an interview. He wrote back saying he would see me after the trial.

I didn't get my interview with Sam until well after the trial, until after he had been released from prison and was together with his second wife, a German blonde named Arianne Tebbenjohans, who had been his prison pen pal. Sam and I met again shortly before he died. (Arianne had divorced him and moved back to Germany, and Sam was on the verge of a third marriage.) Reporter Harry Stainer and I met with Sam in the backyard of his home in Bay Village to talk about his traffic arrest in a small Ohio town. A photographer and I followed his trail through southern Ohio, where he was barhopping with a bunch of his ex-convict friends. He didn't want to talk about it, remarking only that I wore a purple suit during his first trial. We never ran the story about this phase of his private life. It all seemed too sad, from doctor to . . . well, nothing.

The first trial wound down and finally ended on December 21, with an optimistic thread coming from the Sheppard camp that Sam would get a "Christmas verdict." Deliberation took five days, and the jurors came back with "guilty in the second degree." The Sheppards—Sam and his family on the rear bench—were stunned and shattered. The jurors slipped away, refusing to talk to reporters. Much later Juror No. 4, Bill Lamb, said the first vote, after sixty-five days of trial, was 6-6. He described the jurors as "very nice people, good heads. Nobody was demanding or domineering." Each day, he said, someone changed his or her mind. "We wanted him to be innocent, but we just couldn't come to that conclusion. . . . In the end the man was guilty. There was no debate in any of our minds. That was the only verdict we could come up with."

In 1964, just shy of ten years after Sam's second-degree murder conviction, the U.S. Supreme Court overturned the verdict of the 1954 trial. The appeal was led by a young, hotshot, Boston lawyer, F. Lee Bailey, who won a retrial because the defendant was denied a fair trial due to the "circuslike" environment surrounding the trial. *Plain Dealer* reporter Terry Sheridan and others covered the second trial, but I was in the courtroom when the verdict of "not guilty" came in and when Sam slammed the table with his fist and shouted his innocence and yelled for his wife Arianne. F. Lee Bailey crowed for years about this victory. He would have had less to boast about had he put his alcohol- and drug-addicted client on the stand this time around. Had Sam sat in the witness box this time around, Prosecutor John T. Corrigan had a big surprise awaiting him: a convicted bank-robber-turned-FBI-informant as a rebuttal witness to Sam.

Corrigan confided to me that he had deputies bring Edmund Eugene Flott, aka Frenchy, from the state penitentiary to testify to confidential conversations he and Sam shared in their prison cells. Later, retired police captain George Sperber gave me an original carbon copy of Flott's statements made to both the FBI and Sergeant Lockwood. The statements indicated that Flott would reveal damaging testimony about Sam's state of mind while he was serving his sentence. Flott said Sam sketched out a plan that he was to carry out when Flott was released. Flott was to contact both

Spencer Houk and Sam's old friend Lester Hoversten and force each man to write, under threat of death, a confession to the murder of Marilyn Sheppard. Once Flott had the confessions, he was to kill the men. Sam promised Flott that a prominent Cleveland attorney would pay "a bundle" for the jobs. Whether a jury would have believed the Flott testimony is speculative, but it would have cast a black shadow over Sam's claims of innocence. I tried to trace Flott, who was placed in the Federal witness protection program for his cooperation with the feds on bank burglaries after he left Ohio's prison system, but had no luck. Relatives believed that he managed a restaurant in Colorado, where he later died.

I covered another murder trial in which F. Lee Bailey represented a client charged with killing his parents. In a bar one night, I cornered Bailey and his legal team to discuss the Sheppard appeal. I wanted to know if Bailey used Corrigan's sixteen points of error he alleged occurred during the first trial for his own case before the Supreme Court, in which he demanded a new trial. It had been a point of contention among Corrigan followers that Bailey did not do original work. We were right. Bailey admitted he used all of Corrigan's points. My fellow reporters and I were angered not only by Bailey's laziness but because so many of Corrigan's points were biased and untrue. There was no "Roman Holiday" or "circus" in Judge Blythin's courtroom, as Bailey described it. If anything, the defense counsel led the Supreme Court Justices to confuse the courtroom with the coroner's inquest, which took place long before the trial and miles away at Normandy School in Bay Village. Virtually all of the reporters who had covered the original case—from Bob Considine to Theo Wilson to the out-of-town hotshots—wrote to the U.S. Supreme Court to correct the record. But the Court made it clear that they thought it was time to slap the newspapers' hands; they thought the Fourth Estate had gone too far in pretrial publicity. Ironically, and endlessly irksome to reporters, was that much of the pretrial "stuff" came from lawyers with agendas.

But this hollow victory wasn't enough for the Sheppard family. Sam and Marilyn's only son, Sam Reese Sheppard, sued the State of Ohio for $9 million for the wrongful imprisonment of Dr.

Sam Sheppard. Plaintiffs and the defense—in this case the State of Ohio, represented by the Cuyahoga County prosecutor's office—employed the latest in forensic technology to retry the civil case. And the Sheppard team introduced a new suspect, Richard Eberling, claiming the former window washer and convicted murderer was the real killer of Marilyn Sheppard.

I had a direct connection to Richard (Dick) Eberling. His roommate at his Westlake home was Obie Henderson, who sat next to me at the *Plain Dealer*. Obie, a crack stenographer, came to the paper from an executive secretarial job at a major railroad company to handle an innovative reporting scheme. (From the road, we dictated stories into tape, and Obie transcribed our stories on the typewriter for the editors.) My husband and I and Fred Mollenlopf and his wife, Martha, and others from the paper were even guests at the men's home. (We didn't stay long, however, once Howard Beaufait appraised the rich furnishings and objets d'art, suspecting them stolen.) Later, after I was working in Pennsylvania, 1989 Eberling and Henderson were convicted of the murder of Mrs. Ethel Durkin, a wealthy elderly woman they were caring for. Obie and I kept in touch until I said publicly that I did not believe Dick killed Marilyn but that he probably did kill Mrs. Durkin because both of them were "greedy." (From what I saw, Dick and Obie craved the finer things of life and were planning a retirement home in Lookout Mountain, Tennessee. Eventually the prosecutor's office hauled back antiques and collectibles from Tennessee, including items Dick had stolen from Cleveland City Hall when he worked there for Mayor Ralph S. Perk.) Obie and I are back in touch again, but Dick and I continued to carry on a long correspondence, and I have boxes of the letters he wrote me from prison. Dick called me shortly before he died in July 1998 to tell me he had been gang-raped in prison after guards had taken away his wheelchair. I first called his minister and then the warden. The minister called, but there was no official response from the warden's office. Upon his death, Dick was buried in a prison graveyard near a fenced pasture with mooing cows, with only a number to mark his grave. At what passed for a funeral, I met Jim Neff, a former *Plain Dealer* reporter (whom I had never known), and in casual conversation he gave me the distinct impression he had a deathbed confession from Dick that would be featured in Neff's upcoming book. But when I later read the book—I was not impressed with it—I was struck not by Dick's alleged guilt but by how, in all his conversations with me and those conveyed in the book, Dick made it clear he lived in a fantasy world. This was the same fantasy world he portrayed to others and to me in his many letters, always talking about movie deals, book deals, and television deals in which he would "tell who the real killer was." He was a sad man living a tortuous life.

Chip Sheppard and his legal team worked hard to clear Sam's name, but ultimately they failed. The State of Ohio won the final Sheppard case through its meticulous reinvestigation and convincing courtroom presentation, including the revelation that the "harp" from a bedroom lamp in Marilyn's room was likely the murder weapon.

Crimes leave a lot of what-ifs. I never wavered in my belief that Sam killed Marilyn. I worked with reporters who insisted it was "only circumstantial," but I say the right man went to jail. While living in Pennsylvania during the final trial, I was contacted by the media for views on the case and stated my beliefs. After this, Chip Sheppard called me from his Cambridge, Massachusetts, residence and threatened me, an incident I reported to the Pittsburgh office of the FBI, because I inferred it was a threat of physical harm. And I also had another harassing call from a member of Steve Sheppard's family.

I did not always see eye-to-eye with the editorial policies of the *Cleveland Press* or like its raw headlines, demanding that someone speak for Marilyn. But I'm reminded of a quote from an unknown jurist that "the press does not simply publish information about trials but guards against the miscarriage of justice."

-30-

-9-

To the Soviet Union

One January day in 1956, Nat Howard bounded into the newsroom, stopping at my desk. "How would you like to go to Russia?" Per his usual practice, Nat had asked a cabbie what he wanted to read in the *News,* and the guy said, "Russia." I owe that faceless cabbie for a most memorable assignment.

Stunned, I asked: "How? What do you have in mind?" I was jolted by Nat's enthusiasm. He had given me assignments all over Ohio, in Washington, but never overseas! To go to Russia, the Soviet Union, and into the Communist world, that jolted me. I hoped he was not kidding—he wasn't. The cabbie had been in Berlin when the city was divided into American, British, and Russian zones after World War II, and he wanted to know now how the average citizen lived and what the people talked about. Nat was pleased, he said, with how I handled the assignment with the Jackson family, and he figured I could do a similar job in Moscow. His confidence in me was humbling, but what I did on the East Side hardly compared with talking to non-English-speaking Russians.

My head buzzed with the problems ahead—travel, language, communications, contacts—but I knew I could do it.

This was a big story, which meant research and planning. There was no time to lose, so I headed straightaway to the newspaper library to bone up on current events in the Union of Soviet Socialist Republics (USSR). And I didn't brag about the new assignment. Nat didn't call it a secret, but we realized that we would encounter a great deal of red tape (what else?) to get into the country. It seemed superfluous to send up rockets about a story that was only in the throes of birth. Nat never called editorial conferences to discuss ideas, but he floated them with managing editor Barry Mullaney. Nat was basically a one-man band when it came to picking a reporter and letting him run with a story. If big money was involved he had to persuade the board of the Forest City Publishing Company, which operated both the *Plain Dealer* and the *News,* of the venture's merits. Indeed, I. F. Freiberger, board chairman, initially hesitated to approve the $5,000 for the trip, not because of money but because he perceived dangers to a young woman alone in a Communist country. Eventually the board came through and the staff learned of my assignment, and I understood the natural resentment of several male counterparts, many of whom held high military rank in World War II and had served in the European and Pacific theaters. But Nat had picked me, and I had to prove myself.

I lost not a minute on researching with supercharged zeal. My first steps involved making calls to overseas travel agencies and the U.S. State Department to learn of any restrictions on travel to the USSR. A follow-up call to the Soviet Embassy in Washington, D.C., produced slim response other than my submitting a letter of intent. Our newspaper library had old clips on Five Year Plans and World War II stuff but nothing about ordinary people, schools, hospitals, or factories. I had to remind myself that the Soviet Union was a closed society. I read that one hotshot reporter, Walter Duranty of the *New York Times,* never wrote a word of Stalin's purge of millions, mostly the kulak class, who were comparable to our educated entrepreneurial class. What a tragedy! It took decades for that story to be printed.

Nat wanted the focus to be on people, their living conditions since the devastating war, and the struggles they had to deal with to create a stable society. I pored over the Cleveland Public Library's large Eastern European collection, which was unusually rich because of the city's ethnic culture. Heavy academic tomes were numerous and outdated, although I read some for a sense of Russian/Soviet politics and history. There were rare books written by most British tourist-writers, but again, they were not current. Recent photographs were rare, and the best available were of Soviet men and women taken for *Life* magazine by Margaret Bourke-White, the famous photographer who actually was in Russia during the war, snapping men and women assembling war goods and tractors. I had met her in the photographers' room of the *News,* where she developed her prints of steel works along the Cuyahoga River, which she called the "American Ruhr Valley." She was my idea of a savvy newswoman. I also read short stories by Chekhov and Dostoevsky, to get a feel for the literature and the culture.

Neighbors from Lithuania and Ukraine were helpful yet apprehensive about my trip. These neighbors were "up" on Soviet news, grim though it was in the 1950s, including the turbulence between the United States and the USSR. In 1953 the United States had detonated a hydrogen bomb, and in 1954 the USSR had exploded a hydrogen bomb. Soviet expansion into Southeast Asia forced the United States to create SEATO, the Southeast Asia Treaty Organization, a sort of NATO. President Dwight D. Eisenhower, a hardliner, however, failed to help freedom fighters in Hungary when the Soviet tanks moved into their lands in 1956. The Second World War was still a fresh memory, and I relied on local veterans, including cousins, who fought with Gen. George Patton's army in France and Germany and with Gen. Mark Clark in Italy. Nat was also a good tutor, being up-to-speed on international relations. He had served on the Wartime Censorship Board in Washington, D.C. He also had a fantastic memory for details. To my distress, the Soviet Embassy was almost a lost cause, but they deigned to send an application form and a request for a biography. The State Department simply sent measly one-page summaries on population, food output, steel production—all outdated material.

Nat gave me the assignment in January, and weeks started passing without any news. I memorized the Cyrillic alphabet. I badgered the Soviet Embassy. I even called a few congressmen and State Department friends. Then one day in March, out of the blue came a letter from the Soviets with a departure timetable and instructions to contact Cosmos Travel Agency in New York City. It was approved by the Soviets for flights and handled the conversion of dollars into rubles. But the waiting wasn't over yet, and I continued my studies while at the same time writing features, obits, shorts—not sitting around like a prima donna.

People eventually stopped asking about the trip. Still, I called on airline stewardess friends to learn the art of packing one small, soft suitcase, the only one allowed. The girls taught me to roll garments in nylon stockings, which saves space and is wrinkle-free. Pack nylon everything, they said, because it's easy to wash and dry. Take lots of toilet paper, stuff shoes with it. Take sink and bathtub plugs. Fill a sock with lots and lots of American pennies as souvenir gifts. Good stroke! I eventually packed one gray and white flecked wool suit that I made. A buyer at Halle's recommended several cashmere sweaters that were lightweight and warm. Three pairs of nylon panties. One black nylon half slip. One Black Watch plaid raincoat. One crushed knit ribbon hat. An extra pair of eyeglasses. Toothpaste, aspirin, shampoo. An extra pair of shoes. When I actually left Cleveland Hopkins Airport I wore a heavy brown tweed suit with a brown velvet collar, a gift of my sister-in-law, Marguerite O'Donnell. I wore that suit almost daily, as the raincoat was too light for the cold Russian May weather. Tucked into the suitcase were English-Russian and French-Russian dictionaries. I carried a small Hermes typewriter and a 35 mm camera a cousin had bought from a German soldier.

Finally, my departure day was April 26, 1956. There was no band, no hoopla, only a photographer and my mother and brother to see me off. Jack said: "Don't worry. If you fall in mud, you'll come up clean. As always." I simply wanted the Capital Airlines plane to whip me to New York, board Swissair, and get to Moscow. But Swissair, both in New York and in Zurich, Switzerland, gave me red-carpet treatment. They assigned Agent Eric Haupt as a per-

The author at the National Hotel Moscow, overlooking Red Square and the Kremlin. Ca. 1956; author's collection.

sonal guide, and they earned a bit of publicity over a young American reporter traveling alone to the Soviet Union. Eric escorted me to an elegant, modern, Zurich hotel, where I luxuriated in a deep feather bed for a brief nap before we hustled off on sightseeing tours of the city and the breathtaking Swiss countryside. For three days—because Aeroflot, the Soviet carrier, had me on "hold"—Eric and I ate at fancy restaurants and visited historic buildings. Finally the flight-bumping was over, and Swissair was approved to fly to Prague and to connect to Aeroflot on April 30, 1956. Eric handed me a Swissair bag packed with Swiss chocolates. The comforts of the West were behind me as the plane skimmed toward Czechoslovakia and the Communist world. I wasn't scared, exactly; apprehensive, yes. I wasn't sure my stomach would hold food.

The Iron Curtain seemed to wrap around me in the solitude of the Prague airport, where I sat out a four-hour layover. I watched high-priority passengers, some in clerical robes, others in colorful African costumes, board the Moscow-bound flights. The airport was clean with a bare restaurant, a showcase of Czech glassware, and vacuum cleaners. Waiting, I picked out my diary on the Hermes and listened to Billy Eckstine sing "Bitter with the Sweet." I was feeling homesick already. An Italian woman, seated nearby, shared a cheese sandwich with me. She, her husband, and two teenaged daughters were headed for the Italian Embassy in Prague. She was amazed I was traveling alone because, she said, most travelers to Moscow are in delegations. Finally, the handful of passengers, all men except for me and another gal, boarded Aeroflot. The other female passenger was a French girl, young, breezy, attractive, with yellow shoes and matching handbag. We landed in Vilnius, Lithuania, at 8:15 P.M. on April 30. It was dreary, and rain bounced off the metal-roofed buildings at the airport. My first taste of the Soviet world was at customs, where officials in shiny blue serge suits with red piping at the collars began questioning me.

"Who asked you to Moscow?" The English was stilted.

"No one," I said.

Then, again: "Who asked you to Moscow?"

Bulganin's name came mischievously to mind. Stalin's too. "No one," I said. It was a standoff. Either lack of vocabulary or sheer bewilderment ended the quiz. Then I understood. Customs was familiar with delegations of Czechs, Poles, Chinese, and Africans. But a single American female was a rare bird.

Other passengers disappeared into a vast barnlike building while I was detained to fill out forms about furs, jewelry, and foreign currency. I forgot to mention my pennies, but I presented my Intourist money coupons. A silver bracelet was of special interest. "Gold?" "Nyet." He gave it back but kept two gold rings, one with tiny seed pearls that my mother had given me for good luck. He didn't touch my luggage, typewriter, or camera, and eventually I got the rings back.

Waved off to the second floor, I went under an arch with a huge bust of Stalin, over a red carpet, past walls hung with more portraits of both Stalin and Lenin. After just cold cuts on the plane, I was hungry but settled for soup. My companions were two huge Hungarian men, wearing heavy sweaters under suit coats. The French girl with the yellow shoes was en route to Bandong, Indonesia, as an interpreter for a Communist youth conference. Back on board and Moscow-bound, the mood switched from somber to holiday. A young Russian officer offered me an American cigarette, but I had been warned not to take cigarettes because of a black market connection. I didn't smoke anyway. The officer got the pack from an American at an international meteorological conference in Geneva, Switzerland.

Soon we saw lights below us here and there and then a blanket of twinkling lights. It looked like Christmas. It was not the Kremlin, I learned, but Moscow University on a high hill overlooking the city. We circled several times, landing smoothly at Vnukova airport, a half-hour drive from town.

On the windy and rain-swept night in a dimly lit airport, there was no one to meet me. I had expected Stanley Johnston of the Associated Press, but he was not there. Big disappointment. A female Russian doctor looked me over cursorily; I was on my own. My male companions had been swallowed up in the darkness of the port and vanished. Oriental passengers were asleep, hunched, heads on crossed legs on the floor. I collected my bag and was directed to a tall blond man at a counter. "Do you speak English?" I asked. "Yes, and who are you?" Then, "Your name is not on my list. We have no hotel for you. No transportation." Where was Stanley? I tried to explain the delays and asked him to call the

AP at the National Hotel. He had already told the French girl she could not call Paris and that she should sleep on the floor until the plane for China left in twelve hours. Inspired and desperate, I scoured the bottom of my bag for a handful of pennies. I dropped them on the counter. The blond guy scooped them up and told me I could ride to Moscow with a pair of Czech men. "You don't mind, do you?" I nearly kissed him.

It was 3 A.M. May 2—the day after the famous Red May Day— when I saw the huge, red, illuminated stars on the spires of the Kremlin walls. The walled citadel was twenty times bigger than I had imagined. (I wonder how German bombers in WW II missed it!) The old fortress was shadowy and dark as my taxi sped across the Moscow River Bridge, into a roadway in front of the National Hotel. A concierge took my passport and escorted me to room 227, a huge sitting room with heavy, dark furniture, an alcove bedroom, a balcony overlooking the Kremlin, and a tiny bathroom. Pulling aside plush maroon curtains from the windows I gazed on a pink, blue, silvery dawn. It was the Moscow of picture books in the heart of the Communist world. I breathed a deep sigh of relief—the first part of my mission was completed. I left the curtains wide open as I crawled into bed and drifted into a deep sleep, my rosary in my hands.

Sayings from childhood hummed in my head. Dad always said: "Go for it. Seize the moment." Mother's was: "If you don't do it, no one will do it for you." Those remnants of childhood got a Russian airing that May morning of 1956 as I awoke to see reddish-brown Kremlin fortress walls. I was alone. My grasp of the foreign language was rudimentary—my vocabulary consisted of basic words (hotel, eat, bathroom, and street). But I had a job to do and so pushed forward.

After failed attempts to locate Stanley Johnston, the AP bureau chief who had left me stranded the night before, I set off into the biting cold in my flimsy rain coat. Few cars passed as I crossed the wide boulevard toward the forbidding Kremlin walls, and there were no pedestrians. Passing through an open gate into the Kremlin's courtyard, I wandered around for some time before a uniformed guard caught up with me. He saw my press identification card, and I explained, with gestures, I was staying at the National Hotel across the road. I was simply walking, I said. He kindly escorted me back through the gate as though I were an important visiting guest. Again, I was surprised at the lack of traffic. True, I had arrived after the annual May Day parade, but this was the capital of the world's second superpower.

Back at Stanley's door I was surprised to be greeted by an attractive, slender blonde—Josephine, a former secretary to General Lansdale of the U.S. Atomic Energy Commission, I soon learned. She was "Stanley's lady" and introduced me to Stanley, who was still in bed in pajamas, recovering from a "big bear" of a hangover from May Day celebrations. Graciously, Josephine loaned me a fur coat to wear on our walk to the classy Argave restaurant for lunch and a talk. Two high-ranking Soviet officers who spoke English invited us to join them, but wisely Josephine declined. Big Brother, she said cryptically, is watching. We ate great potato soup and "bifstek" and drank hot tea, and she primed me on who the Americans were in Moscow . . . all eleven of them.

Within hours Josephine and Stanley had organized a party for "the girl from nowhere." Stanley thought it amusing that I came from Cleveland rather than a big city such as Chicago or Los Angeles, where their dailies were better well known. Who ever, he asked, heard of the *Cleveland News*? Gradually, between bites of chopped, hard-boiled eggs, onions, black caviar on toast, cheese, and sips of vodka, I sorted out the guests—my new colleagues. Howard Norton, a Pulitzer Prize winner from the *Baltimore Sun;* Irving R. Levine and Dan Shore of CBS News; Edmund Stevens of the *Christian Science Monitor;* Jack Raymond from the *New York Times;* Franklin White of *Newsweek;* Bernie Cutler of UPI; and Roy Essoyan, also from the AP.

After the cold war began to melt, newspaper and broadcasters sent their hotshots to open Moscow bureaus. (I wanted to rush a wire to Nat Howard about the company I was in, but Stanley had already wired that I was safe and sound at the National.) When I say "melting," I must qualify it. I was the third American newswoman admitted to the USSR in the thaw. Dorothy Thompson, the famous American journalist who covered Europe from

Ice cream and Eskimo Pie vendors on the street near Gum Department Store, Moscow, 1956. *Cleveland News* photograph.

her Paris apartment during World War II, was the first American newswoman there. She was the brainy type, analyzing the bizarre Soviet politics, Five Year Plans. Helen Waterhouse of the *Akron Beacon Journal* arrived sometime in 1956, but I never saw her. She was famous for interviewing Yugoslavia's Marshal Tito during the Second World War. This was 1956, yet the cold war ended officially on December 8, 1987, when President Ronald W. Reagan and Russian Premier Mikhail Gorbachev signed the Intermediate Nuclear Forces Treaty, leading to the destruction of 4 percent of the nuclear missiles—859 American and 1,836 Soviet. In his book, *The American Century,* Harold Evans called the treaty "an exhilarating prelude to the end of the Cold War."

This tiny group of seasoned reporters smiled smugly when I told them of my assignment—to talk to the "man on the street." They laughed and told me "Good Luck!" These reporters had staffs of secretaries and interpreters in their hotel room offices. The interpreters read Soviet publications and fed the stories to these journalistic luminaries. Admittedly, access to Soviet leaders was almost impossible. They relied on the never-ending parties, given by various embassies, to meet the leadership and actually pick up stories from human sources. I didn't have the time or the means for a staff. I set out alone.

My first stop was the Intourist Bureau, which handled guides for visiting firemen. I gave them a list of the places I wanted to visit and the types of people I wanted to interview. The manager, Mr. Popov, was dumbfounded. He shook his head when I told him I wanted an interview with Madame Bulganin, Madame Furtseva, and Madame Khrushchev. He said: "You will write letters. Our women do not come before the public as yours do," Popov said. Popov assigned me instead to Intourist guides, which began my assignment in the USSR. This was not my last encounter with Soviet bureaucracy. Ekaterina Furtseva ranked near the top in the Communist Party, and hardly anyone in the Western world ever heard of her. "Our women do not come before the public as yours do," Popov had said, but Popov assigned me Intourist guides, and that began my assignment in the USSR.

True, I met Soviet hotshots in Moscow, and frankly I was impressed with them and their stature in the government in that historical time. They had led their country through a major war and its aftermath. But three Russian women stand out in my memory of that wonderful assignment in 1956.

In Moscow, visiting schools and factories and private apartments, I was kept in tow by various Intourist guides, who left superficial impressions on me. One woman tearfully returned my gift of nylon stockings because her husband refused to allow her to accept gifts. She was in tears when she returned them. He must have thought it was patronizing. Once when I was with a male guide I ducked out on him while he was busy shopping in a state food store and found my way alone into the apartment of a physicist. I didn't really get to know these guides as persons; they simply translated language for me. It was very impersonal.

My days were fleeting and my anxiety was growing over my story production. I begged Intourist for permission to travel, and, surprisingly, they agreed. My colleagues were flummoxed, too. I flew from Moscow to Stalingrad, where I would eventually travel on the Volga River to Rostov-on-Don and then to Kiev before returning to Moscow.

Stalingrad was in the swirl of a dust storm when our plane landed, and my first impression of the city was therefore dispiriting. Huge windows of my hotel were plastered with sand—the scene was how I imagined our old dust bowl Oklahoma once looked. My guide was not on hand, so I gratefully used the facilities of a big bathroom (which had no shades or curtains) and waited again while a delegation of Chinese ate before I was allowed into the dining room. Before I was seated I watched the kitchen help, like hungry locusts, grab all the leftovers. Finally, Olga arrived. In a shiny, navy blue suit, nearly ankle long, wearing a dark blue hat, Olga was the saddest, most sorrowful woman I had ever met. She was slight of stature and worn out. It was tough to extract some of her personal history, but when I began to realize what the German army had done to conquer Stalingrad, and the bloody response of the embattled Russians who fought the Germans to their deaths, I soon understood why. I was overwhelmed with the horrors of World War II that took place on the very land I was standing. It was years later that I read more on the siege of Stalingrad.

I was able to interview Olga, who quietly answered questions as she took me to the waterfront where a memorial had been built. She pointed to the marsh across from the Peace Statue. "Bodies of Germans still lie in the bog," she said. And worst, Olga and many of her friends still lived underground. They dug underground homes, using empty food tin cans that were connected together for flues to carry smoke into the sky from their dirt lairs. The town had rebuilt its science center, its memorial, and the vast concrete steps to the river, but housing was not a high priority. I was ashamed to be staying in a clean hotel with a big bathroom, running water, and roof.

Olga took me to the Central House of Architects, where the director gave me lessons in distinguishing the economic features of communism and capitalism. Rents were cheaper there than in America. Electricity and gas were cheaper. He painted a glowing future with schools, nurseries, stores, and single heated garages for automobiles. Olga desperately wanted me to see the new planetarium, a gift from the Peoples' Republic of East Germany, where four Intourist guides on duty described themselves as "materialists." I admit to being impressed with the circular, domed lighting, which created the Milky Way and Little Bears along with night shapes of Stalingrad's landscape silhouetted in the circle. Lastly, Olga rushed me over to Lenin Hospital, a five-hundred-bed, reconstructed facility for industrial workers and their families from the Red October steel plant and a tractor factory. The director said he had "wonder drugs" for the common cold, and he used the Pavlov method of reflex action for pregnant women. I quietly and politely heard out these various administrators—I was a guest in their country, not an inquisitor—but I wanted to ask Olga why she was still living underground.

It was with relief that I boarded the steamer *Alexei Tolstoi* for a boat ride down the Volga and Don rivers from Stalingrad to Rostov-on-Don. The passengers were in a jolly holiday mood as we boarded and were assigned rooms. In the dining room, where I stood out like a neon light with my American suit and shoes, a Russian naval officer asked me to help him read *Robin Hood.* Two gentlemen invited me to share a snack in their tiny stateroom. By the time I arrived, they had slipped into striped pajamas—common Russian loungewear—and offered me snacks of smoked salmon and vodka. Before I tasted a bit, a Russian teacher pulled me away from them with the words, "Ne kulturney." I had made a major faux pas in her eyes by associating with Armenians. Prior to this incident, I thought the Soviets had a classless society. Dumb me!

Miss Alexandra Zavodskaia was a French teacher at the University of Chernotsy and said in no uncertain terms "not to associate with Armenians." A statuesque blond who wore her hair in a bun at the nape of her neck and had piercing green eyes, Alexandra adopted me as an arm-holding, deck-promenading companion. She was writing a paper on word derivations, tracing developments from Greek or Latin origins to common usage in French, German, English, and Russian. She was a real brain.

Walking the deck, we saw cattle and sheep grazing on the passing hillsides and farmers working: tying up tomato plants, tending vineyards at the river's edge. The Don River was quiet and narrow, and we could almost peek into the wooden houses along the shore. Horsemen rounded up cattle, and I called them cowboys, like our men in the Texas plains. Alexandra loved repeating the word "cowboy" with various inflections. Her father had been an engineer in Baku, Azerbaijan, and she had lived in many cities around the Caucuses Mountains. We hit it off almost immediately. We pored over a world atlas, picking out cities she and I knew. I picked out Lake Erie and Cleveland, New York, Chicago, and Washington. She knew virtually nothing about North America, and her main ambition was to "see France." When it was time to eat, she wrote down my food order for me. When I said "cake," she wrote "torte," and the boat's chef baked a special cake that was layered with jelly. The whole dining room shared it. Later when I asked about a shower, it was again "nyet" because it was for both sexes. Alexandra was extremely modest. Her unstylish skirt and blouse were cut full, with a high neckline. She also had a jacketlike sweater and winter coat. Once I knocked on her state room and embarrassed her to be caught in a green cotton slip. She hurriedly wrapped in a dress.

I hadn't the faintest clue what to expect in Rostov, but an Intourist guide, a young Russian housewife, quickly took me and Alexandra to "the best restaurant" there. Having been startled to hear "The Lady in Red" over the ship's radio and "Tea for Two," it no longer surprised me when I heard at the restaurant "Besame Mucho," which was written in 1941. It was the current hit in Moscow in 1956.

We got royal treatment at the restaurant. The manager asked two men to vacate a table for us, and the chef heated bowls of borscht. The room was crowded with couples who were drinking and dancing, including Red Army officers. The dancing pairs didn't swirl around cheek to cheek but were more formal, and when the music ended, males escorted females to their seats. The room was shabbier than the National and Grand hotel rooms in Moscow, but a ceiling chandelier lighted up every corner of the rococo-walled room. My Intourist guide ordered the famous Rostov "Don Cossack" wine made from grapes along the Don River. She said the wine was traditionally consumed when their men went to war, like the English custom of drinking from a stirrup cup. Alexandra and I drank from a Russian stirrup cup and were also honored with the famous Cossack dance by an agile officer. It was great fun.

Walking to our hotel later we saw Soviet police arm-in-arm with Chinese policemen on patrol. Our guide had led us through a congested district of tightly packed houses and dirty streets. She described the area as a Jewish-Armenian neighborhood. None of the Russians I met had more than formal and courteous conversations, and none asked about race or religion in America. That was odd, and I wasn't about to volunteer anything. I didn't ask about their philosophies either. But I wanted to, although I was cautious.

When Alexandra asked to stay in my room, I thought she was afraid. Of what, I didn't know. We were both weary, and neither of us chatted much before falling asleep. I was astounded in the morning when I awoke and found her gone. We never saw each other again or communicated. I thought about writing to her at the university, but a wiser head suggested I may cause her trouble.

My next stop was Kiev, the capital of Ukraine. When I arrived the sunny day and a different atmosphere brought up my spirits. Women were more stylishly dressed than I had seen in Stalingrad and Rostov. There was more of an air of national pride in the way people walked and the expressions on their faces—some actually smiled at me in my give-away American suits and shoes. More women wore makeup and a pin or flower in their hair or on a jacket. Before I met my new guide, the hotel manager had filled my room with bouquets of freshly cut lilacs. The fragrance was so overwhelming I put them on the small balcony. It was a really nice touch. Olga, my new guide, was a twenty-five-year-old, plump single mother with long curly, shiny brown hair and fluffy bangs. After trying unsuccessfully to interview a housing expert there who had once visited Cleveland, I found myself being led around by Olga to parks, gardens, and cultural spots. I could barely face another statue of a Ukrainian soldier war hero.

I asked why Ukraine wasn't independent—my Ukrainian friends back home had wanted me to ask that—and Olga said: "We are independent. We are autonomous." She said, "We can secede from Russia anytime we want. We are a voluntary organization." It was just recently, in 2005, that Ukraine finally had a free election.

Kiev was a beautiful city. There were new apartments to replace the bombed ones, and the exteriors were made of domestic ceramic tile. Theaters, shops, and libraries were open. Hotel plumbing worked, and beauty parlors were open for business. The huge Vladimirsky Cathedral was filled with parishioners for 10 A.M. mass. (I had been at mass in Moscow once with members of the French Embassy in a tiny chapel near Moscow's huge prison.) Old women in white, newly washed, and ironed babushkas were in the majority. There were stately old men with white handlebar mustaches. No teenagers. The cathedral occupied an entire square block. A fat, squat, sandstone structure in Byzantine style, the cathedral's domes had not been restored. Four American tourists and I joined the throng of worshipers. At times we were elbowed out of our front-row standing locations. We were entranced with the priests, both frail and bewhiskered, and the younger ones, fresh and pink-cheeked. Two young priests wore satin brocaded robes over pale blue silk tunics. Before the service a big ZIS limousine deposited the head patriarch, a small, round priest with flowing gray whiskers. He marched inside, followed by a retinue of more priests. During the ceremony the congregation never stood still, bowing and praying and kissing a relic entombed in glass. Elderly women wiped the glass with kerchiefs after the kissing. Later I irked Olga because I bought an Eskimo pie from a vendor and ate it. She scolded that she "didn't eat ice cream in public."

I wandered a bit on my own and snapped as many pictures as I could, until a policeman took my film. Shooting a photo of an old monastery, I had also snapped the background, the Dnieper River, which was a no-no. I had no idea there was a hydroelectric plant in the background. Later I saw a similar photo in a book by photographer Margaret Bourke-White, who shot it during the war.

Kiev played host to a delegation of Oklahoma farmers, guests at my hotel. I hooked up with them and found one way to visit a "model" farm and a tractor plant. That was a bonus, as I was able to shed Olga and go along with the men and their guide. The farmers fed us soup from huge pots over an outdoor fire. We had been joking about Potemkin villages on the bus ride there, and sure enough we found that only the fronts and sides of the farm houses had been white-washed for our visit. That is what the old Soviets did when Russian royalty visited the hinterlands to make the kings and queens believe everything was hunky-dory. What amazed the Oklahomans were tractors, based on the John Deere American model, stored outside the plant. The plant turned out production but neglected to bring train track spurs to haul the tractors out.

En route to Moscow (as an exhausted traveler who was ready to fly back) I met another young woman, Antonina, with whom I later carried on mail correspondence for seven years. She was the plane stewardess, and she seated me in the rear, near her seat. Russian stewardesses did not wear the chic outfits ours did but simply a navy blue suit. Her English was excellent, and before long I learned she had been born in Shanghai to a Russian mother and Chinese father and partly raised in a Catholic-run school. When China started sending Russians back home, her mother was returned to her native Kiev. Antonina's husband, however, was not allowed out of China. She had married a Frenchmen in China, but he was not allowed in Russia. Thus, with her language skills, the young, pretty stewardess was assigned an airline job that brought her in and out of Moscow. She had a son to raise, and in her letters she described her living conditions, schooling for her child, and how, later, she was reassigned as an interpreter in Kiev or wherever they needed her. We wrote about books and theater and family things. We both knew our letters were opened and read by our governments by the way they were resealed. At one point I was contacted by the CIA for information about her and about a physicist I had met in Moscow. He was the guy whose apartment I had visited when I left my guide shopping. The physicist, I was told, had defected to the United States. After Antonina's letters stopped, I contacted a friend of hers in San Francisco, who told me she preferred not to write to me anymore. I still remember how happy Tony (as she asked me to call her) was when, leaving the Kiev plane at the Moscow airport, I threw all my cosmetics and a gray cashmere sweater under the airplane seat. She had told me how she missed luxury things like cosmetics and fine clothes. I wouldn't miss a thing I left for her. We actually exchanged books, and the one she especially liked was written by Anne Morrow Lindbergh.

Back at the National Hotel in Moscow after the swing around the Volga and Don rivers and Kiev, my nightly headquarters was Stanley Johnston's hotel room. Including him and the other reporters in Moscow, there were only eleven of us. Since they rarely traveled, they quizzed me on what I saw in Stalingrad, Rostov, and Kiev. Their daily production was gleaned from Soviet publications, translated by their Russian secretaries. They attempted to file reports on a regular basis, and each night those with copy to file walked to the telegraph or censor's office, in a converted building not far from the National Hotel, where they shoved their typewritten copy through a slotted grill in a curtained window. It was usually around midnight, and we had to sit around and wait for the okay. More often than not, the copy was returned with huge gashes of black ink through sentences and paragraphs. Those with portable typewriters redid copy for the censor's approval. When I saw this operation, I advised Nat Howard that I was opting to write when I returned. My copy, with candid observations, would never pass this outfit. In my notebooks I had copious notes describing women in long, drab coats, many sweeping streets with old-fashioned brooms and selling Eskimo pies with carts. (Stalin reportedly loved Eskimo pies.) Hardly a flattering picture. Even taking pictures of these ladies was frowned on by Intourist guides.

It was May but dreary gray and cold. I wanted readers of the *News* to see the long lines at the state grocery stores where shelves were stocked only with bread, eggs, tea, and short supplies of meat. There were no vegetables, although there were outdoor markets with makeshift stands where bundled-up merchants sold shriveled carrots or anemic heads of cabbage. A few of us shopped there. I wanted the freedom to describe limited conver-

Modeling a Uzbekistan embroidered cap for a German photographer at the Moscow Circus, Moscow, 1956. Author's collection.

sations with guides. Readers would be interested to know that polyclinics, neighborhood health centers, were staffed by female doctors. So many Russian men were killed in the war that there was a noticeable shortage of men in skilled jobs.

My Intourist guides hemmed me in on approaching an average citizen on the street or in a store, and I grew frustrated with failed attempts to meet real people. That is why on that one occasion I ditched my male guide and broke a lot of rules by following a woman home from the grocery to her high-rise apartment. Russians had an unbroken social rule—you do not visit anyone without an advance courtesy call. This frail lady, hauling two bags of groceries, walked into the lobby of a high-rise—another favorite of Stalin—and I followed her up in the elevator to her door, much to her discomfort, especially when I explained who I was. The door was opened by a husky man, shocked to see his wife with an American. To my shock, he spoke English in response to my hurried explanation. He courteously invited me into the small kitchen for tea. Although we were nervous we quickly established a thread of familiarity. After I explained that I was from Cleveland, Ohio, hometown of industrialist Cyrus Eaton, the man told me that he had attended one of Eaton's international Pugwash peace seminars in Nova Scotia. This middle-aged man, the physicist, wrote his name in my notebook. Whatever his work, he and his wife were given a coveted dacha, or recreation home, several miles from Moscow, and his ambition, he said, was to visit America one day. We talked the usual "peace" thing, impressions of Eaton. He couldn't have been nicer. His wife never reappeared, and I noticed small items of laundry hung over the kitchen stove. Several years later when the CIA contacted me, inquiring about the gentleman, I learned that he had defected. All I knew I had printed, and I gave the CIA agent my notebook with his name and address. I wondered how many defectors lived in the United States with new identities and information about their technical work in the Soviet Union. This encounter intrigued my reporter friends, who also advised caution on going it alone. So anxious for stories, I forgot I wasn't on the streets of Cleveland.

Before I got to Moscow in 1956 my colleagues there had really big stories. Traitorous British spies Guy Burgess and Donald McLean had surfaced in Moscow after defecting from the west. The day after I arrived the Moscow press office held a brief press conference at the National Hotel to announce, "The spies came home." I briefly caught the end of it—not realizing at first it was a big-time story—and looked over a table with a collection of books and spy paraphernalia that the traitors had brought with them. In 1951 Burgess was recalled from his post as secretary of the British Embassy in Washington, asked by the Brits to resign for "disorderliness of his life." Both Burgess and McLean had been warned that British and American counterintelligence was closing in on McLean, especially. The pair fled England and vanished, turning up in Moscow in the spring of 1956. McLean had held the post of first secretary to the British Embassy in Washington, D.C., and he was accused of supplying the USSR with "secret material relating to the formation of NATO." In Yuri Modin's 1994 book, *My*

Five Cambridge Friends, he wrote of Burgess: "Homosexual seduction was his forte and almost a reflex, an entirely clandestine gay society provided excellent practise in conspiracy and leading a double life." It was said that McLean "truly believed in Communism." President Harry Truman was to find out how duplicitous McLean was before the rest of the world read about him when he met with Josef Stalin in Potsdam in 1945. Truman whispered to Stalin that America had "a very powerful explosive," but Stalin didn't bat an eye. Events later proved he knew of the atomic bomb due to the espionage of Klaus Fuchs, a British scientist, and Donald McLean. The nefarious Burgess and McLean ended sadly their lives in the Soviet Union.

There was another major story breaking around our small group of Americans, but because of mystery and secrecy it was not revealed until August of 1956 (although the *New York Times* claimed it "leaked" some of it in June). Historically, this event is called "Khrushchev's Un-Secret Speech." Problems with a closed government, censorship, and translation kept this eye-popping story secret for weeks. On February 24 and 25, 1956, the CPSU (Communist Party, Soviet Union) Congress held a secret session that barred even representatives of the fraternal Communist parties from attending. Khrushchev delivered "a 25,000-word denunciation of Stalin's alleged 'cult of the individual.'" It was the most startling attack on Stalin's legacy to date. What a story! No wonder my little forays into shops and factories were so trivial to reporters investigating this coup. Khrushchev, in the speech later obtained for publication in the West, said: "We cannot let this matter get out of the party, especially to the press. It is for this reason that we are considering it here at a closed congress session. We should know the limits; we should not give ammunition to the enemy; we should not wash our dirty linen before their eyes." My reporter colleagues were still working on "the rumor" of this speech when weeks later I was leaving for home. In August I read about it in a publication titled *Turning Point.* "We are not in the least interested in proving the K secret should not have leaked to the *New York Times* on June 5, 1956. On the contrary, it was designed for leakage; the point is that K found it opportune to collaborate with international capitalism for the reeducation of international communism along the Khrushchevite lines." In other words, Khrushchev was the real reformer, moving the USSR along to capitalism. Gorbachev took the report later to its dramatic conclusion when Ronald Reagan was our president. My hotshot newsmen got these truly earth-shattering stories. I got the "people" ones. What an exhilarating news time.

Also when I returned to Moscow from Kiev, U.S. ambassador Charles "Chip" Bohlen sent word to me. We had a meeting behind the doors of the embassy (guarded by U.S. Marines) that was all about my tours to a Kiev farm and a tractor plant with a delegation of Oklahoma farmers. Bohlen was a handsome, elitist type with strong Philadelphia and Washington social and political ties. He and fellow diplomats were restricted to limited mileage, rarely leaving the city. He was especially interested in the widespread flooding I had seen from the air as we flew into Kiev, which was known as "the bread basket of the Ukraine." Flooding meant major crop losses, and Bohlen was unaware of the bottled-up production of the John Deere tractors due to lack of transport—trucks or rail—to move them.

The ambassador was gracious, offering a Marine chauffeur for the trip back to the National. But the off-duty Marines instead invited me into their barracks for a beer and to listen to American records. The one song I'll always remember listening to is "I Could Have Danced All Night," because we danced around the room like kids on a picnic. It was so great to hear American English and have a brief encounter with these young soldiers.

I wasn't getting world scoops, but I did get into a few private homes. Actually, the first week there Edmund Stevens of the *Christian Science Monitor* threw a Russian Easter party at his home, a small log cottage across the Moscow River from the Kremlin. He was married to a beautiful Soviet woman, and their red-haired, teenaged daughter was the only American in the Moscow ballet.

After my stealth visit to the physicist, Intourist arranged another visit, in the same high-rise, with an honored mother of the Soviet Union. She was definitely handpicked and scripted. She was Mrs. Antonina Grigorievna Balashova, a much publicized thirty-nine-year-old mother of eleven, though some were step-children. Her husband, Poppa, welcomed me heartily into their spacious, four-room apartment, where I learned that Mrs. B. was a frequent speaker to women's groups and had been featured in Soviet magazines as a "patriot." I was offered wine, tea, and cakes while we looked through photo albums of the family. Poppa was a construction worker in the Ural Mountains when he married Mrs. B., his second wife. He had worked all over the Soviet Union, including Siberia. He worked on a project "near Alaska," also on the Dnieper dam in Kiev. I had met another engineer at a Moscow factory who had worked at Eaton Axle in Cleveland on a worker-exchange program in the 1930s. That surprised me. Mrs. B. asked about abortions in American, and Poppa said Stalin was okay at first, but then he became "neglectful, neglectful, neglectful." He asked if Tennessee senator Estes Kefauver would be our next president. That surprised me, too. They autographed books for me and gave me their home telephone number.

Despite the limited family contacts, I couldn't help feel these connections were superficial, or strained. I could not risk cordial relationships by being pushy or arrogant. I was aware that we were watched almost everywhere. Lady editors at a women's magazine asked how many pairs of shoes I owned and how many servants cleaned my home. That was real conversation. I gave them my verbal picture of home where the biggest thing I owned was an automobile and where I sewed my own clothes. Did they believe me? Who knows? We were on different levels of communication, each with our own skewed perceptions.

The best times, where you felt like letting your hair down, were at foreign embassy parties, usually held to celebrate a national day of their homelands. These were the few places where reporters and diplomats spoke directly with Soviet leaders and their top underlings. Stanley Johnston took me along to parties at the Afghanistan and Argentine embassies. We more or less crashed, he said, since there was no formal invitation. These estates were behind iron gates and fences, and little children clung like rag dolls to the outer fences watching the grand people in their grand dresses and suits enter. At the Afghanistan party I met the pot-bellied Communist leader, Premier Nikolai Bulganin. He gripped my hand firmly and had an intense glare. My first thought was, "This guy is a bear, a big Russian bear, and an American wolf!"(After my series appeared in the *News* the Associated Press picked up the story about "Wolf" Bulganin.) A tray of king-sized champagne cocktails was slipped under his nose—one for him, one for me—and we clinked our glasses "to peace." My chances were slim that this would be a prolonged meeting, so I immediately asked him to arrange an interview with Ekaterina Furtseva, the number one Communist woman in the Soviet government. "The premier," the interpreter at the premier's side said, "does not wish to discuss interviews."

I moved around the room with a crush of diplomats and their wives, always feeling Bulganin's eyes following me. What should I have asked him? The Soviet hierarchy did not have wives present. Their guests were young women from the Bolshoi Ballet, scrawny dancers standing around like wildflowers, pretty decorations. Besides Bulganin I met Foreign Minister Anastas Mikoyan, Vyacheslav Molotov, Marshals Zhukov and Bagramian, and Andre Gromyko, deputy foreign minister. Conversations were stilted. At the Argentine party Bagramian called Marshal Zhukov—the hero of Stalingrad—over to meet Roy Essoyan, an AP correspondent and an American Armenian. I watched Marshal Zhukov in lively conversation with Ambassador Bohlen. Few reporters wrote of these parties. They didn't want to be banned from future ones, but at least they saw the leaders in the flesh. My impression was the Russians loved these affairs.

Any social or private life for us reporters was rare. Our reporting talents were highly geared to stories, and there was not a moment to lose. But one evening before dark Jack Raymond of the *New York Times* and I strolled to Gorky Park like natives for a ride on the Ferris wheel. We were at the top when the wheel stopped, and we laughed and joked. It was a mildly warm May night. We waited, and we waited. We saw no one. The wheel was fixed, stuck, and darkness fell. Jack claimed he saw couples copulating in the bushes beyond the wheel. Several hours later, two or three maybe, a mechanic fixed the problem. Had someone played a trick on us? With the paranoia that goes with being a minority in a foreign country, we thought so. We quietly walked back to the hotel. Dan Schorr of CBS brought back diaphanous white nylon blouses for his secretarial gifts when he returned from Stockholm, Sweden, where he had taken a bunch of laundry. He was reprimanded. No one wanted to break rules, be deported. One *New York Times* reporter had earlier been kicked out for dollar manipulations.

I overstayed my planned time in the USSR by several weeks. Stanley failed to obtain a visa extension, as promised, and I became an illegal guest. Trying to leave was harder than getting in. Finally through the Soviet press office I got a flight from Moscow to East Berlin, which was fine, but the East Berlin guard, checking my passport, ordered me back to Moscow. I refused to move an inch from my seat in the lounge. Tired, worried, and determined, I sat to wait them out. I said "Nyet" and "Amerikansky" to every question. Hours passed, six, seven. Finally an American diplomat with his wife and children walked in. Upon seeing my American clothes (the real giveaway), he spoke harshly to the East German guards, called the AP bureau chief in West Berlin for a chauffeured car, and my crisis was over. A few more hours of waiting for the car and I was whisked past the officious East Berliners.

After food, drinks, and sleep at the AP apartment-office, I raced to the Kurfursdendamm shopping stores for a summer cotton dress. I had left most of my clothes in Moscow for anyone who could use them. I bought a beautiful two-piece dress, narrowly striped yellow and black. The skirt was full with a bouffant underskirt. It was great after all those sweaters and woolen suits. The AP filed a story of my airport adventure, and *The Radio Voice of America* interviewed me about my stand against the East Berliners. I wired home a brief explanation and said I was heading home. Nat Howard, however, had other plans. He asked me to call our publisher's executive Charles F. McCahill, in Paris, who took me to a private Catholic convent school where his late wife had been a student. He had helped build a memorial in her name, and we attended the dedication. That night at the Folies-Bergere, we sat behind actor-dancer Fred Astaire and a male companion, who walked out during the performance. The star male performer, dressed in drag in a long, red, sequined gown, sang, "I'm Selling What I Used to Give Away." The next morning Charlie and I went

Colleagues from the *News* welcome home the author. 1956; author's collection.

to Sacre Coeur. He went to confession. I didn't feel the need. Then home, for me.

You bet Cleveland looked good, even after a huge wind storm had blasted through the area, uprooting a number of trees in Lakewood. The city seemed small, almost insignificant after the vastness of Moscow and West Berlin and Paris. I was on a big high over the assignment and faced the huge challenge of converting notes into stories. Nat had lined up a major speaking engagement at the Hotel Cleveland, where I faced an audience of five hundred, anxious for a firsthand report on the Soviet Union. The last several months had been a roller coaster ride, and my good medical doctor supplied me with one Seconal to guide me through that first speech. I later gave about two hundred more. Before settling down, I was a guest of the Overseas Press Club in New York City, where I again tasted the camaraderie of overseas correspondents, a breed of their own. I was so tempted to dream about being one of them. But my cautious nature clicked in. Before leaving Moscow, Franklin White of *Newsweek* had thrown out an idea that we ride the Orient Express to Siberia. My God! What a temptation. But my cautious nature said, "No, you have a job here." And I settled in and wrote a long series on my rare assignment.

Every newspaper reporter should—must—go overseas before settling into a career or marriage or both. Overseas assignments should take precedence over romance, marriage, mortgages, or children. It sounds tough, but take it from someone who has been there. It's worth it.

I changed mentally and emotionally after the trip to the Soviet Union in 1956. There were more international news, more politics, more biographies, and more history tomes in my life. An atlas and dictionary were my bedside companions. I attended lectures on foreign affairs, and, sadly, I found my old friends frivolous, even boring. In Moscow I'd met students who had read great literary works—Dickens, Galsworthy—in English and who had the world's languages and histories and literature as part of their lives. Most of my Intourist guides spoke French and German. At home my friends cared little about these things. They cared about intimate things in their tight circles. Does foreign travel make a person snobbish? Or just more sophisticated, more aware?

It was late coming, but I was maturing.

-30-

-10-

Me and the Cleveland Indians

*W*hen editors at the *News* wanted stunt stories to use as circulation grabbers, they knew they could count on me. I'd driven a Walker Bulldog tank, played a department store Santa Claus, and even dusted a millionaire's office in Terminal Tower. Reporters' lives were and certainly still are (perhaps now to an even greater degree with 24/7 news) at the beck and call of bosses with crazy ideas. At the old *News,* we had a saying: "Ours is not to reason why. Ours is to do or die." I didn't know any reporter turning down jobs just because they were ditzy; we usually found them fun, breaking up the humdrum of police rounds, obits, or writing those little shorts about club meetings. But I never thought I'd find myself watching through binoculars from a clandestine perch on the rooftop of the Shoreham Hotel in Washington, D.C., couples necking and copulating in their rooms below. Spying was not the assignment; rather it was a by-product of a trip with the Cleveland Indians.

In May 1967 Nat Howard hatched a plan to send me on the eastern swing of the Cleveland Indians baseball club. I was all for it. I loved baseball. In my tomboy days I played softball with my brother Jack and his friends in the streets. My father took us to the old League Park on Lexington Avenue whenever the Philadelphia Athletics (the As) were in town, because we were shirttail relatives of Connie Mack (Macgillacuddy). (My Irish grandparents, from Mulranny, County Mayo, settled in the coal-mining town of Cumberland Gap, near Wilkes-Barre, Pennsylvania, along with other relatives, the McDonalds, McHales, Macks, and other immigrants.) Connie Mack autographed league hardballs for us, and had Jack and I not worn the skins off them on the street, I could collect big money today for those treasures. When the huge, new Cleveland Stadium was built, replacing League Park, we saw lots of games there, as another relative was a major contractor on the job and we got free passes. We watched the spectacular farm boy from Iowa, Bob Feller, pitch against the New York Yankees until a game was called by darkness. I was a devoted reader of sports pages and listened faithfully to Jack Graney's radio play-by-play. Yes, I loved baseball. Still do.

I caught up with the team in Baltimore after locating a hotel near the ballpark and getting my long brown hair done at a nearby beauty shop, which I found was "home" to the burlesque girls and strippers, thus explaining my slightly higher and more-lacquered-than-usual hairdo. I hooked up with a few of the team members who were hanging around the hotel lobby, killing time, wandering from the newsstand to the street, some reading sports pages or just doing nothing. None of them was particularly friendly or impressed with this reporter's presence. I needed a story, and killing time with these guys just might produce one, so I hung out in the lobby, too.

I had an eerie feeling this was going to be a desperation assignment. Would I or would I not get a story? Hal Lebovitz, the *News*'s traveling sportswriter with the team, looked askance at me and offered no help. By now I was used to this attitude from male reporters and therefore wasn't deterred. I chatted with two pitchers, Don Mossie and Ray Narleski, and they invited me shopping. We hit the arcades, where the guys picked up souvenirs. One found a cardboard box with a spring-loaded lid. Open it quickly, and out popped a satin brassiere. Great gift for the wife, one said. They bought funky stuff to send home. And I tagged along with other players to a special tailoring shop that catered to ballplayers who required special orders due to their extra muscles and size. The tailors remodeled older, dated jackets and trousers with wearable life in them. Sportswriters also took advantage of tailoring perks, which were often free. There weren't stories in these trips, at least ones that I considered to be of interest to the readers. A strikingly handsome young player, called the "Bonus Baby," whose name I forgot, went to the racetrack. The boys said it wouldn't be a good idea to write about "the kid" at the track. Gradually, I learned self-censoring of a kind. All I really wanted was an inning in the dugout. I wanted the readers and fans to know what players shout, what coaches say, what the catcher says to the home-plate umpire. Was I dreaming?

I almost got my wish in Baltimore until Kerby Farrell, Indians' manager, passed the word along that "The boys don't like it. They said this ain't no ladies' aid society." The umpires said jokingly, of course, that if I was in the dugout, they "couldn't see it." I was, however, welcomed into the press box in Baltimore and Washington, D.C., where there were some grumpy sorts who were less than thrilled to have a woman around (to them the only women that should be in the press boxes were the Western Union telegraphers). And I was aware that my presence put somewhat of a crimp in Bobo Newsom's usually exuberant entrance. As he swung into the press box, one sportswriter yelled: "Language?" He clearly didn't know I'd grown up on the police beat.

I had invited Cleveland Indians' slugger Roger Maris to join me at the Baltimore Memorial Stadium press box. He was out of play on a minor injury. When outfielder Maris and I cheered over a hit, one of the grumpy writers said; "If you want to cheer, get out of here." And we did. I liked Maris a lot. He was quiet and gentlemanly, and he eventually beat Babe Ruth's home run record of sixty runs. I filed a short story about this event, but I didn't cry over it being kicked out, because in 1957 the press box was as all-male as a Saturday night poker game. For me, the news action was off the field, because the regular beat guys were naturally covering on-the-field hits, runs, and outs.

One night in Washington, D.C., infielder Vic Wertz invited me to a spaghetti dinner after a night game, and I felt like I had arrived when Vic and his friends talked about their hometowns and how they made it into the big leagues. I should have suspected something else was up when we returned to the Shoreham and he asked if I had a flashlight. Flashlight? "Meet us in the lobby in ten minutes," Vic said. Vic and a couple other players and I rode the elevator to the top floor and then walked up a dank stairway lit only by our flashlights to the roof. I was game, I guess. From the players' jackets came binoculars, and the fun was on. They focused on the uncurtained rooms of amorous guests who were at play, so to speak. To this day I'm pained at what we did, how it would have reflected on the team, on us, on the hotel. Oh my god! I was trapped. These guys knew I couldn't write a word, and they were so frisky and delighted with themselves. They were holding their bellies with laughter. I guess this relieved the boredom of road travel. And you can bet that it was not the topic of the day at breakfast.

We moved on to Boston where on May 21 I was officially banned from the press box. The *Boston Daily Globe* had hired me to write about it, and the story made page one. "Boston sportswriters are sissies. They banned me from the all-male sanctuary—the Red Sox press box—because they are afraid to establish what they consider a dangerous precedent. Women reporters are by tradition here in Boston persona non grata in the press box." The men didn't want me, an outsider, to shatter their rules. Getting banned meant that members of the Boston Sports Writers' Association voted on whether they should or shouldn't allow a female reporter in. The vote was five to four against me. *Globe* sportswriter Bob Holbrook, chairman of the local association, said members were meeting on this explosive issue when he arrived at Fenway Park that day. "I might have to resign over this. In fact, I feel like it." Suddenly *I* was the story, not who won the game or who pitched. Earlier I made history at Washington's Griffith Park when I became the first woman to sit in a press box. I sat with Bob Addie of the *Washington Post,* who had his three-year-old son with him. It must have looked like family day.

At Yankee Stadium in New York I struck out again. Joe Trimble of the *New York Daily News*, chairman of their writers' association, was determined to perpetuate female discrimination in the press box. At that point, I didn't care. The Yankees gave me a seat alongside the dugout, a spot better than any in the upper deck. I wrote in the *Boston Globe* that I'd be content to return to city-side duties at the *News* after this eastern tour but that I'd be a bigger and better fan of the Indians. I caught the team spirit from the rookies coming up, kids like Maris, Kenny Kuhn, Russ Nixson, and Rocky Colavita. These young men had spark and potential.

While I was writing nice little features, the male writers were doing numbers on me. Jerry Mitchell of the *New York Post* wrote a five-column piece with the headline: "No Wonder the Indians Look Better." That cracked me up. His take:

> Ordinarily one making an eastern or western trip with a base-ball club would pack a couple of suits, an extra pair of shoes, six shirts and ties, three or four pairs of shorts, and maybe an extra can of tobacco. When one member of the Cleveland entourage packed for this here now eastern swing however, the following items went into a big suitcases: 4 pairs of panties, two pink, two blue; 4 brassieres; 5 slips; 5 pairs of white gloves; 8 pairs of nylon stockings; 1 girdle; 4 pairs of shoes; 1 pair of bedroom slippers; 2 nightgowns; 2 pairs of baby doll pajamas; 2 negligees; 1 round straw sailor hat; 7 cotton dresses; 1 cocktail dress; 2 bikini bathing suits; 1 umbrella.

Heck, I didn't own much in those days. I only recall one raincoat, two dresses, four sweaters, two skirts, nylons, two pairs of shoes, makeup, fat stenographer notebooks, copy pencils, and a small Hermes typewriter. So there!

Joe Trimble told me that everyone was happy about having me around except Indians manager Kerby Farrell and Jimmy Schlemmer, writer for the *Akron Beacon Journal*. Jimmy complained a lot. Joe Trimble wrote: "Miss O'Donnell is young, dark-haired, brown-eyed and exceedingly pretty. She has a fashion model figure. She makes the Indians look better than they've looked in many years. In her 12 years on the *News*, she has done police reporting, rewrite, features, and last fall went to Russia and did a series on life on the Vodka Belt that won a Newspaper Guild award. The young lady, in other words, is a major leaguer."

The *Post*'s Jerry Mitchell in his article said that Lebovitz tried to pave the way for me. "We're sending a girl reporter on the trip," Hal told pitcher Early Wynn. "Will you take care of her?"

"I certainly will," said Wynn, a Saturday journalist himself. "With pleasure."

"Good," said Hal, showing him a picture of Grandma Moses.

"On second thought," Wynn said, "Bob Lemon [another pitcher] would be able to help her better. Here comes Bob." Then Bob saw the picture and said: "I'd better not. My wife's making the trip, you know."

These guys had a sense of humor. Travel arrangements provided a roomette on one of two special train cars. We rode busses to parks. The players kidded a lot, wrote a frisky song no one was bold enough to sing to me. "She's a good sport," said Gene Woodling, an Indians infielder. "Takes everything in stride," said Eddie Stankey, an Indians coach. We even went to movies together. One night after a Yankees game, Yogi Berra, the Yankees' catcher, invited a bunch of us to Fernando's Hideaway, where he had a "piece of the place." It was a blast. Everybody had a few drinks and let their hair down. We danced and sang with the entertainers. Farrell treated his guys well, although I wondered about discipline, but when you win, you deserved fun. But what did I know?

It was a whirlwind trip, and the most memorable part happened in Boston where a couple of Boston sportswriters tried to arrange an interview with slugger Ted Williams. He was my hero (after Indians Bob Feller). Williams, tall, handsome, and an ex-Marine, made his bat sing with his powerful swings. He moved like a ballet dancer at home plate. Williams balked at the interview, telling the Red Sox public relations chief: "Let me up." So with no help, I waited prettily near the Red Sox dugout during batting practice at Fenway Park. I called out to him on the field after he had taken a few practice hits. "Why don't you like sportswriters?" I yelled at him. I got Ted's attention and whistles from the other players

The author and her baseball hero: Red Sox home-run hitter Ted Williams, Fenway Park, Boston, 1957. Associated Press photograph.

as he walked over to me. He responded with expletives, lots of them, but I wasn't gong to stop. "Why don't you like sportswriters?" (The regular beat sportswriters had said Ted refused to talk to them.) I explained that my job was feature writing, covering the Indians was an editor's idea, and I'd been banned from press boxes, getting a hard time from the boys in the box. "I wouldn't let those guys throw me out. Go on up there. Don't let them push you around," Williams said. Easy for him, to say.

During this brief exchange, Williams was leaning on the park rail near the dugout, touching my left arm. We were both unaware that an Associated Press photographer snapped our picture, one that made news in Rome, Paris, and Tokyo newspapers. (Later the *News* carried it with my story.) I begged Ted for an interview later in Cleveland, but it never happened. Boston reporters said Ted resented them trailing him at night, reportedly because he was dating a teenaged girl. I knew nothing about his private life, but he was a hunk. He was tall and handsome with not an once of fat on him, and he had merry eyes with wrinkly crows feet around them. When he realized the photo was taken, he hollered: "What will you write under the picture?" I shrugged. Editors wrote cut-lines, not reporters. Jackie Jensen, Ted's roommate, came over and said: "Ted is a lone ranger. He doesn't hang around with the rest of the team. He goes back to his hotel at night, reads, watches television. He's a funny guy. I don't blame him the way he feels about writers in Boston. They give him a rough time." Jensen said Ted wanted privacy. These were the days before tabloid journal-ism, and I thought what a heyday tabs would have had with the party at Fernando's Hideaway. No reporters I met filled columns about players at racetracks or saloons.

The Williams photo made page one in the *News* on May 22, 1957, with the caption: "Doris confers with Ted Williams at Fenway Park." At this time in his career, he was batting .394. My reporting batting average was a bit less; at least I had a bit of a story about the great slugger.

Once Kerby Farrell asked me, "Why don't you get married and raise a family instead of bollyfoxing around with ballplayers?" Well, Kerby, then I wouldn't have had so much fun, nor would I have made so much extra money on my Indians trip. Getting paid for guest columns in the eastern newspapers was truly unex-pected. And later the bible of the sporting trade, *Sporting News,* offered more money. They wanted "the last word" on the adven-ture. I wrote: "Personally, I'd rather see a son of mine drive a bus than be a baseball writer. This conclusion is forced upon me after traveling with the Cleveland Indians on their eastern trip recently when I broke through outdated barriers into two press boxes and then was banished from two others. As a matter of fact, I might line up with Ted Williams, who is convinced sportswriters are schmoos, claiming divine rights to the sacred precincts under the eaves of ball parks. But when the Boston problem child thumbs his nose at the boys for their literary hatchet jobs, I charge baseball writers with discrimination against the fair sex of their profession." My *Sporting News* essay went on to describe sportswriters as "snobbish hermits" who were out of step with the changing world of reporting. Ladies in journalism were here to stay. What were the guys afraid of? Hadn't sportswriters read their own papers, catching bylines of such top-flight reporters as Maggi Higgins, Ruth Montgomery, Phyllis Battelle, Doris Fleeson, and a bunch more? I knew the writers' decadent tower was to banish female drones—gabby wives, gum-chewing girlfriends, and camp followers—but editors were growing more conscious of women readers. Until I made the trip, I never gave a thought to the sacrosanct male press box. Hal Lebovitz didn't say a word, neither did Frank Gibbons, baseball writer for the *Cleveland Press*. And I thought they were my friends. But it was Gibbons who had me and Maris tossed out. It was the writer for the Akron paper who was the most antagonistic. For years, I later learned, he wasn't permitted in a Cleveland ballpark on orders of management!

"I suppose I should forgive the guys in New York and Boston. Baseball has endless statistics to dull the minds of sportswriters in the press box," I wrote for *Sporting News*. "They often sound like arithmetic historians and tend to reduce all humanity on the playing field to decimal point averages. My conclusions go for ballplayers, too. I wouldn't want my son to drop out of school in the eighth grade because someone discovered he could throw a curve or hit a ball out of the park. I'd rather he neglected his muscles than his brains. I think driving a bus is an honorable job. My closeup experience with players and portable typewriter boys shows a keen eye for the dollar . . . free stuff and money on the side, stuff for magazines. Some of the glamour of the game tarnished for me when I saw how commercial everything was." Well, frankly, I was stretching things a bit, but so were the guys, and this thing was getting to the contest and gender stage. My fictional son would be a top-notch newspaperman, or maybe a lawyer, someone who made more money than a reporter. Bob Addie of the *Washington Post,* who'd written a few pieces of women's foray into the sports world, wrote me:

> The sexes became embattled, the press boxes preserve their virginity with the exception of Baltimore and Washington. J. G. Spink of *Sporting News* created some controversy, you and I got checks and nobody changed nobody's mind—as the eminent grammarian, Yogi Berra, would say. I knew you'd take it all in the commercial spirit in which it was written—but you know sportswriters are a lot more sensitive than they let on. I imagine poor Ed McAuley [*News* executive sports editor] and Hal Lebovitz, have been dragging their waffles ever since your wrist-slapping of free-loading. You tell those guys it's in the courts [where the "real" reporting took place and which I once covered, by the way] to throw you a bone now and then.

Nice guy, Bob Addie. And he was right. I had to take my lumps from McAuley and from the *Plain Dealer*'s top sportswriter, Gordon Cobbledick, who said that I had "no place" with the guys. The Ohio Associated Press paid me to write about "being in the doghouse of the Baseball Writers' Association of America," which was demanding an apology from me. In the AP Log, I wrote: "The ballplayers, cool at first, gradually defrosted enough to answer questions. For story fun, I had hoped to divert a few of them from sleep, good food, gin rummy, poker and movies, to take them sightseeing, culturally, that is. It was a lost cause. Indians Manager Kerby Farrell said: 'You ain't taking my boys to any art museum. The Smithsonian, O.K. But no art museum.' Was he afraid of the nudes? He surely couldn't imagine a little hike around the National Art Gallery would hurt. Sadly, I report, I wound up in a fun house with star players, trying to be a sport about the novelties, with far from subtle innuendoes."

Returning by plane to Cleveland after the circuit, Indians' pitcher Mike Garcia slipped me a box of chocolates. But it was Dan Daniels, president of the Baseball Writers' Association, who had the final word, actually interviewing me on my home turf, the newsroom. As Yogi Berra said: "It ain't over 'til it's over." The headline on Daniels's story was "Dan Daniels Fails to Blunt Gal Scribe's Needle"— Subhead: "BBWA Head Defends Scribes, Doris Gets Last Word." In *Sporting News,* June 12, 1957, Daniels addressed the news to me that the Association "is limited to males. On special occasions, nonmembers are permitted to work in the press box. But there never has been any provision for women. It is conceivable that the time has come for BBWA to amend its constitution and permit women to join it. I agree that some of the greatest and finest writers in American journalism are women. But women are not wholly qualified to be baseball writers. The way the game is reported today, locker-sniffing player interviews and talks with managers are ultra-important, especially on an evening newspaper. Your *Cleveland News* is in that field."

Daniels also said that I "had a lot of slants of baseball and baseball writing which came of a very short trip on which she scarcely was able to get a true insight into the problems of the writers, the many difficulties surrounding their association with the job which has been getting more and more onerous with the spread of night play; possession of the notion that a baseball writer is so low grade that he will sell his soul and his integrity for a can of beer and a sandwich." He said I was shouting injustice when I had nothing to holler about on a one-shot one-trip, one-stunt baseball reporting adventure. I'll give Dan that, but I read more sports and found stories innocuous, about as critical as if they had been written by the club's press agents. Writers lose objectivity. They are guests of big-time, money-making clubs. Clubs handle travel and hotel accommodations, but I hoped they did not do their thinking, too.

Daniels concluded: "Well it was a lot of fun talking with Miss Doris O'Donnell. She likes Cleveland. She loves her career. But I still feel that she must think that baseball writers are a pretty cheap lot of soul sellers." We parted friends.

Neither my editor nor I anticipated the flap. For me it was just another stunt story for summer reading. My little escapade, however, has become a kind of legend among baseball historians. Today the baseball history books cite not only Babe Ruth as a legend but also, yes, you guessed it, Doris O'Donnell. I've been contacted by half a dozen of them. One asked if it was true that in Boston, the guys set up table with flowers and candles for me in the press box. Not a chance.

-30-

- 11 -

Reporters and Politicians

*D*on't socialize with politicians.

As a reporter I never said that to myself nor did any editor tell me not to. I like politicians, and I even liked the game of politics. My mother had been a Democrat ward leader, bringing me along with her to dozens of rallies where I handed out literature for judges and congressmen. My father's brothers were politicians—one was Cuyahoga County sheriff, another was appointed postmaster of Cleveland by President Franklin D. Roosevelt. My father's brothers were strong union men and officials of local and national unions. My father's cousin was a U.S. congressman (a Democrat, too). At one time I was president of the *News*'s chapter of the American Newspaper Guild, which was very Democratic. Reporters, by the rules of the culture, were to be professionally pristine. We read editorials in our papers where management supported favorite public office–seekers by political gender. We observed media space and television time devoted to political races. With the muddle of relationships between media and public officials, I made personal and professional choices to be neutral. I grew up in the newspaper business when editors liked to make trouble to get at the truth. The chase was exhilarating, despite tiresome hours on paper trails about devious schemes with taxpayer dollars. Politicians were fair game in their public roles, although I believed in their privacy. More transparency was needed in town halls, city halls, state capitols, and congress. A reporter's job was to expose the powerful and greedy once in office. And as a reporter your family background had to be buttoned up in your pocket.

Only the brain dead ignore politics, which are the life-blood of American life and the newspaper business. For the fun of it, I sought out a favorite author, William Greider, to get his take on the modern press. In 1992 he reported that

> Thomas L. Friedman, the *New York Times* correspondent who covers the State Department, played doubles with the secretary of State of Oman. Brit Hume, who covers the White House for ABC, played tennis with the president [President George Herbert Walker Bush]. Rita Beamish of the Associated Press jogged with him. The president and his wife stopped at a media dinner party at the home of Albert R. Hunt, bureau chief of the *Wall Street Journal,* and his wife, Judy Woodruff, of the MacNeill/Lehrer News Hour. Hunt videotaped the scene of his children greeting the chief executive at their doorway. Andrea Mitchell, who covers Congress for NBC, is often seen in the presidential box at the Kennedy Center because she is—in the news gossip's euphemism—the "constant companion" of Alan Greenspan, chairman of the Federal Reserve Bank board. [She is now his wife.]

These media types have moved on to other jobs by now, but you get the drift. Clearly news hotshots cozy up to political hotshots "for the story, for access to the core of power." And yes, I lunched with councilmen, who never paid my tab. I never played golf or tennis with them, and I managed to keep lines of communication open via lots and lots and lots of telephone calls.

Familiarity between media and pols is an offshoot of the beat system used by papers. Editors assign beats to reporters who they believe develop the most news from a particular beat. Police reporters know cops; city hall guys know the mayor, city council, department heads; the state house reporter knows the governor and his staff. How well? That depends on the reporter. I was a beat reporter on a number of occasions, but more often I was a general assignment reporter, which gave me roving room. My tack was to get to know these people, to let them know me face-to-face, name and paper, but on stories involving theft activities, the questions were strictly on a professional basis. Somewhere along the line newspapers have slipped into printing reports from "anonymous" sources or from "background" briefings. The public has no clue who these sources are (shades of "Deep Throat") and whether they are reliable. The boom in communications resulted in an explosion of spinning and biased views from partisans all angling for television media time. Further, in my view, stories are muddled by larding what should be a straight news report with all kinds of incidental, and controversial, statements. In my era, reporters wrote straightforward, clear, accounts of, say, the governor's budget or the merger of major steel companies. This story stood alone as news. Then, a full-blown sidebar gave the opposing or conflicting views, and there might be an analysis piece, graphically marked with a special border to draw the readers' attention.

Too many front page stories are jumbled messes. Readership of newspapers is down, of course, due to the rise of free news on the Internet, but the quality of writing has been degraded. Readers want plain, clearly written stories that are easy to digest and easy to understand. *USA Today* tries to provide this, and bloggers on the Internet have become "citizen journalists," shoving their cogent views into the public meeting place. Somehow letters to the editor have diminishing punch. Not all the criticism is laid on reporters. Public servants are less available, more arrogant. There are walls between the press and the public servant. There are spokesmen and unlisted phone numbers. Sheer arrogance. But this is no excuse for sloppy, lazy, fuzzy reporting. So ends my sermon for this chapter.

In my retirement—I hung it up on February 20, 1996—while going through boxes stored in my shed, I had decided to write my reporter's story. That was interrupted when I accidentally was talked into a civic project by neighbors. And that was something I never intended to do. I had lived with a mother who was never off the phone, always at the beck and call of neighbors and friends fighting city hall. And I had had my fill of covering countless public zoning meetings, dozens of political meetings and hearings, and what seemed like millions of speeches. Nonetheless, I became involved.

The village fathers in my community moved to permit a new National Guard complex, including five units being transferred to Summit County from Cuyahoga County, to occupy twenty-plus acres at the intersection of our road, which caught our neighborhood flatfooted. We knew nothing of the Guard's plans on tax-free land or that its twelve hundred personnel would arrive monthly with cars and military vehicles. The personnel would exceed our own residential population. The village in which I live is a piece of the historic Western Reserve, and it has given westerly borders to the Cuyahoga Valley National Park. The impact caused a group of old and new residents—including newcomers with homes in the half-million-dollar bracket—to clot into an angry citizens' group, which held nightly meetings, formed committees, and gave assignments. Old residents felt enough taxable land was gone. New residents built in the area for its bikeways, rural atmosphere, greenery, and conservation goals. But there was a deep divide between voters and village administrators.

I suddenly found myself doing the citizen-thing I had reported on in my earlier years as a reporter. I was an activist, working with neighbor activists, veterans of other causes, who knew the ropes. They were organizers—they printed flyers, petitioned door to door and to newspapers and local television stations for coverage of street rallies on Sunday mornings and evenings at the firehouse. What the activists didn't have, I did—I was on a first-name basis with public officials, U.S. congressmen, and senators. Never before had I asked these officials for anything of a personal nature or used a newspaper position. Now, using my former reporters' pull,

Interview with Sir Charles Darwin in the Greenbrier Suite of the Chesapeake & Ohio Railroad. Standing, far left, is Howard Skidmore, public relations man for the railroad. 1959; author's collection.

I got our message to these public figures. One U.S. congressman, currently on the House Committee on Appropriations, was able to withhold funding for the project. Over the years, I had covered his numerous campaigns but never even had a cup of coffee with him! Another important figure was a prominent businessman who years ago I had investigated in a home-building venture. It was more than gracious of him to hear our story. He was in position, since his firm was a major land developer, to assist the Guard in locating another property. Thanks to the turnout of citizens, we won. At firehouse meetings the citizens had sat through hours of listening to pros and cons, with the pros presented by U.S. Army brass from Washington, D.C. One said it would "take Congressional action to defeat the project." And we got our "Congressional action." We did.

During my reporting years with the *News* and *Plain Dealer* we, as reporters, were discouraged from joining community councils or serving as officials of civic organizations. The *Cleveland Press* encouraged its staffers to serve on decision-making boards of area councils, giving these reporters "scoops" on major community developments. Author William Greider deplores today's reporters who seek personal glory and in doing so refuse to use reporting skills to challenge power—power of government, business, labor, etc., on behalf of readers.

At the *News,* where I worked from 1944 until it was sold to the *Press* and folded in 1960, I was on general assignment, mainly features on military affairs, industry, obituaries, social news, and people news (for instance wedding anniversaries, reunions, ethnic celebrations). Gradually I was teamed with veteran reporters to cover civil and criminal courts and city hall. If regular beat people were ill or on vacation, I got to cover them singly. At the *News* I was teamed with Webb Seeley, a tall, handsome, ex–University of Michigan football player. He had street savvy, a wide acquaintance with judges and lawyers, and was generally well liked as a straight-shooter. Our assignment was to study the municipal court system relative to the enforcement of building codes. Were codes enforced? If so, which judges enforced them, and what were the penalties? Which judges dismissed charges of code violations? The focus of the story was to determine whether lack of enforcement abetted the growth of slum housing in aging neighborhoods.

Webb was a great legman. He plunged into court records like a cat at catnip. Once we had a clean shot at the records of housing judges, we divided the work: he gave me the figures, I wrote the stories. This was the first time I saw the power of the press. The judges, we found, were not the culprits. The building department was. The inspectors were asleep at the switch, ignoring gross violations of building codes or accepting bribes to tear up violations. The end result was the resignation of the building inspector, and the mayor was forced to upgrade and shake up the department. Webb and I won a handful of awards from the Press Club of Cleveland and the Ohio Newspaper Women's Association.

Webb Seeley became a legend in his lifetime. On occasion, he binged. On one occasion he bolted into Central Police Station, armed, shooting out clocks until the police—his friends—handled him with care and took him home. Another time he was among a handful of male reporters invited to a Lake Erie cottage party after a baseball game between Cleveland councilmen and visiting Chicago councilmen. The host was the Cleveland council president. In the course of the party—where drinks and party girls were abundant—Webb and his friends were photographed by a minion to the council president. Because this pair couldn't help but boast about the party, Webb, Jack Small of the *Press,* and Murray Seegar of the *Plain Dealer* saw the salacious photos. Weeks passed before Webb spotted the minion in the lobby of the criminal courts building. Webb lost control, snatched up the diminutive figure, and tossed him across the floor as he once threw a football. The limp body hit a circular marble column and was carted off to St. Vincent Charity Hospital. There was no lawsuit—not even a story.

I was among the few *News* reporters hired by the *Plain Dealer* in 1960, where I began a career in investigative reporting, winning another Press Club award for a series on zoning. The newsroom climate at the morning paper wasn't as congenial as the old *News,* and when I was offered a job as public relations director of the Cleveland Zoo I took it. It also paid more money. It was an exciting change to edit a new publication, work with television studios on animal projects, and eventually engage with zoo officials in future plans, when the county was to be the zoo's parent. Again, I was offered another public relations job—and another pay increase—at University Hospitals. Well, why not? I liked new challenges, and I frankly enjoyed seeing life on the other side, since many public relations people gave the impression of being superior to mere reporters. What I found were clusters of restrictive rules regarding intercourse with newspapers. It was appalling how a major institution controlled its news. It was with great, great relief when Tom Vail, publisher of the *Plain Dealer* invited me back. I virtually flew there. By contrast to the other world, the newsroom was a butterfly of freedom. Jan Mellow, the top and talented reporter at the *PD,* welcomed me back. "But remember, I'm the star here, not you," Jan said. That was fine with me. Jan and I became good friends. She taught me how to knit socks.

Unfortunately she died young. My fondest memories of Jan are of December 1954 at the old Criminal Courts building where we awaited a verdict from the Sam Sheppard murder case. He was the doctor accused of murdering his wife in their Bay Village home on July 4, 1954. Jan, a cigarette rarely out of her mouth, played poker for hours with the out-of-town correspondents in a vacant courtroom until the verdict came in. It was a scene from *The Front Page*. She was a real pro.

On November 22, 1963, President John F. Kennedy was killed, and away I went to Dallas, Texas, to mop up that story after Bud Silverman, who had been traveling with JFK, went back east for the president's funeral. By 1964 I teamed up with Fred Mollen-kopf and Harry Stainer for other investigations. By then that was all I wanted to do. Fred and I worked on voting fraud, and Harry and I worked on a federal commutation of Ohio's top drug dealer. But the best part of working investigations was getting out of the office, meeting real people, the chase. And stories came from the darndest places. Filling in at city hall, I found myself eating with secretaries of department heads at a nearby quickie restaurant. Conversation was usually "girl" talk, but one day there was talk about the city sidewalk commissioner's picture in the business section of the morning paper. He was honored, in an advertise-ment, for his entry into a million-dollar insurance club. Whoa, these girls said, how could he do both? Fred and I talked it over and presented an idea to managing editor Ted Princiotto. How did this guy on the public payroll earn this award? Where to start? Every city hall in the country has a system, but how to unlock it?

The sidewalk department, tucked into a corner on the second floor of city hall, was cluttered with desks and shelves filled with volumes of ledgers, in disarray. Many were filled with engineer-ing drawings for every foot of sidewalk in the city. Fred and I were clueless when we entered, but we had a letter to the editor about a cement contractor hired by the city to replace sidewalks along a main residential street. We had a starting point to locate that street and that contractor, but we couldn't find either. God bless Phoebe Lunn, a clerk who, we found, watched us with glee as we stumbled along looking for drawings of Broadway. One night she called me at the paper, describing herself as the "tall, heavyset woman with the braided bun in her hair." We hadn't even noticed her. "I'll help. I'll put the volumes that correspond to the work order that corresponds to the contractor," she said. We had a long chat. Her grandparents, the Barrys, were from my grandparents' former home in Westport, County Mayo, Ireland, and much later she gave me a snapshot of my grandparents' cottage. Phoebe, with a bad marriage behind her, had earned a law degree and chose to work in a public job for the pension. Her only daughter was in a convent. She unlocked the mystery of the ledgers. Fred and I found work orders, the city council approval of contracts, the contracts, and the names of the cement contractors.

Rather than rush to print, we roamed the neighborhood where the old sandstone flagging had been torn up and replaced with tons of wet concrete. Fred and I talked to homeowners, steel-workers from nearby mills, in their well-kept homes and yards. They did not want new sidewalks. The walks were not broken but had perfectly intact flagging. They complained to their city councilman and then to City Hall. They were angry because no one responded. Our boss agreed to hire an engineering firm to run test cores on the concrete that replaced the sandstone since the neighbors saw skimpy amounts of poured concrete. Drawings specified the inches of cement required.

While waiting for results from the engineering firm, Fred was invited by the major contractor's son to lunch at a prominent downtown grille. The son brought a lawyer, and Fred brought me. Interesting lunch, since the son had run a profile on Fred, and the conversation got to "how could he afford to be a newspaper reporter?" Fred had a wife and seven children, but how did this guy know that? The son kept referring to our low-paid jobs. He didn't include me—I was wallpaper. Fred had a short fuse, and I encouraged him to leave before he mopped up the floor with the son. "Pretty close to a bribe, wasn't it?" I asked Fred.

Test cores verified complaints that the contractor cheated on the depths of cement poured, which were far lower than specs on draw-ings. Now we wrote our story with pictures of citizens, sidewalks, and cores that brought a flood of complaints from other people and business owners about cheating contractors. The mayor and city council finally reacted. The contractor was fired. The sidewalk commissioner resigned. The department was to be restructured.

A regular beat guy should have handled this story. In fairness, a beat guy rarely had time. This story took hours and hours of paper trail and personal interviews. We got tons of mail from citizens and from executives of plants victimized by similar scams. I read a piece by Chip Scanlan of the Poynter Institute in Florida who said every newspaper writer needs a tightrope, a net, a pair of shoes, a loom, a Bible, a zoom lens, six words, an accelerator pedal, scissors, and a trash can. The "loom" thing caught my eye as I spin and weave. Scanlan said: "What do journalists do? We make connections for people. We connect the police report at the station house to the red bungalow in the neighborhood on the other side of town. We connect city hall with the sewage project that's been delayed for months, tying up traffic and disrupting lives. Raymond Carver, the writer, said for him 'writing is just a process of connections.' Things begin to connect up. A line here, a word there.' Are you weaving the connection in your stories? In your reading? In your life? Ask yourself what lines connect. Turn your computer into a loom that weaves stories." Well said. The sidewalk story answered all his questions. The headline on January 30, 1965, said it all: "Walk Jobs $424,000 Over Limits." Fred and I felt pretty good, and we were happy with our Press Club awards. Forgotten were hours of hand copying figures and records. There were no photostat machines, and we couldn't take records out. Many days our lunches were a carton of milk and a bag of chips in city hall's rotunda.

The story shook up a lot of city departments, we were told, and we soon had lots of new tips. Fred and I figured even an accountant could not untangle the network of contractor-friendly city councilmen relations, but we looked into one tip involving "Mr. Big," Jack Russell, Ward 16 councilman. Somehow Russell had learned about a fire retardant paint used by the U.S. Navy on its battleships to protect their innards from combustible fires. So he introduced an ordinance mandating all commercial building with basements to have ceilings painted with this product. The catch:

Russell was the sole franchiser of the paint. By the time our story was ready to print, the city law director killed the legislation. Our bombardment of questions forced a red alert at city hall, Russell got wind of the story, and the deal died aborning. We caught Russell with another scheme that connected his fire alarm business with the city's own fire alarm system. Thud! How did this go unnoticed at city hall? We only found out when a nursing home caught fire and both the city firemen and Russell's alarm reps answered the fire call. Russell's business had twin tie-ups with the alarm boxes dotted on city streets. Fred and I wondered how many more hidden operations lay in the bowels of city hall. Our editors had other assignments for us, but these were important investigative experiences. We were unpopular with the beat guys for finding dirt on their turf. Councilmen were cool. Recently, one of those city councilmen, now a fat-cat lawyer, hugged and kissed me and invited me to lunch to talk about "the good old days at City Hall." Huh?!

Fred, Harry Stainer, Webb Seeley, and I had unique reporting experiences because we had exposés printed in bold headlines—and we always personally faced the public individual we reported about. We covered and knew well our hometown, and our stories had impact. Public figures (on public payrolls) resigned jobs because of us. We were not afraid to face the people we wrote about. I wonder if that is true today.

-30-

-*12*-

Where Stories Come From

*W*here do stories come from? Editors and reporters have tons of ideas—some good, some bad. So there's a lot of decision making in newsrooms and at daily editorial meetings. Editors weigh pros and cons: How much time is involved? What's the focal point? Can we spare a reporter or two? Does it have reader appeal? Reporters and various editors "pitch" their ideas against another set of reporters and editors. In the long run, the same questions must be answered, because a newspaper is a daily product. It's a fresh product on the doorstep each and every morning. It's a daily miracle, bringing together a band of men and women—news gatherers, copy readers, photographers, technocrats—who fill those pages day in and day out and, importantly, on deadline. And do not forget the advertising salespeople who fill big chunks of space around those sometimes skimpy inches of stories and photos. Aggressive editors—there are lots of them—demand daily doses of dramas, exposés, and graphic art to sell the newly minted product. Then there is always the unexpected—the death of a president, a devastating hurricane miles from the newsroom, a tornado in Ohio, a brutal murder of a doctor's wife, an explosion wiping out blocks of houses near the newspaper plant. All the "stet" news is thrown away, replaced virtually within minutes with crisp new stories and blockbuster photos, again on critical deadline. What an exciting place to be—that newsroom. I have lived that world, almost a fantasy world, many times. It's unforgettable. But the pressure is on daily—in spades.

When Fred Mollenkopf partnered with me on investigative reporting (and my male colleagues were not gender conscious but very professional), we had options, this story or that, based on titillating information we were given or heard from tipsters. Evaluation was routine before wasting time on a wild-goose chase. Options included complaint letters or personal phone calls to editors about this or that situation a reader wanted investigated. Fred and I checked many of these; some paid off, others were vendettas, personal feuds. Between us we had developed lots of friends around town who favored our paper over the competition, the *Cleveland Press*.

Among the most memorable of our collaborations involved Alex "Shondor" Birns, Cleveland's number one racketeer who later died an ignominious death when his car was bombed and mass goers at St. Malachi's (a Near–West Side Catholic church) found pieces of his body in the exterior walls. Fred and I knew Shon as the greeter and bouncer at the Theatrical Grille on Short Vincent, the hangout for the town's cops, lawyers, judges, gamblers, wiseguys, and "easy" girls. It was like Shon's story came out of, well, almost thin air. We were working on a pretty good investigation about voting fraud involving men and women appointed to various public boards, handling city business. They were required to be Cleveland residents but instead, many lived in suburban cities and in counties beyond Cuyahoga, the home county of Cleveland. This tip came from a disgruntled man, not reappointed to a city board, who learned his successor lived in Geauga County. Slim lead, but we pursued it and struck gold. Half these prominent board members were non–city residents. File card by file card Fred and I searched "city" addresses and checked against the "real" addresses of these mayor-appointees—a long and time-consuming chore. Ultimately our series of stories resulted in an exposé of a dozen individuals in violation of state election laws and in the resignation of prominent election board members who were also leaders of the local Democrat and Republican parties. This was followed by an investigation by the Ohio Attorney General of wide-scale voting fraud. It was at the election board that Shon's story landed.

Due to the election board's file system and security policy, Fred and I stood against the filing cabinet, pulling out cards to copy. We spelled off each other, and when Fred took a break, I worked alone. That's when Tom Crisafi, a board inspector, in his tobacco-coarsened voice whispered he had something for me. "Meet me in the hallway," he whispered. What he whispered had my heart pumping. The numbers' (gambling) hoodlums had moved their rackets' headquarters from the East Side into the ground floor of the building in suburban Parma where his brother had his real estate office. Who was it? Tom said it was Shon. That did it. Shondor Birns had successfully stolen a big chunk of the numbers' business from the black East Side hoods, the major operators.

I finished the card file and still no Fred, so I stopped at the Criminal Courts building on my way home for a chat with Cuyahoga County prosecutor John T. (Jack) Corrigan. We both grew up in old Brooklyn and went to Our Lady of Good Counsel grade school. His sister, Mary, was my classmate, and we palled around, roller-skating or ice-skating. Jack, a decorated World War II veteran, was a straight shooter on the job, and he had once embarrassed Mary and me after mass one Sunday. In the eighth grade, Mary and I painted our fingernails fire-engine red. At the communion rail one Sunday morning, Jack spotted us, our hands in chapel-mode, fingernails in full flag. After mass he said: "Those nails. Never again." Chastened by this righteous young man, we didn't repeat the communion rail ritual. Now, facing him across his desk, I gave him the crude map Tom Crisafi sketched of the building and the parking lot setup where the hoods gathered late each day with their haul from numbers' operations. He said: "I'll keep this and have someone look into it." I was pretty nosey about what he did with the map, but Jack Corrigan was tight-lipped.

I learned later that Corrigan had called the Cleveland police chief, who assigned detectives from the Special Investigative Unit (SIU) to investigate the tip in cooperation with Parma police, since the building was on the Parma side. Setting up photographic surveillance, the police worked days to establish an operation—the men parked cars, entered the building, and got license plate numbers to check against known gamblers. Corrigan was required by law to get a court order to legally raid the offices in the building. The prosecutor formally presented his case for a raid before Common Pleas Court judge Hughie Corrigan (no relation to Jack Corrigan), and the judge insisted on knowing the name of the informant, who of course was me. Prosecutor Corrigan refused.

After a judicial dust-up between the two Corrigans, a court order was finally issued, and the raid was scheduled for a propitious time picked by the two police forces. At this point the cops tipped Fred, not me, to the raid, giving the *Plain Dealer* time to get a photographer at the scene when the police moved in. The next day, we had a story of the raid with photos of Shondor Birns and his aide, Edward Keeling, moving material from the car trunk to an office. Fred was there when a seven-man raiding party, led by Capt. Leonard Benedict of Parma and Sgt. Thomas Dever of the 5th Cleveland Police District forced their way into a twelve-by-twelve-foot, paneled office. They found Birns seated at an adding machine with a hatful of clearing house slips. Keeling was flushing more paper in the toilet. Police said it was the office tabulating headquarters for a big numbers' operation. Birns and Keeling were arrested, and Sergeant Dever found $400 in cash along with the slips in paper bags. Birns and Keeling were booked by Parma police, and later the case was presented to the Cuyahoga County Grand Jury.

Fred and I got a bonus on the Birns and Keeling story when Captain Benedict told us another office in the same building was rented by Vulcan Basement Waterproofing Company to a "Joe Allegro" from Tom's brother, John Crisafi. Later Fred and I followed up on Vulcan, because this business hired ex-cons to sell waterproofing to many Parma homeowners whose homes were later burglarized. Police theorized the sales pitches were used to "finger" houses for hits. We also wrote stories on Vulcan, and, as is customary in writing crime stories, we usually wrote sidebars on the characters. In this story we told how in July of 1963 Birns had been questioned in the gangland slaying of a financial manipulator, Mervin L. Gold. Gold's body was found in the trunk of his car in an isolated suburban area. Gold was involved in the theft of stolen, negotiable, high-priced foreign bonds. Shon's name was pretty much a household word, so whatever he did was news. And more news followed the raid when weeks later the Parma case was thrown out on a technicality by Judge Hughie Corrigan. That was no "informant"! Rumor on the street was Birns paid up to $30,000 to kill the charge. Who could ever prove it?

Fred and I threw ourselves into the Vulcan story, based now on many complaints to the Better Business Bureau of sales pitches by the team of Vulcan salesmen, followed by house break-ins. We contacted many unhappy victims, who said waterproofing estimates were made, no work was done, and the homes were burglarized. Several other suburban police departments gave us similar stories, including that the salesmen were on prison parole. Our story ran in the morning *Plain Dealer* with our bylines, and virtually before the ink was dried, the editor was called by a lawyer from New York City, threatening a suit, but nothing ever came of it. We had reported that Fiore C. Bucci, president of Vulcan, was paroled from an Ohio Penitentiary in 1955, after serving time for possession of burglary tools. We found that Vulcan Industries was named in the McClellan Committee hearings on organized crime in congress in 1958. Branch franchises for the basement waterproofing business were spread around the country, and the firm was known to hire former criminals in major cities in America. That business dried up after our exposé. Fred and I were often asked if we were ever threatened. We never said we were, but we did get a garden variety of complaints from readers.

Today's reporters have Google, computers, and lots of public records accessible via computers. All we had then was a pencil, a pad, a notebook, or copy paper. And we didn't have cell phones but pay phones. We also had to pay cash for copies of public records when they were available, and often they were not. Our editors demanded paper trails from us before stories were cleared for publication. We typed our stories on small sheets of paper, interlarded with carbon paper. Spelling mistakes were xxx-ed out as we couldn't spare the time to insert fresh paper to correct an error. I usually typed the stories, with Fred at my side suggesting quotes, figures, or inserts. If we were on deadline, we worked like mad. If the story was a time-release, or "hold" for quotes from persons named, we prepared it for an editor, and sometimes sections of the copy were rewritten for clarity or to prevent libel.

Deadlines varied from paper to paper. At the morning *Plain Dealer* our deadline was early evening for a pre-11 P.M. edition. At times the *PD* held stories for later runs to prevent the 11 o'clock television news from cheating by picking up our stories without credit. Television was quickly becoming a competition for the print media. On street assignments or covering celebrities or political candidates, we found ourselves in the second tier, shoved aside by television cameramen with huge packs of equipment and ropes of wires all over the floor. Politicians were learning the art of instant television coverage and quickie news bites—things the print media couldn't produce. At one mass interview in a downtown hotel, my photographer, Perry Cragg, a wise, old veteran of the news business, tired of being shunted off, sidled to the left of a speaker, facing the television cameras. He spread open his heavy tweed jacket to expose a huge round button. It read: "Fuck you." There was stunned silence and then roars. Perry had killed the television frames of our uppity competitors. Everyone got a lesson that day, and you can bet a story came from that.

-30-

-13-

JFK—The Murder of the Century

*W*here were you when President John F. Kennedy was killed? That question is invariably asked of my generation, plain ordinary citizens who were shocked, numbed by the assassination on that fateful day, November 22, 1963. I cast myself as a plain citizen, but I was also a newspaper reporter doing my job that day, speaking to aspiring journalists at Lakewood High School. Students were eager to ask about gathering and writing stories for a daily paper. They were so much like me as a high school newspaper editor—ambitious, hungry for a future reporting career. My speech was intended to invigorate these young people to see the potentials ahead in the communication fields, not only newspapers but also in magazines, radio, television, or advertising. My message was: if you can write, you can write your own ticket.

Driving back into Cleveland, I was buoyed by the students' lively reactions. They energized me. Then driving across the Shoreway Bridge a radio bulletin shattered my euphoria. President Kennedy had been shot. Clutching the steering wheel with knuckled hands, I blurted, "They got him." Who "they" was, I didn't know. The cry came from my gut, an instinct that the president's enemies were his killers. My thoughts fixed on the newsroom—who was handling the story? It was afternoon, and beat reporters wouldn't be in for several hours unless they heard the news and raced in.

When I got to the office I found the city room in bedlam. Editors, reporters, and the copy desk people huddled in conferences, making decisions, giving orders. In these news-breaking circumstances, high pressure is on the folks in the library who are charged with gathering vital photographs in files for makeup editors, already dummied-up page layouts, with major emphasis on the front page. As a morning paper, the *Plain Dealer* had the luxury of time. I stood, hesitating on the edge of the excited scene, noting a television set on a nearby desk. We never ever had a television in the newsroom and now there were several at various locations. Boy, what a bow to the competition. I badly wanted a piece of the story, but I was patient, waiting until assignments were given, almost like military orders. Finally, managing editor Ted Princiotto called me. "Get ready to take the story from Bud." "Bud" was Alvin Silverman, our Washington, D.C., correspondent traveling with the president in Texas. I instantly found a desk, checked out the typewriter, gathered stacks of half-sheets of paper, pencils, a phone. No headsets. We cradled a phone into a shoulder and typed.

Silverman was on a routine presidential junket with the usual contingent of Washington press corps. Nothing special, except Jackie Kennedy was traveling with her husband, and she always made good photo copy with her classy wardrobe. Silverman was Cary Grant handsome, articulate, too. I had taken dictation from him before. I was a speed typist, along with good shorthand skills. My female generation prepared ourselves with skills in case we were forced into secretarial jobs. Bud was the ideal suave reporter. He dictated in short, concise words, creating instant images, pictures, moods. He rarely fumbled. I waited for his call from Love Airfield near Dallas, where the president had been shot and where Mrs. Kennedy had now boarded a plane with her husband's body, en route to an airfield near Washington, D.C. Bud, finally on the line, described the presidential motorcade in downtown Dallas, the dramatic and appalling scene, the president's head shattered with bullets, apparently shot from a nearby building. The press bus raced after the president's open car to the hospital, where Kennedy was pronounced dead, and then to Love Field. Vice president Lyndon B. Johnson, he said, was sworn in as president with Jackie Kennedy at his side. Bud saw the dried blood on Jackie Kennedy's hosiery as she boarded the plane, and his voice cracked on the line, a phone line he had fought over with other reporters. He had the last phone booth at Love Field. Tears came to my eyes, picturing the perfectly groomed first lady with dried blood on her clothing. That's an image never erased.

Bud began his story: "Dallas, Texas. In a small classroom at Parkland Hospital in the northwest section of the city, I learned that the President of the United States was dead. Malcolm Kilduff, associate White House press secretary, called the press corps together at 2:36 P.M. [Cleveland time.] John F. Kennedy died at approximately 1 P.M., Kilduff said in a voice barely under control. He died of a gunshot wound in the brain. Details are few." A copy boy snatched the short "takes" from my hands, hurrying them to the city editor. I heard: "Tell Bud to keep going. We need more." Bud kept talking, and I kept typing.

Now, in 2005, chills run through my body as I write Bud's words, the ones I typed in 1963:

> The president had been on the back seat, completely motionless, when he was brought into the hospital. One hand was on his head. Mrs. Kennedy, who had been riding in the back seat of the presidential convertible, was uninjured. She was holding her husband's head and she helped three Secret Service men wheel her husband into the emergency room on a stretcher. Vice-President Johnson arrived and he was holding his chest. Rumors flew that he had suffered a heart attack, but this was denied. Texas Gov. John B. Connally, also in the presidential car, was hit in the left side and wrist, Kilduff said. The president, Kilduff said, was not dead when he arrived at the hospital. But he did not regain consciousness.

As I took dictation, I was sick to my stomach. The scene was stark, vivid. Our president, our young president, was dead!

Bud's story, loaded with details, shared the top of the *Plain Dealer*'s morning news with a national Associated Press story. The headline over Silverman's byline was: "Kennedy Is Murdered—Johnson Takes Oath." I had typed so fast, words flying onto paper, that I had to read the printed story to relive the scenes. Mrs. Kennedy at Love Field wore the same dress she had on all day. The fabric was a rough-weave, vivid pink, with a matching pill-box hat and black blouse. Dried blood spots covered the dress and stockings. After a brief swearing-in ceremony for Johnson, he embraced Mrs. Kennedy, "Okay. Let's get this plane back to Washington, quick," he ordered. My typed copy filled four newspaper columns. My right shoulder ached from cradling the phone. Editors ordered Silverman back east to cover the state funeral along with other *Plain Dealer* Washington bureau staffers Phil Goulding and Ed Kernan. Other staffers called prominent Clevelanders for reactions. Princiotto looked at me. "Get ready. You're going to Dallas."

I stayed glued to the AP copy coming into the city room about the sniper, a twenty-four-year-old American who had lived and worked in Russia and married a Russian girl. He was in custody. Eventually he was identified as Lee Harvey Oswald of Fort Worth, Texas, and he was "pulled screaming and yelling from the Texas Theater in the Oak Cliff section of Dallas shortly after a Dallas policeman had been shot to death." Kennedy's death was on everyone's mind. As I left for home, every available reporter was on the phone developing story angles. Talk about a team operation. We all realized that we are never a one-man band but part of a team.

I drove home in a trance, playing over the tragedy. Why was Kennedy killed? What was I supposed to do in Dallas? I was scared. This was big-time news. I was worried, but I mentally sketched plans for the trip, the job ahead. Kennedy was such a part of our lives. My mother, a Democrat ward leader, had attended the Kennedy inauguration in Washington, D.C. We had more photos of Kennedy on our walls than of our family. Mother and I were among a cheering mob at Euclid Beach Park when Kennedy campaigned in Cleveland. My memory was of a slight, young man with a huge

Irish smile, a mop of auburn hair, quick with a quip, at home or on stage. His campaign was full of hope for the country. He had overcome personal hurdles of health and of being both Irish-American and Catholic to win the nomination. He had his critics. Some of my friends said "Kennedy's old man" bought the nomination in Chicago with a fortune made from Depression-era bootlegging. That and other rumors didn't bother me. To me Kennedy was a military veteran, like my brothers and cousins, and his pretty wife was a former newspaper photographer who wore simple, classic linen frocks. Nothing beats seeing a candidate in person, and Kennedy's Euclid Beach presence remains with me.

Now, he was gone. Did the killer kill a Catholic? An Irish-American? A Democrat? Did the Russians kill him? The Cubans? The Mafia? Racists? Theories were—and remain—all over the place. Personally, I will never believe the Soviets allowed Oswald to leave Russia with a Russian wife unless he was programmed for a special mission, maybe killing our president. These thoughts muddled in my mind, and I recall little about packing. I traveled light, figuring I could always buy toothpaste or nylons on the road. After all, Dallas was not Africa. In 1944 a friend and I drove cross-country to California, but Texas was virgin territory to me. Before heading for the airport, another drama filled the television. Jack Ruby, a Dallas nightclub operator, had shot Oswald in the hallway of the Dallas police station. A single pistol bullet from Ruby's gun smashed into Oswald's left side below the chest. Was Texas still the Wild West? My nerve ends tingled, yet I could barely wait to get there. I thanked God for the police beat stint.

On out-of-town assignments I wore simple skirts, sweaters, and flats, things needing little care. A raincoat was standard gear, along with a big purse, pens, pencils, steno pads, lipstick, aspirin, and an extra pair of eye glasses. The *Plain Dealer* was not stingy on hotel arrangements, and I had a room at the best hotel in downtown Dallas. The hotel bulletin board announced a breakfast for leading civic leaders. I stood meekly in the doorway, listening to speeches from this group of hotshots. A program named the Dallas executives, leaders from the trendy Nieman-Marcus department store, and the Chamber of Commerce. What I heard was startling:

there would never be a memorial on the Dealey Plaza, the shooting site for Kennedy. The message from these Southwestern businessmen was confusing to a northern Democrat who had voted for Kennedy, along with her entire family. It was a former mayor, called "Mr. Dallas," speaking from the podium, who forcefully opposed a memorial to the slain president. This was chilling. How was I going to cover the story? I was an intruder at this meeting and had no idea if it was covered by local reporters. Who among this group would talk to me? I grasped the significance of this national tragedy, how it affected the proud city of Dallas, how it tarnished its commercial and political reputation. My plan of action before I heard this news was to interview the mayor, police chief, and some citizens. Now the plan was shattered. I didn't know a soul in Dallas with the exception of two newsmen, one of whom was a columnist named Greene, and the other was Felix McKnight, an editor who had been in the Soviet Union in the late 1960s with a group of Texas farmers.

McKnight was courteous, providing background on public officials and the city's commercial leadership. Before the Kennedy visit the *Dallas Morning News* carried stories about political splits, fractures among the town's top Democrats and disagreements over sponsorship of the visit, and the parade route. Apparently it was a last-minute change in route plans that took the cavalcade through Dealey Plaza, past the book storage building. And who knew in advance of the change of plans? Another one of the mysteries of the assassination plot. Other rumblings were between the extreme right-wing factions and moderates. There were differences between the Connally and Johnson Democrats, too. A witches' brew of political turmoil awaited Kennedy. I wondered if his aides had scoped out this disorderly political climate. Facing this, I retreated to my hotel room and sat at the desk with phone and telephone directory, checking out labor union listings, which were few and far between. Dallas employers, unlike in Cleveland, were virtually union-free. And few labor leaders were less than candid about working conditions for union members. Unionists told me black ministers were more candid, and they were. City officials refused interviews. Finally at city hall I sat outside the offices, gathering news crumbs from visitors and other reporters. Each night I wrote a draft for later stories.

One of my stories ran December 10, 1963: "This is a city where the 57-year-old mayor, Earle Cabell, is under 24-hour police guard and the Police Chief Jesse E. Curry, no longer talks for publication. It is a city of fear, confusion, and distrust. 'I didn't want the guard,' Mayor Cabell said, 'but there were . . . rumors or tips that my life had been threatened. The chief is so jittery about it that to please him, I have a guard.'" (Dallas police recorded threats against Curry.) That was what I got from the mayor after hours outside his office. On a nearby bench sat two detectives, guarding him. Newsmen called Chief Curry a "nice guy," but that was before the deaths of Kennedy and Oswald. Now he wasn't talking to anyone. It took a while to identify "Mr. Dallas," R. L. Thornton Sr., at the breakfast. He said: "For my part, I don't want anything to remind me that a president was killed on the streets of Dallas. I want to forget." Cabell told newsmen "not to pay attention to him. He's an old man." Others did form a memorial committee after some soul searching. Chamber leaders called for "business as usual," and Dr. William Tate, president of Southern Methodist University called for "fair and considered treatment of others . . . even our adversaries."

Few flags hung half-staff along streets. No black crepe hung from windows along main highways. Ropes of silver tinsel, sparkling angels, and myriad lights festooned Main Street at night, and the bright Texas sun splashed over glittering store fronts by day. I walked through Dealey Plaza, a few yards from the highway where the presidential motorcade was attacked. The grass was matted from feet of curious spectators, many with cameras taking pictures of the six-story Texas Book Depository Building. At first police theorized shots came from the fifth floor, as employees had seen Oswald in the building at various places days before the shooting. Afterward there was a consensus that three shots came from the sixth floor. The Warren Commission concluded that a single bullet wounded both Kennedy and Connally and a third went astray. Yet today forensic experts still disagree about the flight of the bullets, some claiming they came from a government building and others believing they came from an area above an overpass. Will we ever know the truth?

All of us visiting reporters followed the news in Dallas papers, describing November 22 as "Black Friday." They printed statements from the mayor that Oswald was not a Texan. Lee Harvey Oswald was born in New Orleans, Louisiana, lived in Fort Worth, Texas, the Bronx, New York, North Dakota, Japan, and Minsk, Belarus. The man in the street was resentful and defensive of "outsiders" like us. The very vocal right-wing conservatives were angry, claiming the press "blamed us." Right-wing literature said: "Oswald, from jail, admitted he was a Marxist." Mayor Cabell blamed the press for "unrestrained" activities just prior to Ruby shooting Oswald in the jail hallway.

But the real focus of the newspapers was on the controversy surrounding Kennedy's visit. My story on December 13, 1963, stated: "No one can say that President Kennedy wasn't warned about Texas—Dallas specifically—being enemy territory. The day he arrived in Dallas, Nov. 22, he was greeted by a crowed of well-wishers at Love Field, but also by an editorial and a full-page advertisement, loaded with emotion-packed innuendoes in the morning newspaper." The *Dallas Morning News* editorial said: "Dallas hopes, Mr. President, that your brief interlude here will be pleasant. The *News,* along with thousands in this area, has disagreed sharply with many of your policies, but the opposition is not personal. In all good humor, we should remind you, you're in territory with substantial Republican representation." Texas Governor Connally, a Democrat, received 70,479 votes in Dallas while his Republican opponent, Jack Cox, received 95,988, which changed the once Democrat majority to now Republican. The publisher of the 121-year-old *Dallas Morning News,* E. M. (Ted) Dealey, was remembered well for a remark he had made to President Kennedy at a White House luncheon in 1961. Dealey said: "We need a man on horseback to lead this nation and many people in Texas and the Southwest think that you are riding Caroline's tricycle. The general opinion of the grass-roots thinking in this country is that you and your administration are weak sisters." The *Chattanooga Times* said Kennedy told Dealey everyone was entitled to his own opinion, "but the difference between you and me, Mr. Dealey, is that I was elected president of this country and you were not. I have the responsibility for the lives of 180 million Americans which you have not." This story grew out of proportion. I heard it many times. Pro-Kennedy people said it showed the "inflammatory" attitude of this influential paper. Another story featured Connolly and Texas senator Ralph Yarborough, both Democrats, fussing over their seating arrangements for the Trade Mart luncheon, which featured Kennedy. Yarborough even balked at riding with Lyndon Johnson but later relented. Baxton Bryant, a former Methodist minister and congressional candidate, demanded a motorcade route that was not in the original plan.

Conflicting stories everywhere. The mayor took heat from all sides, speaking against a minister who said children cheered over the death of Kennedy. The mayor said the same minister told children there was no Santa Claus. Do you laugh or cry over this stuff? But this guy, Rev. William A. Holmes, was on national television saying, "Dallas is a city where fourth-graders in a North Dallas school clapped and cheered when their teacher told them of the assassination." It was nutty. Rabbi Levi Olan of Temple Emanu El told me, "It was a good time to get the feeling of the community. It's like seeing a patient with a fever." Bruce Alger, the Republican congressman, said, "Dallas is a conservative community where businessmen vote with their pocketbooks. They don't like to pay taxes and they don't like government to be so active." Everyone had an opinion.

This was a tough assignment, and in phone calls with Princiotto he urged: "Keep going. Keep going." Other reporters in Dallas shared my problem. We dined together and swapped stories. Some said, "Dallas is a sick city." Others called Oswald "a Marxist." A Dallas labor leader who refused to allow me to print his name said the Dallas Police Association was dominated by the multimillionaire H. L. Hunt, and a lot of cops were on his payroll. Hunt sponsored a controversial radio show and joked about Ruby's makeshift jail cell. Another reporter and I visited Ruby's nightclub, where there was a real jail cell. Ruby's Carousel Bar did big business. Jokesters said Ruby "arrested" patrons, held them in the cell, and called the cops. Weird! Felix McKnight said he had thrown Ruby out of his office weeks before, refusing to run one of Carousel's ads.

In Fort Worth, Texas, I met Kenneth W. Ryker, a former master sergeant in army intelligence, now running the Freedom Center in a storefront. Folks in Dallas said Ryker's followers were virulent anti-Communists. His literature protested "the left's smear campaign against the John Birchers, Billy James Hargis, Herb Philbrick and himself, Ken Ryker." He treated me like a dumb student, saying, "Kennedy should have been cited for breaking the law by trading with Communist bloc countries." He said the objectives of communism "have been the policies of the U.S. government in 1963." He lost me. At the *Fort Worth Star-Telegram,* Mabel Goulby suggested: "If you're going to do something useful, trace the Communist background of Jack Ruby." She studied files of congressman Martin Dies and his hearings on un-American activities in 1938 and linked Jack Ruby to a "Jack Rubenstein, founder of the Revolutionary Youth, a Communist International organization." She gave her material to the FBI. We had zealots like her back home. I got headaches.

Fort Worth reporters talked of a wild party the U.S. Secret Service guys attended at the local press club the night of November 21. Nothing was printed about the drinking. Years later I met an agent who was there (and now in Cleveland) who was adamant that there was no drinking party. Agents were dispersed around the country after the president's death. Fort Worth reporters laughed at my ignorance of Texas politics—of Lyndon Johnson's big business connections and how he had stolen his senatorial election from Pappy O'Daniel. It was obvious my Texas history page was a blank. As the saying goes, "all politics is local." It was no wonder the Dallas paper warned Kennedy of the atmosphere. My stories weren't kind to Dallas, and when Cleveland was wracked later with race problems, the Dallas papers did a number on our city.

Since 1963 there are few Kennedy books I have left unread. Having been in the Soviet Union in 1956, I found it inconceivable that Oswald, once in the U.S. military in Japan as a radar specialist, and a Russian linguist, could have entered the USSR, worked, and married there without KGB contacts. It was rare to treat an American with kid gloves and rarer yet to allow one to leave with a Russian wife. This is not to say there were not other sinister plots by the Cubans in retaliation for the Bay of Pigs fiasco, or the American Mafia that was anti-Kennedy because of attorney general Robert Kennedy's nationwide war on organized crime. Where is the truth? Somewhere, somehow, there is or were people at the core of the Dallas community who were terribly frightened to death at the assassination of a president in the heart of their proud city.

-30-

-14-

"Burn, Baby, Burn"

$\mathcal{T}$hinking back to the Hough riots of that hot July 1966 gives me a chill. It was a scary time. At the time we had one black male reporter on the *Plain Dealer* news staff who refused to cover what turned out to be a full-fledged, five-day orgy of rioting and burning. "I work for whitey," he said. "I can't go." So I did.

Walking down Hough Avenue, on the inner East Side of Cleveland, behind rumbling Ohio National Guard tanks and with councilmen George Forbes and Morris Jackson, we shrunk into our long coats, collars pulled up, hands in pockets. The way we bundled into our clothes and hats an onlooker wouldn't have known if I was as black as George and Morris or not. Each of us, we admitted later, was certain any moment a bullet would sink into our backs. The tanks wouldn't protect us; neither would the police sharpshooters on the roofs of buildings in the canyon of commercial buildings and slum apartments. It was with relief, coupled with high-pitched nervous laughter, that, halfway down the street littered with debris and broken glass, we ducked into a small shop, its window plastered with a handmade sign: "Soul

The disorderly streets of Cleveland's East Side during the Hough riots of 1966. Author's collection.

Brother." As if that message to the rampaging African American citizens would grant safety and sanctuary to this humble black merchant. He looked me over, fearfully. Forbes, laughing, said: "She's half-souled." If only that quip could paint out the cloud of fear hanging over the entire Hough area, with its crumbling tenements and blighted mansions, chopped into bulging rooming houses owned by wealthy suburbanites.

I don't know if I was the first or fifth choice of reporter the city editor assigned that morning to test, for a story of course, what was happening in Hough after nights of rioting and vandalism. The town was now under the microscope of police and city officials who were searching for clues to the source of the disorder spreading like wild fire through a neighborhood once home to prominent Cleveland families now gone to newer affluent sites. The shifts in population in Cleveland had been under way for many years, beginning when the city fathers experimented with ethnic cleansing of old inner-city streets, burning clapboard houses with gingerbread trim to erect concrete, block, public housing for the poor. The original housing belonged to the founding families of the historic Western Reserve. The next tenants were immigrants from Germany, Ireland, Italy, and later southern Europe, including many of Jewish background. Pushed by innovative urban renewal—where property was taken from owners by eminent domain—the population dispersed to greener pastures.

With World War II Cleveland became an industrial magnet for Southern blacks, yearning, too, for greener pastures and good-paying jobs in steel mills or war plants. These checkerboard moves, overseen with professional smugness by social architects, were viewed with horror by the city's safety forces and a few academic types, who were wondering when push-shove social engineering would explode. Already Detroit, New Jersey, and Watts in Los Angeles had burned, leaving blackened shells and corpses and a community in guttural rage against what rioters scorned as a heartless white society. Hough was a tiny cracked mirror of Watts, where smoke was seen for miles as chanters' voices joined the spiraling vapors with, "Burn, baby, burn." Were these chanters getting even with social planners, greedy developers who shoehorned these Southern migrant-strangers into the worst housing in the city's marketplace?

Of course I took the assignment eagerly. Police reporters were the first on the scene the first two nights of the riots, secure in a police communication bullet-proof van within earshot of gunshot and smoke. My city editor had said: "You know the area, the councilmen. Call them. See what you can do." This was how Forbes and Jackson became my companions.

I liked to believe my association with the African American community was alive but tenuous. I had lived with a black family in the late 1940s and kept ties to various families. I covered area council meetings, many chaired by rising black politicians who were working diligently for new housing, neighborhood safety, and new schools. I also covered city council meetings, writing many, many news stories of efforts by young African American councilmen (also rising young attorneys) such as George Forbes. Morris Jackson later served in the state legislature. Other of these promising young men served in city administrative posts, and one councilman, George White, became a federal judge. There was no shortage of leadership, rising like a big bowl of yeast bread, in the Hough and Glenville areas, which African Americans inherited from white flight. Luckily for me, Forbes and Jackson were game for the walk, and that became a story, along with a snapshot of this fiery eruption on July 18, 1966.

Police pieced together this scenario: a black patron at the Seventy-Niners Cafe, in the heart of Hough, was refused a glass of water in a saloon with the sign that read, "No water for Coloreds." Apparently this thirsty patron didn't belong to the Hough Area Council, eager do-gooders uplifting schools, parks, streets, and libraries. The patron was joined by a bunch of young hoodlums, smashing the cafe windows with bricks. Once that was demolished, they roamed the street, which was mostly a white commercial string, vandalizing window by window. By night, gangs, gathering strength, moved into the tenements, burning and destroying, forcing their fellow citizens to the rubbish-littered streets. As night fell, newly formed police SWAT teams, headquartered in the mechanized bomb-proof vehicle, plotted to cordon the damage, tightening a noose and killing roving mayhem. Fire bombs were thrown. Shots by snipers sailed out of apartment houses—a young black mother was killed while standing in the window of one of them. Crowds cut the fire hoses of firemen watering street fires that had been set. Twelve policemen were injured. Police feared rioters would outrun Hough, and eventually an armed black man was killed near Mayfield Road by two white men. Farther away in Shaker Heights, a black man was killed in a drive-by shooting.

The newsroom on the morning of the second day was in shock, editors passing out assignments like generals sending troops into battle. Reporters went to talk with Cleveland mayor Ralph S. Locher, to Police Chief Richard Wagner, to various city councilmen, and to activist city leaders. My assignment was the walk down Hough, where I later described the fear, tensions, shattered storefronts, and bins of garbage and rubbish strewn about. We tiptoed around debris on the sidewalks. The worst part was the smell; the awful, dirty, smoky smell of rubbish, paper, and asbestos burning. It was like barbecue smoke only worse, and the smell clung to our clothes and hair. The scene never really washed out of my memory, coming back to me year after year when I covered fires throughout the city.

After writing my story in the newsroom, I joined a meeting of editors, who were brainstorming about recent events in the African American community and sorting out kernels of activities involved in the mix of this social upheaval. The theme of the meeting was: How did it happen? Before this flame-out, urged on by African American councilmen and with the desk okay, I visited various headquarters of black activists, some of whom marched, military-fashion, on city streets with wooden replicas of rifles and carrying freedom banners. It was the police chief's theory that the JFK House was the pseudo–military training center for unemployed youths. The JFK House on Superior Avenue was named for Jomo Freedom Kenyatta, and possibly John F. Kennedy. The police subversive unit, which was comparable to similar police units throughout the country, amassed data on a growing number of black activists as well as their publications supporting Chinese and Cuban revolutions. The operators of the JFK House were Harlell Jones, Ahmed Evans, Lewis G. Robinson, and their band of followers. Robinson and his white wife, Beth, had recently cut sugar cane in Cuba for Fidel Castro. In the cellar of the house were Black Power posters with arms outstretched, holding rifles.

My story was pure reporting; what I saw, what leaders said. After the story appeared, a delegation of white ministers protested, claiming harassment. My editors countered with: What else can we write but what the reporter saw with her own eyes? Personally, I doubt any of these guys ever visited 8811 Superior Avenue, but to be fair, churches had opened doors to the bulging growth of black citizens, even though it was more patronizing than understanding.

Thinking back, our city room meetings brought together threads of the Black Power movement, its various leaders, and its goals. I first met Robinson and his wife when their group formed the United Freedom Movement in the early 1960s, demanding desegregated schools. They had sit-ins at the school board, where I walked over prone bodies entering and leaving the school board building. I ran into their group when the school board broke ground for a new public school on Lakeview Road. Along with the Robinsons were white ministers Rev. Bruce Klunder and Rev. Charles Rawlings, all of whom were attacking school board policies. At the site, police formed a human chain, restraining protesters from the muddy site where a bulldozer surged over clumps of mud, enlarging a huge excavation. Suddenly and unexpectedly, Beth and Klunder broke through the chain and slipped into the growing hole. Klunder raced ahead as the bulldozer moved forward. People shrieked, "Stop! Stop!" Klunder was flattened and died under the bulldozer's mud-caked treads. We—cops, housewives, children, reporters—stood like statues. The scene was bizarre but real. Shakily, I tried to make notes, pulled my mud-sucked boots from the hillside, and raced to the newsroom. These were days without cell phones, and I didn't even bother with a pay phone, I drove like mad while the crazy death seared forever in my mind. Police cameras caught the scene on film. I still have the photos. While writing, I got a call from Rawlings, inviting me to a "victory" party at a downtown hotel. He was affiliated with the Ohio Episcopal Diocese. I asked my boss: "Shall I go?" "For God's sake, no. He's sick."

During the summer and fall of 1963, we reported on the United Freedom Movement on and off, with its clamorous demands of the school board to end de facto segregation. Promises came slowly, and finally the board agreed to bus a small percentage of black children for a forty-minute period each day. Protests continued at two elementary schools and moved on to a third, in the Italian-American community of Murray Hill. Murray Hill is a tight Italian conclave, known during the prohibition and Depression days for a series of bloody assassinations, the "Corn Sugar Wars." Bootleggers had illegal stills in their homes and were making illegal hooch with corn sugar. The morning of January 30, 1964, I was called at home to stop at Murray Hill on my way in. "There's a rumor of trouble at the white public school, Memorial."

United Black Brotherhood demonstrators at the Cleveland Central Police Station, 1966. The leader of the Brotherhood, Ahmed Edvans, is second from right. Photograph by Ray Matjasic, *Cleveland Plain Dealer.*

By the time I arrived there, a group of citizens, between one thousand and fifteen hundred, lined Murray Hill, not far from the red brick schoolhouse. There was sparse traffic on the road when along came an elderly black man with two elderly white women who were driving east, up the hill. Out of nowhere a tall, husky, white man attacked the drivers' side of the car with a tire iron before a slew of male onlookers could grab the attacker, smashing him to the pavement as the car sped off, but not before photographers caught the attack. Photos in the afternoon *Cleveland Press* brought outrage; reportedly the paper lost thirty thousand of its circulation in the Italian community within a week.

During the mob scene two of the *Plain Dealer* Teamsters' circulation men had yanked me into a small bar, and the bartender poured me a thimble of muscatel wine. The talk there was of machine guns on rooftops to protect families. Incidentally, many of our teamster drivers were Italians. These experiences, Klunder's death and the attack on the car, lacerated my psyche. I hate crowds. I am frightened to death of crowds. Later, covering Senator Ted Kennedy in an old converted night club where Secret Service men cordoned the press with yellow plastic tape, I slipped away, watching events from a cleared exit. I was paranoid of being trampled to death in a fire. At rallies my spot is the nearest exit, and my car is parked, in cleared space, heading out.

The pre–Hough riot days revealed a variety of newspaper editorials begging the growing number of African American professionals to "cool it" with constituents. The pot continued to boil against the school board and against absentee landlords, who collected weekly rents from slums and skirted off to suburban mansions. Cleveland was a divided city. I spent hours and hours with Councilman Leo A. Jackson of Ward 24, a harsh critic of his own black community, especially exploiters of "their own." Black Power was growing, and its voice reached into the offices of big law firms, corporations, city hall, and smoke-filled offices of the major political organizations as the engine of discontent rolled along. It wasn't as though the brains of the three daily newspapers were dead. Each paper delicately poked and pointed at the problems—black/white, urban/suburban, segregation/desegregation, wages/relief, religious/secular. It was a whirligig of good and bad intentions.

After the smoke cleared in Hough and the sooty fires died and left that awful smell of doused wood and wool, I scoured the East Side, interviewing people in all walks of life for a series of stories. White people called blacks shiftless, lazy, no-good drunks, and thieves. Whites with close-knit families did not comprehend the plight of African Americans in a segregated city. And the blacks, trapped in a vicious circle of frustration, distorted the image of whites. As I stated in my story in the *Plain Dealer*, "The Hough rebellion is the tragic by-product of this distortion. It is the burden now shouldered by the teen-ager and the young black men who feel totally untouched by the millions of taxpayers' dollars used to study his problem and to help." Sociologists from Western Reserve University with foundation grants lifted the lid on Hough. Suburbanites gave "one day a week" to Hough. Yet poverty in the town grew, with the medium income below $4,000; unemployment was at 9 or 10 percent; only a couple of men here and there were admitted into the trades or into the construction work field. It was a sad, sad picture. Sometimes I said to my African American friends: "What took you so long?" The Irish, I said, wouldn't have stood for it; yet I knew the Irish fought decades for their due. A quote in Gunnar Myrdal's *American Dilemma* says: "America is free to choose whether the Negro shall remain her liability or become her opportunity."

As far back as the 1940s I was familiar with the black streets, neighborhoods, and the urban renewal areas. In February of 1967 my stories appeared as "Cleveland's Negroes: Frustration/Hope." I talked to hundreds of persons over the weeks. "Cleveland is the most prejudiced [city] I have ever lived in," a former IRS clerk said. In a Superior Avenue beauty shop, a civil rights marcher said: "In a revolution you have to be willing to give your life for what you believe." In a crowded St. Clair grocery store: "A Negro has to decide which side he is on; he can't vote 'white' if he wants to help us." With an ongoing story like this, we, the whole staff, were immersed, although there was still a daily paper with daily demands requiring us to report events of the day. But in the wings, politics took over the front pages, a direct result of public unrest. Leaders were torn by the downtown construction of Erieview against low-income housing, both projects stumbling along with delays. James Lister, the father of the drastic urban renewal projects with his eminent domain hammer, resigned, leaving undone plans for the University-Euclid area and increasing restlessness in Hough's slums. Finally the Housing and Urban Development Department cut off all federal funds, a major blow to the Locher administration and a call by the establishment for new blood in City Hall.

Changes came to the upper editorial management of the *Plain Dealer*. In December of 1966 Tom Vail's two right-hand men, Phil Porter and Barry Mullaney, veteran newsmen and my good friends, retired. William M. Ware, former night managing editor, and Tom Guthrie replaced them. I had known Ware for years, both as an active Newspaper Guild member and, later, in management, as an editor. Walking back from downtown one afternoon, Ware asked me—it was not an assignment he said—to look into the background of a young black state representative, Carl B. Stokes. Rumors abounded of a "dump Locher" movement to replace a white mayor with a black one, and Stokes was in the running. I was to get whatever I could pick up. It was informal, verbal, and remained that way.

Newspapers, like other industries, are not immune to takeovers or the stopping of publication. The *Cleveland News,* where I started in 1944, was "sold" to the *Cleveland Press* in January 1960, and it was like a stab in the back to the loyal and close knit *News* family. Several veteran columnists actually suffered heart attacks. The suddenness of the *News's* decline left a bitter taste among its victims. The *Plain Dealer* and the *Press* hired a limited few, based on actuarial data. I was hired by the *Plain Dealer,* whose many staffers held themselves above the rougher, more competitive *News* and *Press.* But more shock waves hit the newspaper business on March 1, 1967, with the bombshell news: Samuel I. Newhouse, head of the Newhouse dynasty, bought the paper from the Holden estate for $55 million. This was the result of a bitter tug-of-war among various Holden descendants, all of whom, except Tom Vail, were residents of the East Coast. Tom, too, was an old friend whom I met while he was having his journalism internship at the *News.* Now Tom was editor and publisher with carte blanche over the newsroom. While Tom benefited financially from the sale, his dream of a new building on the shoreway east of Edgewater Park and a newspaper enterprise sadly vanished.

A year and a half after the Hough riots an election was on the horizon, and while the Democratic organization stuck with the pragmatic Locher, Stokes, an attractive figure, was backed with enthusiasm and funds by liberals and businessmen. It was no secret that I had discussed Stokes with Porter before he retired and kept a running dialogue with Ware. Porter, in his retirement

Anniversary parade of the Hough riots, on Superior Avenue. Pictured here are Harlell Jones (left), head of the JFK House; Cleveland mayor Carl B. Stokes (center); and Willie Tolbert (far right). Photograph by Ray Matjasic, *Cleveland Plain Dealer.*

memoir, wrote: "Doris O'Donnell, the star reporter who had many contacts with police, the FBI, and with lesser black leaders, had no confidence in Stokes and did not believe his past record as a liquor inspector or police prosecutor qualified him to be mayor. Finally Vail took the bull by the horns himself and decided to go all-out for Stokes in the primary election. Some of his political friends in Columbus told him he'd be sorry later." Vail thought Stokes would unite the city, and in a rush to beat the press, the *Plain Dealer* endorsed Stokes around Labor Day. Stokes won the primary by twenty thousand votes. In November, with both papers endorsing Stokes, he beat the Republican, Seth Taft.

Before the primary, late one night in the newsroom, I took a call from Jack Raymond, the *New York Times* correspondent I met in Moscow, the same reporter who was stuck with me on a Ferris wheel in Gorky Park. Now working for a Washington, D.C., advertising agency, Jack asked me for a rundown on Carl Stokes. "Why?" The agency's account involved the Democratic National Committee, and the bottom line was, Vice President Hubert Humphrey was interested in promoting Stokes for mayor. Not too surprising. Ohio Gov. Frank J. Lausche gave Stokes an in-or-out order: either leave the state or face problems associated with Stokes's "irregular activities" while a state liquor agent. Stokes opted to move to Minneapolis where he hooked up with Humphrey Democrats. At one time, Humphrey was once one of the nation's youngest mayors, and Stokes became a Humphrey acolyte. With few bosses in the newsroom, I took that scoop straight to Vail, who ordered an eight-column headline over my story, news of Humphrey's support of Stokes for mayor. I was not around for Stokes's victory party on election night since the *Plain Dealer* assigned me to Gary, Indiana, to cover a spectacular election—that of another black man, Gary Hatcher, who was elected mayor of that mill town city. These were historic times to be sure.

-30-

-15-

On the Trail of Martin Luther King's Assassin

*D*r. Martin Luther King Jr. was killed by a sniper's bullet in Memphis, Tennessee, on April 23, 1967. James Earl Ray, the number one suspect, was arrested thirteen months later, captured by Scotland Yard at Heathrow Airport, London, England, on June 8, 1968. The arrest and conviction, while it sent Ray to jail, never ended the mystery of King's death. After Ray's arrest, the *Plain Dealer* assigned me to backtrack on Ray's life, to sketch out who and what the man was all about and judge the killer of the nation's civil rights leader. This was a tall order.

I barely knew where to start, so I went to the usual place—the paper's library, where there were envelopes of clippings. Stories carried datelines from all over the world, and sorting them into some sort of order directed me first to Jefferson, Missouri, and its state penitentiary, once home to Ray, the prison bum and petty thief. Ray's escape to freedom and into history books began here. The big question was: How could this ex-con travel all over the United States, Canada, Britain, Belgium, and Portugal without visible means of support in thirteen months? Cops and accountants say cherchez la femme; cherchez the money, too. In other words, did Ray have a godfather? If so, who? Early on in the investigation veteran reporters for major papers posed the question asking whether there was a link between the assassination of President John F. Kennedy and Dr. King. My personal opinion is there was a link: some really kooky extremist sicko. His name or names and perhaps the bagmen I believe are locked in secret Justice Department files that may never see the light of day. Conspiracy theorists trolled these grounds for decades.

My bookshelves bulge with books on assassinations, but in 1968 my mind was wide open. I had a story to find and write. Rookie reporters learn from old hands the tricks to knock over roadblocks as high as Mt. Rushmore. Once, my late husband, Howard Beaufait, covering executions at the old Ohio Penitentiary in the 1930s, faced opposition from prison bureaucracy. He and veteran photographer Perry Cragg ran circles around the prison system by interviewing "cons" and "trustees" working as gardeners and laborers on prison grounds. They pried "prison grapevine" information from these guys.

In 1968 as I wandered around Jefferson City, Missouri, a lively Southern city with its imposing capitol buildings, I began my groundwork for the story. I had been in Jefferson once before as a guest of the all-black Lincoln University to receive an award for my "Cleveland's Negroes" series. Also receiving awards were Bill Raspberry, *Washington Post* columnist, and a *Los Angeles Herald-Examiner* columnist. Seated in the school cafeteria at a long table set with white linen cloth and the best cutlery and surrounded by elite professors and guests and a tall, slender, aging university president, I didn't expect much excitement. But suddenly we were being shoved around by a gang of black youths who were yanking the table spread and tossing dishes and food over the floors and walls. It was a riot.

Everyone fled, and I raced to the lobby's phone booth, immediately calling the *Plain Dealer*. Finally, after many rings, a weary-sounding deskman listened to me and then said, "Call back tomorrow." Stunned, I walked into the lobby, which was now filled with tear gas and state troopers. Eyes stung by chemicals, I stumbled outside literally into the arms of a huge black man, a state legislator. Our group adjourned to a nearby hotel for the delayed event. My rescuer joined us, and we chatted about Cleveland and ultimately the Cleveland Indians' once star whiz-bang pitcher, Satchel Paige.

Unfortunately my Missouri rescuer/legislator was not available on my second trip to the city. I knew no one there. Officials at the state prison, which was built in the early 1800s on sprawling acreage, refused calls from reporters. So I wandered around the capitol grounds, peeking into the neatly manicured gardens through huge, green hedges. Men in prison garb (uniform coveralls) hoed, weeded, and mowed the lawn. Through a hole in the shrubs near the rear building, I called to one guy. He was as scared as I was, but curiosity won him over, and he scrunched down near me under the bushes. I told him my dilemma of being a reporter who was looking for news on Ray, and he had a brilliant idea. "Talk to the guards." "How?" "They live all over town. You can find them somehow. Can't you?" I crawled away and went back to my hotel and to the Yellow Pages for names of unions, ministers, legislators, and newspapers. I hesitated calling any of them, especially the paper. I didn't want to share anything. At the local library, I scanned the directory for names with the occupation "guard." A city directory is the bible for reporters, along with the old Haines directory that listed addresses first, then names and phone numbers. I walked off with about fifteen names of guards in Jefferson City and a street guide.

I hired a cabbie, and we set off early the next morning, striking out at the first two apartments—no answer. But at a small bungalow a woman in a cotton wrapper and hair curlers answered our knock. Surprised at my enterprise, she invited me into her cheery kitchen for coffee. Her husband, the guard, joined us. Lucky for me she was the gossipy type, and she had many stories of Ray's life in prison. I learned that he sold or rented magazines to fellow inmates, and once he disappeared for weeks while guards searched for him in old vents. He had escaped in a bakery truck, knowing the prison routines because he had spent most of his life behind bars and had worked in the prison bakery.

The couple also told me how guards and prisoners made money in jail. Wives of guards worked in the nearby Ralston Purina plant, where the firm added amphetamines to chicken feed, which kept the hens awake longer so they could lay more eggs. (Later, my husband and I called Purina "layena Purina.") The women stole amphetamines for their guard husbands, who then sold it to prisoners, who would sell it to fellow inmates. There was always a way to sell contraband drugs in prison. Did Ray make money that way? They didn't know. And other guard families were less forthcoming; not anxious to be "snitches," as they didn't think it was worth losing a good job. This skimpy material gave me a start on my story about James Earl Ray, an enigma.

My June 30, 1968, story began: "The mystery of James Earl Ray is as cryptic as a jigsaw puzzle whose pieces lie scattered over half of the United States and Canada, and parts of Europe. No matter that Ray—using the name of Ramon George Sneyd—sits today in a London, England, jail charged with the killing of Dr. Martin L. King, Jr." British newspapers questioned whether Ray was a lone assassin or part of a big domestic or international conspiracy. There were more questions than answers about this former slum boy who grew to manhood in American prisons, where he was a loner. Who bought or paid for his alligator shoes? Where did he get the 1966 Mustang he drove in Memphis? Who paid his airfare in the States and overseas? Who kept this escapee "on ice" from the long arms of the state of Missouri for thirteen months, from escape to capture?

Eventually the FBI, with the help of the Royal Canadian police, developed the best chronology of Ray. My humble research, covering three states and Toronto, Canada, put more flesh and blood on the flat image of James Earl Ray, alias James McBride, James Walton, W. C. Herron, James O'Connor, Eric Starvo Galt, Paul Bridgman, John Willard, Harvey Lowmyer, and of course, Ramon George Sneyd. To fill the blanks, I interviewed a wide variety of characters from his prison days, his old neighbors in southern St. Louis, people from his life in Birmingham, Alabama, to Toronto.

Fred T. Wilkinson, director of the Missouri Department of Correction in Jefferson City, finally answered my questions. "Ray was as near a nonentity as any person I ever met. He was innocuous. He was a passive personality. He gave the appearance of indolence. His attitude was 'Here I am. So what?'" Apparently the psychiatrists underestimated Ray. He wound up in Missouri State Penitentiary for robbing a Kroger store in his hometown. He got twenty years for armed robbery and auto theft, and he tried to escape from the courthouse even before he got to Missouri State. There he tried to scale the walls of the prison, which was built in 1836, and he fell into a ventilator. He tried to escape again on April 23 and was missing a month before guards were convinced he was gone. They theorized that Ray, working in the kitchen with white clothes and gloves, slipped out in a huge bread box in a bread delivery truck. He had left $10.36 in his account. A guard said inmates made money on "powder." In a slow drawl, he told me about chicken farmers who kept electric lights on in chicken roosts so chickens slept less and laid more eggs. He also repeated the story that chicken feed now had amphetamine pep pills for chickens. The guard thought the stuff came in from Kansas City and was $60 per pack, which would have made the seller $2,000. Some guys who used it, he said, wouldn't sleep for a week. He saw Ray use it, although the administration denied it. Inmates got regular drug tests.

My office had AP photos of Ray, who was described as white, five-foot-eleven, 175 pounds, and forty years old. He had so many aliases that there was confusion over his real name, which was later cleared up by the FBI rap sheet. This jailhouse "nonentity" had an IQ of 103. He was stationed in Nuremberg, Germany, with the army during the Nazi German war criminal trials, where he read Friedrich Nietzsche and developed a belief in his superman theory. Records listed his mother as Mrs. Lucille Ryan and his grandmother as Mrs. Mary Maher.

Anxious for more material, I debated whether Memphis, where King was killed, should be my next stop or Ray's original home in St. Louis. After flipping a coin, heads directed me to Memphis and its famous Peabody Hotel, where the lobby water fountain hosted live ducks in its pool. King had gone to Memphis a second time to show his support for the city garbage worker's economic plight. Police gave me short shrift. Actually, they were hostile, saying things such as "How dare [I] . . . ." On my own, with map in hand, I identified the location of the Lorraine Hotel, King's last stop. Toward the rear of the hotel on South Main Street was Fire Station No. 2, at the intersection with Mulberry, the road that the Lorraine was on. As the daughter of a late firefighter, I expected friendly treatment from the fire brotherhood. I introduced myself to the firemen on duty and explained my mission, adding: "If I'm not back in two hours, come looking for me." We all laughed, although a serious mood hung over me like a storm cloud.

Walking over to Ray's apartment, I passed a string of small merchant shops with dirty windows and flyers stuck in door handles. It was a seedy section of South Main. As I entered the rooming house where Ray had stayed, I quickly discovered that it provided one with a direct view of Dr. King's balcony. Actually, investigators measured 205 feet and 3 inches for a bullet to fly from a rear window of Brewer Place, the rooming house, to its target, King. By chance, Guy Canipe, owner of Canipe's Amusement Company, let me in to the room. He was a solemn, tight-lipped man and had a dubious honor. After the shooting he had found a bundle, wrapped in some kind of green material, near his front door. When police opened it, a gun rolled out. Canipe was cagey about talking; he had had his fill of reporters. I sensed, too, as I am sure he did, that police were suspicious of people around South Main.

Patrons at Jim's Grill, a restaurant near the rooming house, repeated the newspapers stories while nursing beers. The talk was Ray had checked into Bessie's Place on April 4, 1967. Bessie's was a flophouse that had rooms for rent at $8.50 a week. As "John Willard," Ray took room 5. The man in room 6, just next door to Ray, was Charles Q. Stephens, who claimed Ray was in the bathroom from 5 P.M. to about 5:35 P.M. The window in room 5 faced the Lorraine, where King stood alone, waiting for companions he would never meet. The Grill's manager walked me over to his back door, pointing out the upper floors of the Lorraine, where King had stood on the balcony when he was killed. Canipe's neighbors had spotted a white Mustang near Bessie's before the murder, which was identified as the one Ray purchased in Birmingham, Alabama, where he also bought a rifle.

My next stop was the Lorraine, where the portly black owner couldn't have been nicer or more courteous, no doubt due to his many years' training as a hotel employee, saving every dime to open his own hostelry. The man was still in grief over the death of his wife, who had died of a heart attack hours after King's death. He simply had to show me their ultra clean and tastefully decorated private quarters, including the huge circular bed with its shiny purple satin spread. Watching him, I could feel his tragedy. It was not just King's dream that died, it was his also. Upstairs was a shrine to both his wife and Dr. King. In a locked, glass-faced cabinet were the silverware and plate used by King when he had his last fish dinner. On another shelf were mementos of his wife, including her slippers. We stood silently as he played a recording of King's "I Have a Dream" speech. It was in moments like these when I realized that death was real, not merely a headline or an interview. It was the end of so much—King's mission to help the Memphis garbage workers get raises, and this self-made man, with years behind him of working for Holiday Inns and saving and saving.

We walked over to Beale Street, where the man told me, "Talk to the people over there." On Beale Street? To me, it was the "beginning of the blues," the birthplace of great music and song. I didn't know the significance of that street to Dr. King's murder, but I took the man's advice. The barber on Beale was gracious and chatty; and he was not sold on Ray as the killer of Dr. King. He said that a young black man had come to Memphis days before King returned to help the garbage workers, and this young man had found a job with an undertaker. He was in the Lorraine yard, below King's balcony, the day of the murder. "Either he was the shooter or the spotter," the barber said. The young man disappeared and was never found or questioned. The barber went on to say a lot of union organizers from New York were in town at the time, and King, against his inclination, at first refused to come back for a second visit but was talked into it. The town was scared, he said.

Back at Fire Station No. 2, the firefighters were the first ones anxious to hear my story of the Lorraine, and they were relieved by it. But I was nervous and anxious to write and so went back to my hotel. In the lobby of the Peabody I gathered my notes and drafted my story. And in an effort to relieve my tension, I walked to a furniture store, ordered a Memphis style, glass-topped, wrought iron table with four chairs to be shipped home for our screened-in porch. My gut instinct was to stay for more interviews, but my boss suggested moving along.

So I moved on to Ray's grandmother's house, 1913 Hickory Street, St. Louis. Again I hired a cab to take me to Hickory Street, which led to a doorless, rundown, two-story brick house with faded ancient French architectural influence of seventy-five to one hundred years ago. The tenant, an elderly woman, said Ryan and Maher, his grandmother, were dead, but neighbors had known them. Ray was one of ten children of Lucille Ryan. Mrs. Grade Weiss, who lived across the street, tended bar five doors from the Ryan home and knew a bit of gossip. My approach was low-key. I identified myself as an Ohio reporter who needed some information about Ray. I had the impression few reporters had picked the neighbors' brains, dismissive of Ray's slum roots. Ray was "polite," Grace said. Another neighbor, Mrs. Alice Martin, said Lucille separated from her husband, the children's father, and changed her last name to Ray. Then she lived with a guy named Jack, who was an ex-con. Mrs. Ray was "a wino" but managed to have her clothes dry-cleaned. James Earl was rarely seen because he was serving in the army from 1946 to 1948. Back home he served jail time for drunkenness and resisting arrest. Later, he served time in both Joliet and Pontiac prisons in Illinois for armed robbery and was in Leavenworth, a federal prison, for forged postal money orders. I learned from one of Ray's prison buddies that "he was a real pro. He had money on him in prison. Guys like that are always targets. But no one ever tried to steal from Ray. There was something about him, like he'd kill if you tried anything."

One of Ray's brothers ran a bar, the Grapeview, which was closed, but I found him at his home. Through a screen door I watched him sort out mounds of silver change on the floor. He barely acknowledged me but laughed, kind of squirrelly, and kept counting. Neighbors described him as an eccentric who had a low boiling point. That was a moment when I questioned my sanity. What was I doing there alone? I backed off and went back to Hickory Street, where neighbors said the bar was in the name of Carol Pepper, Ray's sister. I suggested that bar receipts might have bankrolled James if his family was generous or in on the murder, but no one knew. Only once was a racial issue about Ray spoken.

Up the river from St. Louis is the town of Alton, which sits across the Mississippi River. On July 13, 1967, the Bank of Alton was held up by two men wearing stocking masks. The take was $27,000. Ed Pound of the *Alton Evening Telegraph* said: "Ray had nothing to do with it." Ray's ex-con buddy said: "If Ray and another guy got $27,000, Ray got it all. That's the kind of guy he was. He got his money from holding up people who couldn't or wouldn't report it to police. Like the big gambling games in K.C. [Kansas City], things like that." The majority of those I met in Alton didn't believe Ray killed King. They questioned why he would. But I knew Ray was hardly an innocuous or passive person. Family and friends thought he was set up.

Another facet of Ray was on display after he moved to Los Angeles in 1967. First living in a Puerto Villarta, Mexico, motel, he moved to North Serranos, in Los Angeles, hanging out at the Sultan Room bar of the St. Francis Hotel. (I once visited my mother's sister, who lived around the corner from the St. Francis, where we were entranced with the piano player—Nat King Cole.) Ray had circulated petitions for Alabama governor George Wallace, who wanted his name on the California primary election for president of the United States. Ray, using the name Galt, also drank at the Rabbit's Food Club on Hollywood Boulevard, where the manager threw him out for arguing about African Americans with a part-time barmaid. One of Ray's bar buddies said Ray drove his sister and a woman friend to New Orleans on business. They thought he was a "politician." Bar talk had Ray taking dancing lessons and studying for a bartenders' license.

Studying the FBI rap sheet, I found that the feds had Ray in Montreal in July of 1967, and, also in that summer, before going to Mexico, he was in California, Louisiana, and Birmingham, Alabama. For six weeks he lived in a rooming house, banked at the Birmingham Trust National Bank, and bought a 1966 Mustang, and, on August 27, 1967, a Remington 30.06 rifle with a telescopic site.

In Birmingham I scoped out Ray's former rooming house, where the owner told me he was "sick" of reporters, so I moved on to my next stop, the gun shop where Ray, using the name Galt, had bought the rifle. By chance, the store owner was born on Ramona Boulevard in Cleveland, and we chatted about my relatives and in-laws and his family's neighbors. He told me that the feds had questioned him many times about Galt/Ray, who bought one rifle and then returned it for another. There was nothing special about the owner; he was just a guy knowledgeable about firearms, not connected to Ray as a criminal colleague. The shop, near the Alabama National Guard base, was a stone's throw from the Birmingham Airport. It was popular with military-types, the Alabama National Guardsmen, who were part of the volunteers at the Bay of Pigs. I was unfamiliar with "our country's bombing of Cuba," and at the owner's suggestion, I bought a paperback book on the subject that night at the airport—where weather grounded outgoing flights.

Always as I work on stories, topics of interest pop up that force me to deviate from the assignment at hand. As I sat reading on the Bay of Pigs, I met a pilot who knew a lot about it. Actually, it was the topic of conversation among the stranded passengers. Where had I been? The book was the first published account by an American pilot—Albert C. Persons—hired by the CIA to fly combat missions in Cuba. Persons wrote of four friends who lost their lives at the Bay of Pigs in January 1961. Part of that CIA operation was based at Birmingham National Airport. Later, back in the newsroom, I urged our editorial writers to look into the Bay of Pigs and the botched attack and death of American and Cuban refugee-volunteers. It has since become a watershed story of the early days of John F. Kennedy's regime, and it led to more conspiratorial theories about his death. Did Castro kill JFK?

Back on track I next stopped in Toronto, still on the Ray trail. I tracked him to the Chinese compound where he was just another ship in the night to the Loo family. They walked me from their nondescript rooming house to a fabulous green vegetable market;

they were more anxious about food than about Ray. The Loos thought that when in his room Ray drank beer and read magazines, but the Royal Canadian police found he was a lot busier. When Ray was arrested on June 6, I learned from the Cuyahoga County coroner, Dr. Samuel R. Gerber, that the National Association of Coroners had circulated, worldwide, Ray's dental records in the event of a John Doe body popping up someplace. Before the charts were fully distributed, the Royal Canadian Mounted Police (RCMP) had found a Canadian passport picture of Ray, who now was Ramon George Sneyd. C. R. Doey explained to me that "the most remarkable was the passport search." He added that Canadian police had known for years that Communists and fugitives took advantage of the ease with which Canadian passports were obtained. All one had to do was swear that they were born in Canada.

Ray was ordinary, but Doey described certain features—a cleft chin, the hairline, the nose—that were distinguishing. RCMP personnel went through 250,000 passport applications for two weeks, finally finding a picture of "Sneyd" on May 29. Mrs. Loo told me her boarder's birth certificate had come to her house at 964 Dundas Street, Toronto. RCMP tracked Sneyd to two rooming houses, a passport photo booth in an arcade, a travel bureau, and a doctor's office, where he had gone for small pox shots. I was tipped he had had a date with a cocktail waitress—a woman of easy virtue—but she didn't answer her doorbell when I went to ask questions.

I still didn't know how he was tracked in London. Easy, Doey said. He flew to England on May 5 and then applied for a refund on the unused return trip portion of a BOAC airfare. Makes one wonder about the long arm of the law, doesn't it? The inspectors said Ray/Sneyd "showed ingenuity" in falsifying his birth certificate. Ray obtained the certificate by going through old birth certificate records and finding one that matched his birth date. Then he took on that identity. But Mounties were unable to find any library employee who caught Ray going through back issues of newspapers for births printed in 1932. But this was a good story—250,000 passport photos to find one man!

One of my deepest regrets is never meeting James Earl Ray. The paper simply didn't want more; besides, the wires covered the trial for the rest of the nation. Ray died in Brushy Mountain State Prison in Tennessee in 1998 of liver failure. He took his story to the grave, although published books by die-hard conspiracy addicts developed other endings, naming mysterious people he met in L.A. I called a few writers but never could interest the paper in more stories. Investigators testified that the fingerprints on the gun were Ray's. And he was interviewed at length by private investigators and lawyers for the U.S. Congress Select Committee, who investigated the assassinations of JFK and Dr. King. Ray failed two lie detector tests. The committee dismissed the "conspiracy" theories and said its work was "severely" hampered by being unable to examine top-secret FBI files. One committee member said the investigation ended too quickly and failed to explore everything.

This assignment, along with those involving the Kennedy brothers, emotionally impacted me, but not right away. I was the reporter first—a worrying, anxious reporter whose sole mission was to get and write the story. Putting these dramatic events in historic perspective took time. I concluded, after tons of reading, that none of the three assassins, or should I use journalese and say "alleged" assassins (Oswald, Sirhan, and Ray) acted alone. There was too much money and traveling involved; too many opportunities to be tools of those with deadly agendas of elimination. The mood and temper of the country at the time scared a lot of mayors, governors, and law enforcement officials, who just wanted to move one. But for me, the cases remain open.

-30-

-16-

The Glenville Shoot-out

*T*he riots in the ghettos of Hough shook up Cleveland's establishment of Union Club regulars who represented the city's elite and brainy law firms and their moneyed clients. The fires of Hough blackened the city's shrinking commercial reputation, and there had to be a fall guy to hold accountable. That guy was the mayor, Ralph S. Locher, who was considered honorable, personable, modest, and civilized but also a bust as a politician-administrator. Businesses blamed him for his slow reaction in 1965, before Hough, when there was limp holiday season business, particularly because he failed publishers in bringing striking newspaper employees back to work. There were no newspaper advertisements three weeks before Christmas.

Stubbornly, Locher insisted on running for reelection in 1965 against a veritable unknown, a handsome light-skinned black man named Carl B. Stokes. Locher won by two thousand votes, but remnants of Hough ended Locher's career in 1967, when Stokes won on a second try, because city fathers gambled on the radical endorsement of a black man to bring peace to troubled citizens, both black and white. Ultimately, as the years of riots and rage continued, the city's newspaper editors and corporate structure came to regret their big gamble. And I, in my humble spectator role, continued to report daily news from the streets as Mayor Stokes bragged of his guest status in the most exclusive clubs of Cleveland, New York, and the Bahamas. It took a lot of digging by *Plain Dealer* and *Press* reporters to expose cash payments to black nationalists to "cool" the town after Hough. Roldo Bartimole, a former *Plain Dealer* reporter who edited a newsletter, wrote that corporate leadership paid weekly payments to black nationalists to "Keep Peace for Carl." Money went to a summer program, with payments siphoned through the black newspaper, *Call & Post*. The scared corporate types urged Republican Seth Taft to run against Stokes in the fall of 1967, but money poured into the ghetto from the prestigious Ford Foundation, as I learned.

My editors, impressed with New York's attention on us, sent me to the foundation's New York offices to cover monies approved by foundation president McGeorge Bundy. Bundy had told the Urban League in 1966 that "If blacks burned American cities, the white man's companies will have to take the losses." He was an elitist Ivy Leaguer who had been a close adviser to President John F. Kennedy. To me, he was aloof, arrogant, and officious. Author Robert Allen, in a book on "black awakening," said the Ford Foundation "was on its way to becoming the most important though least publicized organization manipulating the militant black movement." Ford's Cleveland strategy was to test the rage of blacks in a traditional political voting environment. A big chunk of money, $175,000, went to Cleveland's Congress of Racial Equality (CORE) for voting registration. Businessmen raised more than $300,000 for other summer programs, and Stokes brought Dr. Martin Luther King to Cleveland to register forty thousand black voters. King's group, the southern Christian Leadership Conference in Atlanta, had a $230,000 grant from the Ford Foundation. Yet this money trail was virtually invisible to the public.

Stokes beat the stubbornly determined Locher in the primary, and he easily beat Republican Seth Taft, grandson of President Taft, in the general election in November 1967. I wasn't around for Stokes's victory because the paper had sent me to Gary, Indiana, where Gary Hatcher became the first black mayor of a major national city. To ballyhoo Stokes's victory and to pat themselves on their backs, Cleveland leaders took a full-page ad in the *Wall Street Journal*. But did Cleveland's commercial and industrial structure, heavy backers of various foundations, buy peace and harmony? Stokes, a former liquor inspector, city prosecutor, and state representative, brought talent to City Hall but only for a short time. Disillusioned with frustrating administrative problems in housing, employment, and crime, many rising African American stars left Cleveland for more stable futures. The blush was off the rose early in the Stokes administration when illegal liquor sales involving the mayor's top campaign aide were uncovered. One good note was the release of federal urban renewal funds from Stokes's old friend, Vice President Hubert Humphrey.

In the summer of 1968 the roof fell in on Stokes when the Glenville riots, engineered in part by some of the characters on the city payroll and beneficiaries of grant monies from those various foundation-funded summer programs, overtook the city. The riots were like a red hot brick, too hot to hold but too hot to drop. It was a "siege," an "ambush," a "shoot-out" between a group of black radicals and white Cleveland cops. It was worse than Hough. Three of the dead and eleven of the twenty-two people injured were cops. One killed was Leroy Jones, a classmate of mine. He walked out of his police car into a rain of bullets the early evening of July 23, 1968.

Glenville is described as the culmination of unrest epitomized by Black Power, Muslim Power, "hate whitey," and "burn, baby, burn" philosophies. I was not there, in the East Side area that was once a middle-class, white neighborhood but was now slipping into slumhood. The few newsmen who were there were lucky to leave with their lives. Police reporters Bill Evans and Bill Barnard called for help after tires of their *Plain Dealer* car were shot out and burned. Police reporter Don Bean, called in from vacation, rescued them in his car. In the newsroom that night it was déjà vu all over again, recalling Hough riots and later parades of armed Black Panthers marching down Hough Street to the JFK House. In Glenville fifty or sixty businesses, mostly small merchants, were looted and destroyed. Losses were estimated in the millions. The fears of shopkeepers, mothers, and children were unimaginable. White friends of mine, who lived not far away in a multiracial neighborhood, told of being hassled nightly by black Muslims when they were merely driving home or picking up a family member whose midnight shift ended at a local factory. One young white man, fleeing an attacker, ran the attacker over and kept on driving. Editors, conferring with powerhouse law firms, were in a state of shock, especially when they learned that Mayor Stokes, barking instructions over the police radio network, ordered all white policemen out of Glenville, leaving streets to looters. The dream of a black mayor keeping the peace turned into a disaster, portending more to come. Today America has sleeper cells of Muslim extremists, followers of Osama bin Laden; back then we had sleeping black Muslim sleeper cells that were awakening below the civic radar.

These unsettling events consumed daily lives; we recognized these were historic times for us, not dissimilar to the Bull Conner days of the South. Everyone on the staff got assignments relative to Glenville, its causes and its future. An Aug. 2, 1968, *Time* magazine post-mortem gave my editors ideas, and we followed with a series called "The Cleveland Police: What's on Their Minds?" for which Dr. Louis Masotti of Case Western Reserve wrote a report titled "Shoot-Out in Cleveland." The report was edited by the Eisenhower Commission. Both *Time* and Masotti said that unlike other random or chancy racial upheavals, Cleveland's was a planned attack.

The scene was sketched: a City of Cleveland bright yellow tow truck stopped at the corner of Beulah and E. 123rd streets, at the edge of the Glenville ghetto, to haul away a junked 1958 Cadillac. Gunfire opened up from every side of the truck. A trucker called for help on a two-way radio, and within minutes squad cars responded, becoming targets of a well-coordinated ambush. Police, equipped with standard .38 revolvers, were outgunned. "It was worse than Saipan or Tinian," said Detective Robert Bennett, a veteran of both Pacific baffles. "They shot at us from every direction imaginable." Three policemen, two patrolmen, and a lieutenant were dead, and another fourteen were wounded, all within thirty minutes. "We were sucked up," said Detective Gerald Viola. "They were waiting for us." Three men, one by one, tried to rescue Sgt. Sam Levy, who had been hit in the chest and arm and was lying in the street. One by one, each was wounded.

The pitched battle lasted four hours, as snipers ran from house to house. A force of one hundred strong, armed with automatic riles, moved from house to yard to garage; flames burst from windows. One house burned; two charred bodies were found later. Stokes, who had just returned from Washington, D.C., as the events began, reluctantly called Gov. James Rhodes for the Ohio National Guard. The riots started at 2:30 P.M. on Tuesday, July 23, and finally cooled down at 8:30 A.M. on Sunday, July 28, when 2,700 guardsmen as well as 100 black cops and 500 black civilians crowded the streets. Anger at Stokes was elevated when the FBI reported that their informants had sensed "trouble brewing" when they noticed that guns were being imported from Detroit, Toledo, and Pittsburgh. The FBI added that requests for a search warrant on the house of Fred (Ahmed) Evans, where the riot started, had been refused by Washington, D.C. Of the alleged snipers, three died and two were jailed. Evans was charged with first-degree murder, along with possession of narcotics and an automatic rifle. He later was sentenced to life in prison for his role in the ambush. *Time* magazine said snipers had failed in "outright insurrection in Cleveland, but created local turmoil and national apprehension."

On the heels of national stories, the city desk sent out the staff to talk to policemen all over town. I was part of the team, and over several weeks I talked to dozens of cops and ended up writing a series on the frustrations of the city's safety forces. Stokes complained to the editors about the series, saying that it was me, the reporter, that he especially did not like. But Glenville was the death knell for Stokes and a tombstone for the black community. Many of the young African American lawyers and businessmen joined the white flight to the suburbs. It also took its toll on the newspaper business. Some stories never made it to print, such as the shooting range for Black Nationalists in Geauga County and threats to poison the city's water supply.

Due to the violence, I learned how to fire a gun. Artha Woods, a black friend, gave me two foot-long hatpins to stick in the left side of my car seat and loaned me a curly haired Afro wig to wear when driving home through the black neighborhood. Phil Porter, my executive editor at the *Plain Dealer*, and I had long talks about the city's racial problems. He saw Stokes's election as the dawn of a new day because the city was 35 percent black. But Councilman Leo Jackson, a foe of the Black Power movement, disagreed with Phil (as did I). Leo made a lot of sense. In his ward, he said, blacks living on welfare, gambling, alcohol, and prostitution were downgrading a good neighborhood. Many stories I wrote, quoting Jackson, were thorns in Stokes's side. Porter said Glenville shook the confidence of whites, who naively believed Stokes was insurance against racial disorder. Porter now called Stokes "a racist." What we didn't know was that Stokes had been named as one "of the radical black comers" by the noted Baltimore writer, William Worthy, in the November 1967 issue of *Esquire* magazine. Worthy said, "The American Negro is dead and risen as a black man of the world, soul brothers to non-whites everywhere. Don't look now, honky, but some of his best friends are the Vietcong." Stokes, we saw, was a man on a racial see-saw, siding with black guerilla brothers and accepting payoffs from whites.

And things got worse for the mayor when newspapers disclosed that Evans and his pals bought guns from Stokes's $4 million Cleveland NOW! funds. So Stokes dumped his police chief and brought in a new one, Pat Gerity. The next scandal to hit City Hall concerned civil service tests for the police department. Copies of the exams somehow made it into applicants' hands in city motels before the official tests were given, and two of Stokes's aides were indicted for the theft of the exams. Gerity was bounced, and Stokes brought in a national war hero, retired Lt. Gen. Benjamin O. Davis, the highest ranking African American in the U.S. Air Force. He stayed briefly but left when he was convinced Stokes was too cozy with undesirables. The next replacement for police chief was William Ellenburg, a Grosse Point, Michigan, cop. Within hours of the announcement, I had a call from Phil Sheridan, an old friend who had worked with Bobby Kennedy in the

Justice Department. "No good," Sheridan said, adding factoids about Ellenburg's checkered career with the Detroit Mafia. Sheridan was the key investigator of Jimmy Hoffa during his years as a Teamsters' national leader. The *Plain Dealer* and *Detroit Free Press* searched and scratched, finally printing stories that named names of Ellenburg's associates with Detroit's organized crime crowd. Ellenburg, within days, resigned and went back home. Stokes looked like a sucker, a conspirator, and a poor politician, Porter told me.

By the time 1971 rolled around, the Stokes charisma faded, and his few remaining corporate friends got him a job with a national television network in New York City. Phil said that rather than pull the city together, Stokes managed to racially polarize Cleveland during his four years in office. News-wise, these were rough years for the whole town; morale was way down.

The next mayor was a white Republican, Ralph Perk, whose political career started as a councilman in the Czech neighborhood near E. 55th and Broadway. Nationally Cleveland was dubbed "the mistake on the Lake," which most Clevelanders did not find amusing. I strongly believe the Glenville story must be told; it is a shameful part of the city's history but also a painful lesson: Payoffs cannot buy racial peace. This was a wake-up call to every one of us. As a good friend, an African American civic leader at her children's' high school, once told me: "We are tired of being invisible. We are the people who clean your houses, take care of your children, go to church, and are invisible." I carried this message to our editors, and I am proud to report that my publisher, Tom Vail, took that to heart. The African American community finally made the *Plain Dealer*'s social pages. These were tiny steps toward the meshing of the two communities; communication and dialogue had begun.

-30-

- *17*-

Johnny Gay's Federal Commutation

*I*t's funny the things I remember about stories. When I think of Johnny Gay, who was at one time Ohio's biggest drug dealer, what comes to mind is my lime-green, merino wool knit dress. It's an odd connection, I know, but that lovely hand-knit dress, hanging in its plastic bag in the back of my closet, reminds me of a rare reporting job that lasted many weeks in 1967. No longer can I fit into this slim garment. Yet, it won't be thrown away or given to Goodwill. Touching its sensuous soft fibers unwinds memories of my daily travel to Lorain, Ohio, with Harry Stainer. We went to discover how Gay had gotten a federal commutation of his drug sentence.

Johnny Gay had served four years and six months of what a federal judge ordered as an "unpardonable ten-year sentence" when he earned his commutation. Our assignment was to figure out how he earned it and what got him the sentence in the first place. Harry drove us daily to Lorain for reimbursed mileage in his paycheck, and, as we didn't need two cars, that was fine with me. Besides, I wanted to knit during these portal-to-portal hours from the *Plain Dealer* offices in Cleveland to this western lakeside city. As a child I skipped crochet and knit lessons, learning beginners' stitches when I briefly left the newspaper business and worked in public relations at University Hospitals. On lunch hours I would watch older women, many born in Hungary and Poland, click-click aluminum needles, turning yarns into gorgeous sweaters. With their help, my first sweater was notable for mismatched stitches, but it was a rewarding experience anyway. This daily commute was heaven-sent. While I hummed along, counting stitches, Harry ticked off targets of our investigation, based on homework in the city room.

Who exactly was Johnny Gay? We learned his background from both Cleveland policemen, working the drug scene with federal narcotic agents, and a few Lorain cops willing to talk. We found court records of Gay's arrest for drug possession and dealing in the 1960s. Newspaper stories about him were skimpy despite his arrest and reputation. Contacts in Lorain suggested we come in "cold" and hit bars (of which there were many) and "soak up" the town's atmosphere. From June until September 1967 and into the spring of 1968, we practically lived in Lorain, a steel-mill town known for its huge tube plant. We also spent hours in Washington, D.C., at the U.S. Justice Department on another paper search of federal pardons and commutations. All told, we wrote nineteen stories on this presidential pardon and commutation procedure, the politics in play, and circumstances that generated forgiveness and reduced sentences. During our operation the biggest surprise was the resignation of the federal officer, the Washington overseer of the pardon program, another impact aspect of our research.

After the series was printed I wanted to pursue the subject on a national basis, to survey pardons and commutations state by state, because so many U.S. congressmen and senators were sponsors of ex-convicts benefiting from clemency. We painstakingly surveyed the years 1965, 1966, and 1967, covering 890 cases, of which 177 bore recommendations of senators and congressmen and well-known Americans. Familiar names were Sen. Hubert Humphrey; Jack Valenti, head of the Motion Picture Association; columnist Drew Pearson; Walter P. Reuther, head of the United

Auto Workers' Union; and a host of others. But managing editor Ted Princiotto ruled against it. He could not spare reporters for another long stretch of investigative reporting on this subject. Harry and I envisioned a Pulitzer Prize, just dreaming, I guess. But my interest in these cases remains strong, even to this day. These stories popped into my mind as I read the furor over President Bill Clinton's eleventh-hour pardon for Marc Rich, a Swiss-based, infamous billionaire who remained isolated in Europe rather than face charges in the United States. This pardon story pops up in various news stories relative to funds from Rich's ex-wife to the Clinton Presidential Museum in Little Rock, Arkansas.

Back in 1967 we reporters were unfamiliar with federal procedures in this field, and the public, for the most part, paid scant attention to who and why presidents granted pardons. In legal terms, a pardon is an exemption from punishment for a criminal conviction. A president grants a pardon, unilaterally, and it cannot be reversed. The same goes for commutations. Those desiring them seek out the smartest, most devious ways to do so. Reporters tracking Marc Rich through various congressional panels learned that his consideration came up a few hours before Clinton left office. Rich was a U.S. fugitive at the time who, in 1983, was indicted in federal court for evading more than $48 million in federal taxes. He was charged with fifty-one counts of tax fraud and running illegal oil deals in Iran during the U.S. hostage crisis. At the time of his commutation he had been living in Switzerland for over twenty years. An investigation, still ongoing, was looked at again by the federal prosecutor's office in New York. It was also found that that his ex-wife, Denise Rich, had donated $1 million to various Democratic causes.

Now, our guy in Lorain, who was sprung by President Lyndon B. Johnson, was a wart in a big pumpkin compared with someone like Rich. Gay was a virtual nonentity until Princiotto handed us an Associated Press list of Americans pardoned by President Johnson in June of 1967. Ted wondered who the heck Johnny Gay was. Princiotto had covered federal courts for years and never heard of him. Our Lorain stringer said: "He's a drug dealer. Cops say he's the biggest drug dealer in Ohio." Wow! How come no one on the police beat knew this? This just shows how provincial a big city paper can be. Our suburban reporters read papers from other counties, both daily and weekly, but none knew of Gay either.

That's why Harry and I drove daily from Cleveland to Lorain and back, talking to Lorain barflies, saloon hangers-on, barmaids, and bartenders to get a handle on Gay. And we did. In smoky bars along the old U.S. Steel-mill roads we were met with cold stares, hostility, and blank looks. Other times we talked with loquacious drunks who were more helpful, but most folks were suspicious of us. Lorain Mayor Woodrow Mathna said: "That takes a lot of pull, a lot of influence to get a presidential commutation. I have no idea who got it for him." Mathna was a wise and entrenched politician in Ohio politics who courted the votes of union steelworkers for Democrat candidates. We worked the "people angle" but spent hours, too, studying and ordering records from the State Liquor Department on Gay's ownership of bars, including liquor license transfers. At the Lorain County Courthouse we searched and copied records of property and deed transfers, relative to bars and personal property. At the U.S. Justice Department we read Gay's records, copying them in the building's lobby, papers spread across our knees. This outfit was not too happy to see us or answer our questions. Ultimately we paid a good price for the entire batch of Gay's federal records.

Into this tangled web of legalese, we traced Gay's liquor businesses, his bigamous marriage, drug dealing, life in a federal prison, and the business affairs of his prominent brothers-in-law, which related to Gay. The story was like eating peanuts—we couldn't stop. We focused on a political angle, the question of political favoritism or money changing hands, and we came up half full and half empty. All roads pointed to the White House, but that was never nailed down enough to print it. The clemency spotlight was on Gay's friends and relatives, those who benefited from Gay's deals and who might again in the future. Johnny Gay got out of federal jail against odds. In the end our persistent probing brought about the sudden resignation of U.S. Pardon Attorney Reed Cozart, and President Johnson temporarily froze pardons and commutations. In 1966, before our probe, Johnson handed out 444 pardons and commutation. In 1967 his score was 245. Our stories exposed the underbelly of the Lorain community and his various business deals between prominent Lorain residents and organized crime figures in Chicago.

Gay's commutation was granted over the objections of Cleveland Federal Court judge James C. Connell, whom Gay bombarded with requests, claiming he had only a dime to his name. He appealed without counsel. In a federal prison in Kentucky, Gay wrote a long biography, sparing no details about his past. He and his family and friends signed documents for an appeal and release. Fourteen Lorain friends and relatives, and a Cleveland policeman, signed the appeal document. These names were listed in justice department forms. In denying Gay's appeal, Judge Connell wrote:

> One can learn something of the mental capacity of a defendant by the way he goes about the business of committing an offense. Of what did Gay's crime consist? He was in the criminal business which requires more cunning and ingenuity than most others, and he brought to it more cunning than others. He was in the business of successfully buying narcotics, finding the sellers; using dupes to make the purchases; then finding the buyers; transmitting to buyers on a successfully financial basis and scale; successfully selling only to those he can trust; successfully selling only to known addicts; successfully avoiding sales to government agents. No one could possibly have worked up the lucrative business he enjoyed and at the same time have been too mentally incompetent that he didn't know what was going on around him, or what he said to others, or what they said to him. The agents had no easy time with Gay, for Gay bought unusual intelligence, caring, perception and generalship to his nefarious business.

That sums up the guy.

U.S. attorney Nathaniel Jones received the Gay file from the U.S. pardon attorney on January 18, 1965, for review. He answered the same day. "The seriousness of the offenses committed, compels this office to the belief that a reduction in sentence at this early date is unwarranted." He said Judge Connell concurred. There was no record that either Connell or Jones asked why Gay's sentence was halved. I guess in politics no one asks pointed questions, understanding the ballgame is between other parties and the president. Harry and I asked the Justice Department public information officer why Gay's commutation was granted. "Ask the president," he said. Other newspapers around the country picked up our story, tracing pardons in their cities to big money contributions to Johnson's President's Club. But no one found the straight, perfect road to prove donations bought favors. "Ask the president" was the stock reply, but no one did.

Court records of the indictment stated Gay bought, sold, and transported heroin and sold specified amounts to a federal narcotics agent. Named with Gay was Curtis Orr and his sister, Virginia Orr, who also sold heroin to agents. Gay pleaded innocent to eighteen counts of drug trafficking and faced a term of ninety years. He changed his plea to guilty on six counts and received a lesser sentence of ten years. Curtis got six years, and Virginia, two years. She served her term at the Lexington, Kentucky, federal prison, where Gay was also incarcerated. Johnny Gay bigamously married Virginia in Chicago on August 23, 1960. Connell said: "Gay made a drug addict out of this young colored girl when he made her his agent for buying and selling drugs, and then married her and lived with her in rooms above his dope den. He fooled her into believing he was divorced."

We desperately tried to reach Virginia, and finally she called us. "It's important. I must see you. I can't talk on the phone." At twenty-nine years of age, Virginia Orr was a tired and confused young woman who told us she didn't know who she was. She thought she was Mrs. John A. Gay of Lorain, because she was identified this way at the federal treatment center for addicts in Kentucky. She said Johnny Gay callously treated her as his wife, even though he was still married to his first wife in Lorain, when he desperately pleaded for presidential clemency from a ten-year "unpardonable" term. Needless to say, she was bitter. Prior to Gay's release, he had written passionate letters to "My Dearest

One" and signed them "Your husband, John." He promised her a home in Oberlin, Ohio, children, and normal family life.

Virginia was illiterate when she came from the South to work in Gay's Broadway Street bar. It was the town's "place of action." Her sister, Bea, dated a bartender there, and through this casual association with Gay, Virginia developed an affair with illegal drugs that also involved her brother, Curtis. "I never smoked, drank, or used drugs until I met Gay," she said. "Now my life is over. I'm ruined. I cannot get a job. When people find out who I am, that I've been an addict, they fire me. I'm tired, just tired. Sometimes I think I can't go on." For Gay's drug deals she made weekly trips to Chicago, New York, and Pittsburgh to buy heroin. Gay arranged them, but she made the phone calls to sellers. At home Gay would "divide the powder [heroin] into two piles and say 'this is mine and this is yours.'" She had a $250-a-day drug habit. John, she said, used "as much heroin as I did." Virginia said Gay was in federal prison when his first wife, Dorothy Dandrea Gay, divorced him. After both John and Virginia were released, she said he bought her a twelve-dollar dress and took her to K-Mart for dinner. She borrowed money from a Lorain policeman to repay loans, loans Gay promised to cover. She thought of returning to Tennessee where she was born, because Gay never meant a thing he promised.

Despite Virginia's claim that Gay was an addict, he asked to be evaluated at Hanna Pavilion of University Hospitals for "psychiatric treatment." But the court system ruled he was an addict and sentenced him to the federal treatment center. There he became a character, switching from Episcopalian to Catholic and authoring a book on changes in the liturgy between the faiths. He was a guinea pig for drug research, including LSD. His supervisors said, "He bucked for freedom from dawn to dusk." He revived an old greenhouse and taught English to Spanish-speaking prisoners.

Harry and I thought we hit pay dirt when the name of Sen. Stephen M. Young appeared in Gay's file. Was the senator his "godfather"? Young said he did not personally intercede for Gay with Reed Cozart, the pardon attorney, yet Young's file had a letter dated June 9, 1966, from the justice department. Gay's letters were sent to Ohio senator Frank J. Lausche and to Sen. Robert F.

Kennedy of New York. Asked why Young's letter was in the Gay file, Cozart said: "The lawyer who prepared it just stuck it there. He [Young] was the only public official we heard from. It was a routine showing of interest, and the lawyer in the pardon department just used it. There was no political interest. This matter was handled routinely. Young didn't actually do anything about Gay." We asked: "But who did?"

We later saw Senator Young in person, and when asked about political pressure or influence, he started to reply, saying, "The National Committee [meaning the Democratic National Committee] might. . . . ," but an aide stopped the senator from continuing. Senator Young did say that John Bailey, head of the DNC, was a John F. Kennedy man and not in the good graces of Johnson to get favors. But Young's aide knew Gay was "a patient" at a narcotics hospital, and he was aware of his criminal past. We were close to a news lead but not close enough. The aide did not know that Cleveland Police captain George W. Sperber, involved with federal agents in Gay's arrests, had said the Lorain barman "was one of the biggest narcotic peddlers in Northern Ohio." That translated into big bucks—if only we could get to them.

When our stories finally broke Ohio congressman John M. Ashbrook, on the House floor, said, "Gay's release was surprising and unwarranted." The wires carried our stories, provoking the *St. Louis Post-Dispatch* to report that in October of 1964 the Steamfitters' Union political fund gave $52,000 to Johnson's reelection and gave more gifts to out-of-state politicians. The paper scrutinized the case of Lawrence L. Callanan, a St. Louis Steamfitters' Union boss, who got a Johnson commutation in 1964.The story quoted a course as saying the commutation was "handled in the White House." They used an anonymous source; we could not. It was *Plain Dealer* policy.

Our final story was an interview with Gay. We saved him until last, waiting until we had met with his in-laws and Virginia Orr. When Gay checked into the Lexington center he was forty-nine years old and weighed 215 pounds; he was balding. He strode out of the center thinner and with a piece of paper signed by U.S. attorney Nicholas D. Katzenbach, which had President Johnson's name in big bold letters and granted executive clemency. The U.S. Pardons Office said his case was evaluated and his sentence found "disparate" in the national picture of first offenders—that group only served five years. Gay ran from us to his mother's trailer in Lorain. For a moment we thought he slipped under the trailer, but he turned up on the other side. His bottom line: "There was a conspiracy, but I broke the law. The sentence was not justified." He refused to elaborate on the conspiracy other than saying it could have involved other dealers. He said he was a master in the Merchant Marines, where he started using morphine. At home he had organized a building company with his in-laws, sold out, bought a bowling alley and recreation center, and began using heroin. He then ran a bar and construction company, and that was Johnny Gay's story. We asked whether he planned a business with Olimpio Giannini, owner of the once prosperous but now seedy Antlers Hotel. Giannini, a prohibition bootlegger, said Gay came to him about a deal in January of 1967. Gay told us, "The old man said, 'I can make money easier than going into that direction [prostitution].'" But in July 1967 Lorain police raided the Antlers and charged Giannini with running prostitutes, including a teenaged girl.

We felt like huge vacuum cleaners, sucking in schemes that crisscrossed with the lives of Gay, his buddies, and his in-laws. We found liquor licenses tying a relative of Gay's to main figures in Chicago's organized crime circles. Our last conversation with Gay was in March 1968, when the state liquor department refused him a deal to manage the S & J Bar at 1624 E. 28th Street in Lorain. Gay was unable to find work.

Harry and I kept eyes on federal pardons. President Jimmy Carter pardoned World War II traitor Iva (Tokyo Rose) Toguri, and, posthumously, Dr. Samuel A. Mudd, who treated President Abraham Lincoln's assassin. The stingiest president with pardons was President Ronald Reagan, who granted only 393 in eight years. He gave solicited pardons to two FBI agents convicted of illegal break-ins of homes of families and friends of suspected members of the radical Weatherman Underground Organization in the 1970s. Near the end of his terms Reagan also pardoned

George Steinbrenner, former Clevelander and owner of the New York Yankees, who had a felony charge related to illegal campaign contributions of the Richard M. Nixon presidential campaign. President George Herbert Walker Bush, in August 1989, pardoned Armand Hammer, the ninety-one-year-old industrialist and philanthropist and Sovietphile. Hammer's record was also for an illegal presidential campaign contribution. He wanted not only a pardon but also to be found innocent. He didn't get that.

Harry and I felt joined at the hip at times. He was a genius at deeds, bank loans, and liquor license records. My forte was people. The wily old gentleman who owned the Antlers talked of "ladies of the evening" in Lorain and his ties to "the Brotherhood." It was not, he said the "Mafia" or the "Cosa Nostra." It was the "Brotherhood." He boasted in an eccentric gangster mode that he was "in," that he "had the book on his 'brothers' in Lorain, Cleveland, Youngstown, Canton." At his age, he was the kind of guy who would make another great tell-all story, that is, if he would talk. But if he had taken the Italian oath of silence, all bets would be off. We were fascinated with this character, but he was just baiting us for fun.

I wore that nifty little green wool dress for as long as I could fit into it. It was an eye-catcher, but creating it on those drives kept my mind working on the story at hand. Harry talked about a lot of scenarios this story had. We had a scare one afternoon when we stopped for a beer at a lakefront joint rumored to be involved in white slavery, with girls brought in from the Middle East for prostitution in northeastern Ohio and western Michigan. After we drank, paid, and were leaving, the barmaid handed us a Polaroid snapshot of us drinking at the bar, which was obviously taken from a camera nestled among the liquor bottles on the bar backdrop. What a town.

-30-

-18-

The Gun That Killed
Bobby Kennedy

*N*ever in my wildest dreams did I imagine, as a newspaper reporter, that I would cover the double assassinations of the ill-starred Kennedy brothers, John and Robert. In November 1963 it was JFK, killed by Lee Harvey Oswald, an American GI and Soviet defector. Then in June 1968, just five years later, Sirhan B. Sirhan, a noncitizen Jordanian, killed Bobby. We Americans tend to shrug off the murders of government leaders in "banana republics," but now, with murders of our own public icons, we were in the shoes of the citizens of those countries. For how long could we be blissfully immune to criminal acts that marked indelible stains on our public lives, our personal souls? Abraham Lincoln and the Civil War were front and center in my mind as I thought about assassination. I never bucked for these assignments and have been forever grateful to editors who picked me—they trusted me not to fail. This is not to say I was arrogant or smug. More often, I was overly anxious and worried as hell.

Up early as usual on that beautiful morning on June 6, I first heard the news of the attempted assassination of Robert Kennedy, who was in the kitchen of a Los Angeles hotel. It made me physically sick. It couldn't happen again! I caught more news stories driving into Cleveland, arriving as usual at 10 A.M. Ted Princiotto, managing editor, called over to me: "Pick up your airline tickets before noon. You're on your way to L.A." Grabbing AP copy off the machine and the morning's *Plain Dealer,* I updated myself on the latest news. There was no time to drive the twenty-five miles back home to pack or to care for my Newfoundland dogs; so I called my husband, Howard Beaufait, whom I had married in 1956, and gave a few instructions. Howard was a veteran newspaperman, familiar with the ins and outs of unexpected assignments. I also needed cash, which was easy to obtain because we always got cash advances. (Plastic was still in the future.) With a loaded purse I headed for Cleveland Hopkins Airport and whatever came next. I felt pretty good, because I was wearing a brand-new navy blue, nylon, seersucker dress my mother had made. The fabric was newly developed by DuPont or one of those big chemical-textile giants. Mother loved the design; so did I. There was a fitted bodice, V neck, and a bouffant skirt over a fluffy bouffant underskirt. I loved that dress. I didn't know that morning that I would be wearing it straight for the next six or seven days. I washed it by hand each night and it dried over hotel bathtubs. Funny how a dress like that inspires a lot of self-confidence, and I'd need it.

Dallas, Texas, and Jack Kennedy were on my mind. This was another national story, and I would be competing with national reporters. Again, I knew my old police reporter skills, honed at old Central Police Station, would be my most helpful tool. On any homicide, cops held the keys to the news. There were cousins and an aging aunt in the Los Angeles area, but calling them would be a waste of time. L.A. homicide detective, Captain Hamilton, was only a voice on the phone when we talked about Cleveland hoodlums involved in West Coast crime, but I was counting on him.

I rarely recall feeling the way I did for this assignment as I did on other plane trips. I wanted to get where I was going. And now that was the Los Angeles Biltmore, a grand old lady of a building, where, before checking in, I talked to the Los Angeles AP bureau and learned that reporters were still on the "death watch," clustered on the grass in front of Kennedy's hospital. I made a quickie stop at the drugstore for the essentials, a toothbrush and other things, and then took a cab to the site, clutching the latest editions of newspapers and my big purse. By now police had identified the shooter as a hotel busboy, Sirhan B. Sirhan, who shot Kennedy in the kitchen of the Hotel Ambassador as Kennedy was leaving a rally. Fellow reporters said news was scarce. The Kennedy sisters were en route or maybe already at Bobby's bedside. Frank Mankiewicz, the Kennedy spokesman, gave terse briefings with some hope that Kennedy remained alive. The mayor of Los Angeles, Samuel W. Yorty, told reporters the presidential candidate remained unconscious. Actually, we learned later, Kennedy, who was campaigning for the presidency along the West Coast, had died that morning. The news pack broke up when the truth filtered out.

News-wise, the next story for the New York senator and U.S. attorney general in his brother Jack's president cabinet was his funeral, which was set for Saturday, June 8, at St. Patrick's Cathedral in New York City. Checking with my desk, I learned my orders: "Ask the cops where this busboy got the gun." Princiotto was a pragmatic reporter, like me. Before his promotion, he was a crack reporter at the federal courthouse with a coveted reputation. I learned a lot from Ted, especially about paper trails. He insisted reporters "follow the paper trail." That meant police and court records, bankruptcy records, marriage and divorce records, anything in writing, anything in the public domain.

Reporters from out of town scattered, many going home or flying east for the funeral. Virtually alone, I taxied over to the central police station, which was as quiet as a morgue. Unfortunately my guy, Captain Hamilton, wasn't available. I wandered around, looking into empty rooms off the lobby, when I saw a guy in civilian clothes, bunched up on a lounge, watching TV. He looked tired and grouchy, and he ignored me, but I stood my ground. Smiling and friendly, I told him my sad story that I was from a Cleveland paper and was looking for Captain Hamilton. He didn't say it, but his look said all reporters were scum. I sat down. I was weary, too, and to my surprise, he talked, and then he talked about the two-faced, snooty Kennedys, about lousy politics, about the city's racial problems, about Watts, the black enclave burned by riots in the 1960s. This was the time to be a sponge. I sat quietly and listened, simply nodding my head.

The man had been on a security detail for the Kennedy visit. He was a veteran detective with a jaundiced eye, made more so by the murder in this district. His bitterness surprised me as he sat emptying his soul to a stranger. Under the circumstances, though, I was a better listening board, than say, his superior officers. So I let him talk about the Kennedys, about their past visits to Los Angeles when they demanded the best police protection, to the point of requesting elite squads of men known to the Kennedys by first names from past visits. Now, he said, the political climate had changed. The blacks had burned their Watts neighborhood with the deaths of black radicals, and angry criticism was heaped on police by the black community. Bobby Kennedy's handlers, sensing the racial climate, specifically asked for "black policemen." "The advance team wanted black cops for Watts," said this grim-faced detective, angry over the political twists. His anger escaped like air from a torn balloon. I waited before I began my questions. Where'd the shooter get the gun? How'd the cops trace the gun so fast? "We knew early June 6 that the gun was a small revolver, a .22 caliber, manufactured by Iver Johnson's Arms and Cycle Works in Fitchburg, Massachusetts, and shipped to an L.A. wholesaler. The computer coughed up the name of the owner." This disheveled man said in August 1965 flames from Watts had lit the coastal skies and communities around L.A. "Burn, baby, burn," was the Watts' chant, forcing lots of people to buy guns. I hung on his every word. Then he dropped a gem in my lap. Not the name Sirhan, but the name Albert Leslie Hertz, a seventy-year-old man from Alhambra, California. The gun was registered to this guy. Who the heck was he? How was he connected to Sirhan? The ball was now in my court, and I knew I could find Hertz.

My heart was pumping back at my hotel, where I replenished my cash and grabbed a cab for Alhambra. I told the black driver I was a reporter from Ohio who knew nothing about Los Angeles and begged him to stick with me no matter how long it took to find this Hertz guy. Luckily, the driver caught my fever, and during the course of several days we were inseparable. And I had cash. This tiny morsel from a dispirited cop put together the threads of a case history of the gun used to kill a man who may have become president of the United States.

En route to Alhambra, I read the papers, which described how a bullet had struck Kennedy behind the right ear, killing the forty-two-year-old candidate. A second bullet struck him in the armpit, traveling to the back of his neck. It was a gruesome image of Kennedy falling on the kitchen floor, surrounded by hotel workers and his bodyguards.

We found the Hertz home, a modest bungalow, less than nine miles from downtown L.A. and fifteen miles from Watts. Through a screen door I introduced myself to Mrs. Hertz, an attractive, gray-haired woman who was cooking dinner. She held the door lightly, with no intention of talking to reporters. The FBI had warned her. Also, reporters heard from Superior Court judge Arthur L. Alarcon that he banned those involved in the investigation from talking to anyone, including reporters. But her guard came down when I introduced myself as a reporter from the *Cleveland Plain Dealer*. She hesitated then confided that a Cleveland couple, related to the owners of the paper, had been their best friends in Panama. I heard her husband's voice in the background. He was ill, she said. She opened the door further but kept the screen door locked. Her husband, an engineer, had worked all over the world—Panama, South American, Korea, and he had been a consultant to an Arab king in Saudi Arabia. She knew from the FBI that Sirhan was a Jordanian Arab. The FBI had run a check on the couple and were not yet finished questioning them. Questions were bubbling up in me. I could barely contain myself, yet I knew rushing this elderly woman would be stupid. I did learn she hadn't talked to any other reporter. I had this story, alone. It was my story, and I forged ahead. I asked her about the gun, and she answered: "Yes, we bought it. We gave it to our daughter. Yes. I am sorry. This is so terrible. I cannot say more. How strangely things turn out. I understand feelings about Arabs. There is so much wealth there and so much poverty."

Meanwhile her husband shouted things about their daughter. They had adopted a baby girl, now Dana Westlake, at Booth Memorial Hospital, run by the Salvation Army in Cleveland, during a brief stay in Ohio between overseas jobs. Thank God for this kindly old man, giving me Dana's address in nearby Altadena in the foothills of the San Gabriel Mountains. It must have been the Cleveland connection. He actually knew one of the retired *Plain Dealer* editors, whom I barely knew (he was pretty old). He said their daughter was educated at Green Mountain Junior College in Vermont and had worked for Flying Tigers Airline in New York City. She and her husband, Robert F. Westlake, were moving to San Francisco, where he was starting a new business. My taxi driver and I found Olive Way, a short, dead-end street that was junglelike with flowering trees and shrubs and obscured eight Spanish-style houses, two of which were owned by the Westlakes. Unfortunately the Westlakes were either in San Francisco or someplace in Marin County, cautious and scared neighbors said. They had taken their two sons, eleven-year-old Bobby and six-year-old Johnny, with them.

Wracking my brains for sources, I gambled that Charley Bates, an FBI agent I knew in Cleveland, was still in San Francisco. He had moved from Cleveland to London to be the FBI liaison with British intelligence before he was transferred out west. Luck was with me. Charley took my call and laughed at my plight in finding the Westlakes. He suggested that I go to a general store in Woodacre, in Marin County, and ask for a blonde clerk who was the shop bookkeeper. Bates said Dana Westlake cashed checks there. Charley said to use his name if I needed to. Luckily my cash got me to Marin County, to the general store, to the blonde at the meat slicer. "No, they've been bothered enough," she said. "I'm an old friend of Charley Bates," I said. She perked up and within minutes I was looking at a cashed check. In the corner of the check was the Westlake name and address. Thank you, blondie, and you, Charley.

My cash was running low, and I was in a dumpy motel, living on milk and potato chips, when I finally caught up with Mrs. Westlake in a tiny office of the *Recorder,* Marin County's legal newspaper, where she handled court filings and legal notices. She was a thirty-five-year-old vivacious woman who spoke in staccato cadence. she told me that she had been awakened at 4:25 A.M. on June 7, hours after Kennedy's death, by sheriff's deputies. She was unaware of the scene at the Ambassador Hotel. Yes, she said, she owned the gun. Yes, she gave it away. No, she didn't know Kennedy was shot. Yes, she gave the gun to Chick. "Chick" was George Charles Erhard, an eighteen-year-old boy who lived across the street on Olive Way. "I'd have been better off if I'd burned the damned thing." Her mother hated the gun, and she took it from her in its original box. Her husband, when remodeling the roof of one of their houses on Olive Way, found the boxed gun, and she gave Chick the gun in September 1967, because he had lots of hobbies and often scrambled through trash to fund them, once rebuilding an old Ford car from a chassis.

So Chick got the gun, which was bought by the elderly white couple during the violent racial fires of 1965. As the old detective told me, cops traced the gun through California state gun registrations. The Hertz registration was on an index of 2.5 million guns. "Mother told me later the police kept them incommunicado from about 1:30 A.M. to 6 A.M. and warned her not to talk to me or they'd be part of the investigation." She added: "Charley Bates interviewed me at 9 A.M. when I told him the federal government had cleared me twice for government jobs, including the Flying Tigers."

Dana called Chick's family for an interview on my behalf, but they declined. However, I found other neighbors who told me Chick was a stock boy after school at the Nash department store in downtown Pasadena. Dana believed Chick told police he sold the gun "to a gay named Joe, with bushy hair."

Joe, another Nash employee, was twenty-two-year-old Joseph Sirhan, younger brother of Sirhan B. Sirhan. These young men lived with their mother and a younger brother in a small, white, frame bungalow at 696 E. Howard Street in Pasadena. They had been in the United States without citizenship since 1957, while the father remained in Jordan. Three clerks at the Nash store had heard Joe Sirhan's reaction when the television flashed a photo of his brother. One clerk heard Joe say: "My God, I know him." Joe told his boss, the buyer in basement hardware, something terrible happened and he had to go home. But Nash officials called police, who took Joe away. His boss knew Joe had served time for marijuana and was on probation and also under a deportation order. The boss said: "Joe was here because he deserved a second chance. But Joe had one problem: he hated Jews. He would say things that were out of line about Jews. I finally reminded him, I am married to a Jew, and his employer is a Jew. I don't think he listened."

The buyer described Chick Erhard as "very possessive." If he needed a part or something, he would sell another thing to get it. He believed Chick sold the gun to Joe about eight weeks before the shooting, around April 22. That week Senator Kennedy and his family were campaigning in Vincennes, Indiana, with their three kids and a dog. Mrs. Westlake said the gun was never fired, but police said Erhard fired it when he drove his rejuvenated Ford to go fossil hunting in the hills. The nephew of an L.A. cop said he believed he saw Sirhan shooting a gun at a San Gabriel shooting range a week before Kennedy's fateful end.

The arrest of Sirhan resulted in anti-Jewish demonstrations by Arab and Jordanian students at Pasadena City College. Newspapers printed excerpts from notebooks police had confiscated. "Kennedy must be assassinated before June 5, 1968." That was the first anniversary of the blitzkrieg, six-day Israeli war in 1967, When Israel subdued, in humiliating fashion, three Arab states— Jordan, Syria, and Egypt. The mayor of Los Angeles said Sirhan wrote eighteen to twenty pages of anti-Israel, pro-Arab, and pro-Communist ramblings in pen and ink. Police guessed that Joe gave brother Sirhan the Hertz gun. Under California law, it was illegal for an alien or a person convicted of a felony to possess a concealed weapon.

I was worn thin on this assignment, not getting much sleep, eating poorly, and bouncing around California like a ping-pong ball. But I was happy to get the story. My L.A. taxi driver stuck with me, even when I spent a morning with two Armenian brothers who had hired and fired Sirhan B. Sirhan. Charley Bates was a big help, too, and in San Francisco the city editor at the *Examiner* had helped me cash a personal check. But I wanted to go home. I badly needed to see this in print. I was writing leads in my head. But Princiotto said:

"While you're there, run over to L.A. Jim Brown threw his Chinese girlfriend through the window of his apartment." I had never, never turned down an assignment, and I reminded Ted that I covered Jim Brown, the great ex–Cleveland Browns football player, when he was charged with assaulting Brenda Ayres, a teenager, during a party at the Howard Johnson's in University Circle. He called me a lot of names, all of which I cannot repeat here, and said, "Okay. The AP can handle it. Come on home." Ted had heart after all.

On Thursday, June 13, the story ran: "Story of a Gun That Killed a Dream." From page one it jumped to a full inside page with photos. The story was later reprinted as a mailer to readers and public officials. And I got a Newspaper Guild award for it. Not surprisingly, my lovely blue frock wore out the miracle fabric—it was tough but faded from laundering, and the threads weakened underarm. Not that I cared to wear it again anytime in the near future.

-30-

- *19* -

"What's it like being a reporter?"

*G*lamour women are few and far between in newsrooms. But they are there. You'll see one or two in a snazzy black evening gown, with pearls and flimsy pumps, accepting a coveted award from her peers. But it's the sloughing behind a moment of fame that is the norm, when a trophy is the farthest thing from your mind. My fastidious editor for this book asks me what I wore, what I thought on the job, what my opinions were. The truth is, I recall few times when clothes meant something. My cleanest, purest, targeted thoughts were: just get that story. I never knew in advance, but I knew, just knew, I'd get it.

My generation of reporters was objective spectators. We reported, looking through a clear lens at scenes in our vision. Our copy, we were taught, while descriptive, was shorn of "I." Later television news shoved the written media around in a fight for readership, moved the boundaries, freeing reporters to slip in personal opinions. Today there is a glut of personal opinion, growing by the day with Internet bloggers. Big changes have taken place from the time I started in 1944 until today. But certain things cannot change. News, especially 24/7 news, still must be gathered by reporters on the street, on deadline.

In the newspaper business assignments are handled daily, routinely, under extreme pressure and in professional, businesslike ways. Under normal conditions, the city editor or bureau chief discusses the assignment, the kind of story he wants, when he wants it, and whether to hook up with a photographer or go it alone until an art date is confirmed. It sounds cut and dried, and it is. Stories are routine on various beats—education, police, courthouse, general assignment. Reporters who are slotted into these beats bear the responsibility of furnishing tips and leads to news breaking on their beat. The story can be as mundane as a speech before the Chamber or Rotary or a major announcement from the mayor or county commissioners. It is also the reporter's job to find the key phrase, the key message of a speech that many times turns into major headlines and controversy. Assignments are doled out in minutes, and reporters are on their own; deadlines drive the day's actions. Going solo means needing a car, money, pencil/pen, notebook, tape recorder, and, now, a cell phone. Newsrooms, by the nature of the beast, require lots of paper, phone books, computers, phones, etc., and they are sloppy affairs, despite management's cubicle rabbit warrens. The cubicle entitles staffers to a privacy of sorts. These little cages sometimes are tiny lunchrooms, despite frowns from bosses. There is no time to eat anyplace else.

Deadlines control the lives of everyone in the newsroom, from reporter and photographer bringing in the news and photos to the copy readers, headline writers, layout people, photo editor, and through the chain that moves the copy, from copy editors, via computer, to the printing presses, which are often miles from newsrooms, to circulation distributors, and finally to the front door. The operation, ideally, is smooth as silk. But then there are the Big News Days, propelling everyone into speed-ups. As a neophyte reporter, I noted the veterans kept extra shoes, raincoats, and umbrellas in lockers. A cupboard held extra pencils and notebooks or other extras, and photographers carried Slim Jims for emergencies, when your gear was locked in the car. These slender rods slip in-between the car door window and the door handle.

Cops frown on them, considering them burglar tools, but we used them anyway.

Early on as a young police reporter, the city desk assigned me the "dawn" beat, calling me any time from 3 A.M. on. That meant I had to have a bedtime shower and decide on clothes and shoes the night before for an early getaway. Honestly, I can't remember worrying about my hair or makeup, although I wouldn't be seen without lipstick. The call sent me to rendezvous with a photographer, usually in a part of the county I'd never been. I kept on hand road maps for four counties and a detailed street index for the city proper, along with an old telephone directory. Reporters on these assignments memorized gas stations with big window clocks along with twenty-four-hour service, phones, and johns. Like military units, we were prepared. In a three-newspaper town—Cleveland had three dailies when I started—competition was fierce, and more than once I owed details in my story to a streetwise photographer who knew the town, the cops, and weaknesses of our competitors. I'll always owe a debt to Perry Cragg, Jerry Horton, Eddie Dork, George Hixson, Bill Nehez, and Dick Misch, to name a few.

Really big stories interrupted home life, birthday parties, and relaxing days off. The reporter was thrilled to be called, but the spouse was not so happy, stuck with the family chores. But that was life on the run. Being a reporter is a profession not unlike being a cop, fireman, or army volunteer. There was the chase, a thrill-a-minute, until the story was splashed across page one, and you did it. Once, on July 20, 1969, a Sunday morning, I saw the headlines on my way home from church. The big headline was: "Apollo in Orbit for M-Day." Below that: "Kennedy O.K., Woman Drowns in Crack-up." Not again, not another Kennedy story, I thought. The managing editor said: "Get going." He didn't ask, "Can you make it?" That was unthinkable! There was no mention of family plans, No mention of my health or anything personal. I was to just go. Naturally my husband and I checked each other's schedule to be sure someone was around to feed our Newfoundlands. Throwing things into a bag, making sure I had personal checks, I was off for Massachusetts before sunset, and by Monday I saw the morning sun at Edgartown, Massachusetts, on Martha's Vineyard. What a glorious site, sailboats bouncing in a light morning breeze; houses with wrap-around railings on front porches; walkers in shorts, airing pets on leashes along quiet town streets.

Catching up with the story meant reading every paper I could get my hands on and making calls to the local AP bureau for back up. In a nutshell, this was it: A car driven by Sen. Edward M. Kennedy, D.-Mass., plunged off a narrow bridge on Chappaquiddick Island about midnight on Friday (it was now Monday), killing a woman companion. My first thoughts focused on the time element—death Friday, details Monday. Why the delay? Kennedy and his buddies were partying at a rented cottage on the tiny island, a ferry boat away from Martha's Vineyard, when the accident happened, and news accounts commented on the time and "damage control," a Kennedy family mode of operation, according to critics.

The dead woman was Mary Jo Kopechne, a twenty-eight-year-old campaign worker in Washington, D.C., who was weekending with girlfriends in Edgartown. The local paper noted that nine hours had passed before Kennedy "exhausted and in a state of shock," walked into police headquarters in Edgartown to give a statement. The senator and his political friends were at Edgartown for an annual regatta. He was expected to be with his wife and children at the Kennedy Hyannis Port compound for the weekend. The dead woman, a former secretary to Ted's brother, the late senator Bobby Kennedy, was staying with five girlfriends from Washington, where they all were campaign workers for the Kennedys. The girls, all single, joined the married Kennedy and his married pals at the rented cottage. In his police statement, Ted said he left the party with Mary Jo between 11 P.M. and midnight to return to his room at the Shiretown Motel. He made a wrong turn, away from the ferry road, and drove onto a humpback wooden bridge and over an inlet when the car went off the bridge. The car sank in the water, landing with the roof on the bottom. He had no recollection of getting out of the car and said he dove in the water repeatedly, without success, to find Mary Jo. He came up exhausted and in shock.

Again I was to report on a national story, just as I had for the assassinations of President John F. Kennedy in 1963 and Sen. Robert

F. Kennedy in 1968. I was a stranger in another small town packed with reporters, flying and boating in from around the country. A Kennedy was forever Big News. Town officials, overwhelmed by the throng of reporters, turned the briefing chores over to Edgartown police chief Dominick Arena, who gathered us in a big conference room, where he fumblingly and cautiously tried to answer questions involving the coroner and county prosecutor's actions.

As pack journalism was never my bag, I rented a car and, via the ferry, went to Chappaquiddick, a piney, woodsy place with cottages here and there and a handful of year-round homes. The ferryman directed me to the party cottage, now locked tight, shades drawn. At a nearby cottage I was greeted by loud barks by—of all things—a huge black Newfoundland, my favorite breed. I momentarily forgot my mission, so upset to see a chained Newfie in the hot sun with no water bowl, running in circles around an iron post. The dog's owner got a lecture from me, and his pet was soon tied beneath a shady tree with a bucket of water. It so happened that this Portuguese man, now subdued but polite, was the caretaker for the Kennedy cottage, which was rented from a family in New York. He didn't unlock the "party cottage" but instead drove me to the island dump. "Look," he said, pointing. A heap of liquor bottles, beer bottles, and picnic plates and debris were piled high at the edge of the dump. He simply confirmed that the party took place and that the Kennedy kids knew the island like the back of their hands. He also told me that the road that led over the inlet was known as "lover's lane."

It wasn't much, but it gave a setting and sense, something the others hadn't bothered with. Several homeowners on the road even talked to me. Of course my competitors were glued to phones, busy locating the party-goers who were by now scattered from the island to Boston and Washington and Cape Cod. Not too many party-goers volunteered information. Some reporters flew to the tiny town of Plymouth, Pennsylvania, for Mary Jo Kopechne's funeral and back again to see whether Ted would be criminally charged. From Hyannis Port, Kennedy, wearing an orthopedic collar, was snippy with reporters, saying he'd talk "at an appropriate time." With that, reporters dug in.

I ferried back and forth and then decided the next action was in Edgartown, where Kennedy would face a judge and be charged with leaving the scene of an accident. There were more than fifty reporters in the courtroom. As sleeping rooms were hard to rent, some guys doubled up in small rooms. They scooped up news like vacuum cleaners; no bit of gossip was too insignificant. We soon learned that Joe Gargan, a Kennedy cousin, had rented the cottage and organized the party. Gargan was particularly close, a sort of caretaker to Rosemary Kennedy, the sister of Edward, who had a mental disability. Practically every island citizen, from visitor to shop owner, was interviewed, including local police and firemen and divers who had almost been swept away in a strong tide while trying to retrieve the body.

This assignment was wearing on everyone until, finally, on Friday, July 26, Kennedy and his wife Joan were in the Edgartown court. I anxiously sat with two hundred other spectators, reporters, photographers, and vacationers; all of us jammed the courthouse to its maximum. Rain and fog kept the Kennedys from flying in, and they had to settle for a half-hour boat trip. Joan, petite and blond, wore a mini-mini skirt. Kennedy, tall and handsome, looked grim, his face ruddy and a bit puffy. His lips were tightly drawn. At his side was Stephen Smith, a brother-in-law. There were no court fireworks. Judge James A. Boyle heard the clerk read the case of the commonwealth versus Edward M. Kennedy. "How do you plead?" Boyle said. Kennedy, so quiet, said: "Guilty." The clerk asked him to repeat it. He did. The hearing took twelve minutes. Chief Arena told the court Kennedy informed him he was the driver of the car. "There was no concealment." Kennedy received a two-month suspended sentence.

On the steps outside the courthouse Kennedy started, "I have made my . . . ," but his words were lost to newsmen who were too busy running for phones. One islander said: "It stinks." A female Bostonian said: "It's sad. But we don't want him as president." I reaped good quotes for my story by the crowd on the courthouse steps. Everyone freely gave opinions, many critical but affected by the unfolding drama of another member of the Kennedy clan. My only concern, as always, was to write the story, get it in print.

There was no time for personal feelings or judgments. It was just another story, but a big one.

The next time I saw Ted Kennedy he was running for president in 1990 and had a campaign stop in downtown Pittsburgh, Pennsylvania. Speaking from the steps of a downtown building, Kennedy was no longer the sleek, black-haired, handsome young Irishman who sailed in regattas. He looked tired. He asked an aide what city he was in. His clothes were wrinkled and untidy. We followed his campaign to Johnstown, Pennsylvania, where he met with seniors and where labor leaders, shouting through bullhorns, gathered people to a union hall. It was a lackluster day; few people clamored to shake his hand. The campaign soon fizzled out, and Jimmy Carter, a former Georgia governor, became the Democrat spear carrier that year.

Months, maybe years later, I recognized the tragedy of this story, especially when Ted Kennedy appeared on television. I wondered whether he felt guilt, how he rationalized the death of that young woman. Not infrequently a cartoon appears in some jokester magazine, about Kennedy, Chappaquiddick, and the upside down car. Lesser incidents ruined other senators and public officials. How proud the Irish-American and Catholic communities were of the Kennedy clan at one time. The Kennedy brothers had so much going for them—an ambitious father, money, good educations, social acceptability. Where did it go wrong?

Senator Kennedy was socially and probably intellectually a cut or two above Bay Village doctor Samuel H. Sheppard. Kennedy got two months' suspension; Sheppard got ten years for killing his wife. The Kopechne death was an accident; Marilyn Sheppard's death was one of passion, elimination. But the Cape Codders, I felt, wanted nothing to tarnish a high-class tourist trade. The judicial system there moved swiftly. I did hand it to Kennedy for pleading guilty when he could have fudged and extended his court case. If I had any judgmental thoughts at the time, it was that the rich get away with things. I never wiped from my memory that bitter detective I met in Los Angeles after Bobby's death. He hated the Kennedys, who demanded special treatment and special security when they campaigned. Before Watts, this cop said, they asked for the elite white cops to save their lives if they were called on. After Watts, Bobby Kennedy wanted "black cops." Ted Kennedy is still a U.S. senator, looking to another term. I turn the television off when he comes on, but my personal feelings wouldn't stop me from covering him again. And I did, at a fundraiser in Greensburg, Pennsylvania. He had flown in to Latrobe Airport in a private plane. Surrounded by staff, he was courteous and smiley but declined an interview and answered no questions. "Listen to my speech later," he said as aides whisked him to a waiting car. Shutdown, I wondered how reporters penetrate the cast-iron skills of celebrities.

-30-

-20-

Investigative Reporting

The Difference between Cops and Reporters

*W*hat makes reporters think they are smarter than cops? There's a long-held view among us, the print media, the tabloids, and a lot of other reporting institutions, that we're better at solving mysteries than cops. Arrogance and revisionism, I think, are twin engines driving this view. There is also the gut element of the "competitive chase" that reporters, with more money and less restrictive strings, can outsmart the guys with badges searching crime clues. Unless there is a bizarre fluke, experience shows that cops start with an edge since they are the first on the scene, first to get a crack at witnesses, first to see forensic results, first to get tips from the public. However, reporters doubling back on crime find witnesses afraid of police and more likely to unload to sympathetic reporters.

I couldn't help muse about this when suburban Euclid police spent hours, days, weeks, even, trying to solve the murder of a Euclid housewife, Marlene Steele, the wife of Municipal Court judge Robert L. Steele. Oddly, during that bitterly cold day of January 10, 1969, reporters literally joined hands in a sweep with police, plunging through knee-deep snow in the Steeles' back-yard, looking for the gun, the crime weapon in the case. And still later my colleague reporter and friend, Bill Evans, and I spent a lot of time, some on our own, chasing down prostitutes and low-class types, hunting for clues that we, though a bit arrogantly, figured police had missed.

Bill Evans, a tall, handsome guy, was our chief police reporter, and when the mystery of Marlene's death dragged on, we worked together exhaustively interviewing people who had been brought to our attention through gossip and tips. As I had learned in the Sam Sheppard case, in domestic homicides, the spouse is invari-ably the first suspect, the target of neighborhood stories. Gos-sip we heard, not unnaturally, linked the judge to an attractive, red-haired court clerk, and tips implied a lurid connection to the underworld of vice and prostitution. This was pretty heady stuff to be swirling around a respectable member of the court on the heels of a homicide. But that's what happened in the wake of the cruel murder of a popular mother and housewife. Judge Steele said that from his upstairs den, on that early wintry morning in 1969, he heard noises downstairs, like "pop-pop." When he went to investigate the noises he found his wife shot to death in a downstairs bedroom. He called police and the murder mystery began to slowly unravel. In fact, it took years.

Covering crime stories in the metropolitan city of Cleveland gave reporters access to police officials on a professional basis. But more often than not, a reporter stood and an officer sat—a pro forma thing with top cops. I can't recall times when the chief offered me a chair. We spoke to courteous, professional, ranking officers in and out of their cubicles, asking pointed question and getting terse quotes or none at all. We rarely got an off-the-record comment. On the flip side, we got valuable tips from frustrated persons close to investigations, who were anxious to see some-thing published. Of course all tips had to be checked before publi-cation, but at least we got pointed in intriguing directions.

The Steele case in Euclid broke the mold. We reporters were grouped en masse in the office of Euclid Police chief Frank Payne, where he waltzed us around with his charismatic personality. We

Interview with Euclid Municipal Court judge Robert Steele hours after wife Marlene was shot to death in January 1969. Photograph by Ray Matjasic, *Cleveland Plain Dealer.*

actually sat with the chief around a large, polished, oval table, hanging on his words. Long entrenched in the city's political and civic life, he was a man in control, he thought, and we were his minions. It was all jocular play-acting, of course, and leaving after an hour or so of bantering and risqué jokes, the cynical reporters said, "Oh yeah. And what did he give us? Nothing. Bullshit." The lone female, I took it all in. Soon, a Euclid police officer, meeting me by design in the parking lot, filled me in on what my male counterparts were actually talking about. It was prostitution, which was operating openly in the town's high rises on the lakeshore part of town and in a popular motel, owned by a "highly respectable" citizen, and in a racy nightclub, patronized by the town's doctors and lawyers. The question was what did this have to do with the judge and his dead wife?

Chief Payne was chitchatting with us, giving us snow jobs, wasting our time when we should be on the street looking for answers. Readers of the two dailies, the *Plain Dealer,* my paper, and the *Cleveland Press,* and daily and weekly suburban papers, were not getting the full picture, only the basics of an unsolved murder. My informant cop said the chief was "scared shitless" when we'd asked about vice in the city, why nobody was arrested, and who was protecting the rackets. This was another big order, a can of worms, for us reporters, when our assignment was covering the day-to-day operations of cops and solving a high-profile homicide.

The city desk called me at home the morning of January 10 and informed me that I was to check out the homicide in the wooded area of Euclid where the Steeles lived in a comfortable, two-story home with their two young sons. Walking through the deep snow, and later drinking hot chocolate in a neighbor's garage, I heard the women talk about Marlene Steele, the devoted mother with a master's degree in teaching and a hospital volunteer. Who could have killed her? Neighbors were frightened, locking doors and threatening to bar windows. I scooped up reaction as the obvious follow-up newspaper story to a crime. Then I got a break through a fellow reporter, Jim Byrne. Byrne, a tenacious ex-Marine covering the civil branch of the country courthouse, was by chance a close friend of Judge Steele's father, who was a highly respected county official. Otto Steele told Jim his son would give an exclusive interview to a "fair and open-minded" reporter, and my editor picked me. Interviewing the distraught judge in the private apartment of Otto Steele, I studied him, sobbing and shaking, retelling the same story he gave police about hearing pops and then finding his wife dead in bed. He chain-smoked and his hands twitched. His best quotes were that he believed her killer "knew someone in the house and knew the house." He said the killing was tearing him inside to have anyone think he did it. His attractive, dark-haired wife had two bullets in her head. Studying him that morning, I waited for him to look me in the eye. He never did; he just blotted his eyes with a handkerchief.

Secrets grow lives in small towns. On January 13 I wrote my first story about Judge Steele's extracurricular friendship with an attractive court clerk. My colleagues described this as the "bombshell" Chief Payne was hiding, as he played cat-and-mouse with us that day. Court aides clammed up, but a tipster revealed the woman was Mrs. Barbara Swartz. Bill Evans and I met casually at lunch with young attorneys who were practicing before Steele

Euclid Police chief Frank Payne (second from right) holds a press conference on the Marlene Steele murder case with (left) *Plain Dealer* photographer Ray Matjasic, the author (center), and television reporter Paul Sciria. 1969; author's collection.

and said the judge and clerk were regulars at popular Euclid bars. And surprisingly both of them freely admitted the lunches, the judge explaining that gossip about public officials is "making big things out of little things." Steele appeared to be cooperating 100 percent with police and even offered to take a lie detector test. The thirty-eight-year-old Swartz, vice president of a school board, said she talked over legal board problems with the judge. She was in the process of a divorce, and her attorney had urged Steele to hire her in his courtroom. The Euclid safety director, Ralph O. Dunker, a former FBI agent, had Swartz questioned along with other court employees.

Bill Evans and I lunched where the judge and Swartz were seen, picking up pieces of information about the couple here and there. Urban (Ruby) Leoni, former Euclid transportation director, said Steele and Swartz were regulars at his bar. Judge Steele then admitted that in the second or third year of the Steele marriage they had in-law problems. One night he found his clothes in the garage, and he and his wife argued over his nightly speaking engagements and political campaigns for office. On many assignments I used a lot of patience, waiting for people to talk. But I couldn't get Steele to shut up about family life, about Barbara being a classmate of a best friend. Interestingly, Jay Swartz, Barbara's husband, was surly and wouldn't talk. But his eyes remained shifty, off in space.

Euclid police, needing help in the investigation, turned to the skills of Cuyahoga County prosecutor John T. Corrigan and Capt. Louis (Lou) Kulis of the Cuyahoga County sheriff's office. Kulis was a former Cleveland cop who was laid-back and dogged. Weapons' experts continued searching ducts and concrete blocks around the Steele house for the missing .38 gun after we failed to find anything in the deep snow drifts. Bill Evans learned of Steele's "kinky" sex life, his photo collection of various male Cleveland athletes, and his sexual foot fetish, which was known by his high school classmates. Evans, via his Central Station police connections, was also being fed information by several waitresses and prostitutes on the side. We were writing daily stories about the investigation, but the sex stuff was taboo. We had nothing to pin it on but gossip.

Then on January 24 Swartz admitted to having an affair with the judge and took a lie test. The judge sent his resignation to Ohio governor James A. Rhodes. Bill and I convinced our city desk we should show blown-up photos of the pair to area motels, seeking identification from hotel employees, based on rumors they rented rooms downtown and in Detroit and attended hockey games in Cleveland and Detroit. I felt pretty silly following motel maids around with these photos; it was like something out of a movie. Evans, a striking male, in the vernacular, a "hunk," was a magnet for barmaids. He had a big quirky smile and came on like Mr. Friendly, a shoulder to cry on. On his regular night-police shift— not on specials like this—he ate at neighborhood joints where "ladies of the night" hung out (they were waitresses since their employers were fringe hoods). One of these waitresses was Marty

(Martha) Prunella, whose husband Arnie Prunella was a known punk-hoodlum who had mysteriously disappeared. She poured out her story to Evans, along with a tip about Judge Steele's off-duty playtimes. Marty and her friends—call girls—worked for "a house" in a suburb on Euclid Heights Boulevard.

Bill and I had lots of freedom on this assignment, moving easily around on vague tips about Steele. We called on the "madam" at her imposing brick apartment near Coventry Road, fishing for tips on her customers, especially Judge Steele. She was a fat, blowsy woman who invited us in as a man scurried off to the back rooms. Rocking in a big chair, she kept her hand within reach of a red phone, shutting it down when it rang. Marty was "on call" from an apartment across the street, and my pal Bill had even loaned her money. He was a soft touch. Bill and madam played question-and-answer games for several hours, and we left with the distinct impression there was a link between Steele and the prostitutes. Madam had no intention of giving straight answers. The case remained unsolved until FBI agent Bob Ressler made the connection between the judge, the hit man who killed his wife, and prostitutes eight years earlier.

Bill and I were straining for daily stories when our boss finally called us off the story. We resisted, believing we weren't finished. Some evenings we hung around a private Euclid club, not as reporters, just as customers, soaking up bar talk. It was "the place" for young professionals and a lot of questionable characters. Bill buddied up with a guy who boasted: "I could drive a Cadillac out of Central Caddy for you tonight." That's the kind of trade this place had. I recognized young lawyers, friends of one of my young relatives, also a lawyer. This guy was pretty loose in describing Steele's "other life"—more unprintable stuff. Since we weren't producing daily stories we had to give up the chase. Our boss was nice and liked our efforts, but he reminded us we weren't cops and that we had to get on with life.

Bill and I returned to our normal newspaper life, he on the night-police beat, me back on general assignment, writing whatever came along. Stories like the Steele murder were the exception, and it never bothered me when I had to return to a general assignment. However, a prominent Euclid citizen once complained to the editors about the "excessive" daily cover stories tarnishing the character of the City of Euclid.

Before Bill and I shut down, we spent an afternoon with Lou Kulis at the sheriff's office, hoping to "horse trade" our notes with his notes and gossip on the investigation into the Steele murder. Kulis liked reporters, and although he was close-mouthed on lots of investigations, he was a walking encyclopedia of the town's criminal element. Bill described Marty Prunella, the call girls, the madam, causing Kulis to hand us a long typewritten memo. It detailed a Lakewood police "bust" of two call girls and their handler or pimp, a guy named Owen Kilbane. Kulis, working with Lakewood police, said there were "people of interest" involved, and the names on the memo included Bob Steele; Owen Kilbane and possibly his brother, Martin; Pete Degravio and possibly a cousin; Marty Prunella and her missing husband, Arnie Prunella; a prostitute named Bunny; Joan Sidota and her girlfriend, Donna, and Donna's ex-husband, Bob Faranacci. There was also possibly a Mrs. De Gravio. Well!

Kulis watched us, our mouths open while we digested all this. We read photostat pages from one of the girls' "trick book," and we recognized names of prominent citizens, lawyers, and judges. This meeting was off-the-record, and we left Kulis with our unpublishable notes. Opening up the yellowing papers in my old Steele file, I reread letters with a variety of tips, ranging from public corruption involving city contracts to high-ranking officers trading traffic tickets for sexual favors. One officer had call girls visiting him "at all hours night and day" while he was hospitalized. One letter-writer wrote that racketeers with previous criminal records worked in the police department. He said Bob Steele "was swimming with sharks." The trail was cold, but someday, somehow, the murder would be solved. Time, Lou said, solved everything.

We never forgot Marlene Steele. Euclid cops remained our friends, and Bill and I covered dozens and dozens of other mundane stories. Lakewood police and the FBI, unknown to us, were doggedly pursuing a prostitution ring in their jurisdiction. The case eventually burst full-blown in the news on April 11, 1977, when

Judge Steele and two brothers, Owen and Martin Kilbane, were convicted of first-degree murder in the death of Marlene Steele. Twelve jurors, after five days of deliberation, found that the trio had hired a hit man to kill the sleeping woman. During the trial, prosecutors described the gunman as Richard N. Robbins, a policeman's son who was also involved in another murder. He turned state's evidence against Steele and the Kilbanes. Robbins was given a new identity to live out his life as federal witness. Steele, in the meantime, actually three months after Marlene's death, married Barbara Swartz. Unknown during long years of investigation—where Steele remained a suspect—was the role of the FBI.

Bob Ressler, a resident FBI agent in Cleveland who worked interstate vice, along with suburban police working on prostitution rings, found one operating in a high-rise apartment in Euclid, a stone's throw from Euclid City Hall. Tracking the young women, who were later arrested in Lakewood, Ressler found them in a major Midwestern city. It's unclear what persuasion he used, but he located Carol Braun and urged her to confess that she worked for the Kilbane brothers. Ressler also found that the vice operations of the Kilbanes were holed up in a once prominent Cleveland Heights hotel and in another suburban motel. Marty Prunella had told Evans she worked out of the Heights operation, and her missing husband was discovered to be a drug courier for the brothers.

Securing bulletproof testimony from his sources, Ressler recreated Marlene Steele's murder. The triggerman was Richard Robbins, who earlier had been convicted of the murder of a popular black folk singer in Cleveland Heights. Facing the Steele murder he confessed to getting paid by the Kilbanes, whom Judge Steele had contacted to do away with his wife. The Kilbanes paid him $1,000 for the hit. Ressler and the Cuyahoga County Prosecutor's office, before taking the cases of Robbins, the Kilbanes, and Steele into court, worked tirelessly with their witnesses, who were alternating between fear and duty, changing their stories, and refusing to cooperate. In the end, they cooperated.

Carol Braun, Owen's common-law wife, reunited with him after the arrest and refused to testify in court, leaving Ressler reading a five-page document about her ten years as Owen's call girl. And on April 11, 1977, twelve jurors in the courtroom of Common Pleas Court judge Joseph J. Nahra found former judge Robert L. Steele and two companions who hired a hit man, guilty. Steele and the two Kilbanes got life. Steele is now dead; the Kilbanes are still in prison. Steele's two sons, now adults, appear regularly before the Ohio parole board to keep the brothers in prison for life.

Bill Evans, never one to give up, spent time on April 27, 1970, talking with a faded beauty and prostitute, Betty Prunella Corena, about her son, Arnie, and his racketeer associates. Showing him her son's notebooks, Bill found the names of Cleveland's number one gangsters. Captain Gordon, of the Cleveland Heights Police, described Betty as "an old hooker" and said she was a pretty good police informant, especially on major burglaries and on one spectacular jewelry heist. Her son did time in California and then lived at the Alcazar Hotel, where Owen Kilbane had lived with Marty, Arnie's wife. Betty said Arnie returned from Nevada, and then he drowned during a Lake Erie boat ride on the Kilbanes' boat. The blowsy woman we met told Bill she cared for Denise Prunella, Marty and Arnie's little girl, and that Marty had her husband "done in." In 1983 Martin and Owen Kilbane and Phillip B. Christopher, a bank burglar, were tried on first-degree murder charges in Prunella's death. Police described him as a "pimp and gambler" who was shot in the summer of 1968, and whose body was weighed down with a manhole cover. The body was never recovered. The trial ended in a mistrial, although efforts are still underway to try the Kilbanes for Prunella's death.

Before Steele was convicted he was in private practice, representing the Kilbanes in a 1973 federal prostitution case. He also represented Rick Robbins, his hit man, when Rick was charged with killing the black singer. Then in jail Steele got a two-year reprieve from his cell when a federal judge ruled the lower court had erred in allowing Ressler to read Carol Braun's statement to the jury. Another federal court put Steele back in prison for life, although in 1987 an Ohio governor commuted his sentence to ten years to life.

Bill Evans died young, before the courts convicted the murderers of Marlene Steele. We did a lot of "cop" work, and had we worked for tabloid journalism, chances are the sex life of Bob Steele would have been headlines long before his trial, eight years after his wife's death. We didn't outsmart the police, but we were right on the trail. Bill believed Marty Prunella was on the verge of telling him big things but was too terrified. It required the unique skills of an agent like Bob Ressler, having the heavy arm of federal prosecution on his side, to get the truth. On the tenth anniversary of Marlene's death Kulis called Bob Steele "a liar" whose details about her death were all "lies." Carmen Marino, the county prosecutor, said, "Robbins was a rotten little killer." To Marino, Steele "was a scheming treacherous human being. We hinted at lots of things in the trial. He protected prostitutes in Euclid, how he shared girls with some other men. The public yet does not have a real appreciation for two sides of Bob Steele."

I learned a lot watching Evans interact with all types of characters, quietly, politely, and respectfully. I honored the confidence of many policemen, watching questionable things in their hometown, helpless to open their mouths. They were our anonymous tipsters. I admired the tenacity of Bob Ressler, a studious observer of mankind with his eye always on the ball. At Ressler's urging, I visited the Kilbanes in state prison, where the brothers were amassing a lode of college credits. Ressler recommended their freedom, considering their cooperation. But the Steele sons put a lock on their freedom. I also learned Bob Steele never stopped talking. He never looked me in the eye either.

-30-

-21-

Career Change

Time to Move on

$\mathcal{I}$n 1970 I had been working full time for twenty-nine years, starting with the Morris Plan Bank, where I toiled as a fresh young bookkeeper. It was a detour from my newspaper goal, but I needed work, and an uncle called the bank's president to hire me. At the same time, I enrolled at Cleveland College, the city's landmark downtown school, where I wrote short pieces for the college paper. One toe was in the door. Then in 1944, my dream was fulfilled, when I was hired at the *Cleveland News,* which folded in 1960. While I worked briefly for the *Plain Dealer,* I left—mostly for a pay increase—then worked briefly at the Cleveland Zoo and University Hospitals in public relations before rejoining the *Plain Dealer* again in 1962. From then until I left in 1970, I covered the best of newspaper assignments—assassinations of President John F. Kennedy and his brother, Robert; following the trail of James Earl Ray, charged with the murder of Dr. Martin L. King; Ted Kennedy at Chappaquiddick and a string of other big and small stories; and then race riots.

Thinking back, it seems I worked my fanny off as superwoman. I wanted it all: a husband, a home, a career, dogs, family. I painted walls, hung wallpaper, mowed the lawn, learned how to shoot a gun, groomed my own dogs, sewed my own clothes—everything I could, all embodied in a full life. I never had domestic help, and to this day I have yet to get a professional manicure. Instead my fingers banged out story after story on typewriters. But this all seemed normal to me. Didn't everyone do the same?

There were twists and turns in life. I married Howard Beaufait in September of 1957, in a hurried ceremony at St. John's Cathedral in downtown Cleveland. The ceremony was hurried because we made a frantically quick decision to marry before driving to Florida due to the death of his stepfather, Rex Uden, and to be with Howard's mother, Dorothy Uden. A city editor and Korean War correspondent for the *News,* Howard was not hired by the *Plain Dealer* or the *Press* when the *News* folded in 1960. He, along with his veteran colleagues, was in shock over the "sale" of the *News* to the Scripps-Howard Press. Actually, all Scripps bought was the circulation list.

Howard had been on the *News* staff since 1928. During his time with the paper many veteran newsmen suffered heart attacks and several died, abruptly ending their careers. Howard was offered jobs in New York City and in Michigan, but he chose to remain in Cleveland. Few *News* reporters were hired by either the *Plain Dealer* or *Press,* mostly based on actuarial considerations relative to pensions. Because I had less experience (and was twenty years younger) than my husband, I was hired by the *Plain Dealer.* Howard, however, an award-winning writer, found writing jobs with the Stouffer Organization, the Heart Society, and other institutions. When he was inducted into the Cleveland Journalism Hall of Fame in 1983—he died of cancer November 3, 1976—he was described as "a creator of strange rainbows" and a sensitive and perceptive writer, winner of the National Headliner Award and president of the Cleveland Press Club for four terms.

When my frustrations over coverage of the Hough riots and follow-up racial news wore me down, I told Howard I was quitting, taking a rest, slowing down, joining the League of Women Voters,

Howard Beaufait and Doris O'Donnell Beaufait at home in Novelty, Ohio, Geauga County, 1958. Author's collection.

and becoming a housewife. He may or may not have believed me, but by a stroke of luck, we shipped aboard the Queen Elizabeth II ocean liner to Ireland after a travel agent friend, in passing, mentioned a cancellation, which we snapped up. Howard was partly reared in London, England, the birthplace of his stepfather, and he studied at the Slade School of Art. With his mother and stepfather, a retired Royal Canadian Air Force pilot, he had crossed from New York to England and back eighteen times. After our marriage in 1957 we had talked of travel but never found time, yet we pitched loose change into a big iron kettle. That was to be our "trip money." The trip was memorable—the ship, the crossing, driving through Ireland, visiting my grandparents' home town, farms, racetracks, nearly buying Irish Wolfhounds. The fresh environment erased the cobwebs in my mind. I could hardly wait to return to work.

After we returned from Ireland both of us, at the urging at an old friend, Jim Byrne, joined the staff of the *News-Herald* in Willoughby, Ohio, in Lake County, just to the east of Cleveland. The paper was owned by Harry Horvitz, a wealthy entrepreneur who also owned the *Lorain Journal*. His father had made his wealth in the asphalt paving business. I was so happy to have Howard back in the newspaper business; it was the love of his life as it was mine. But it wasn't the same as the old *News*. Nothing ever would be, but we had to close the door on the past and start anew.

Howard worked at the copy desk, I on general assignment, although I wound up with direct assignments from Horvitz, who turned out to be a remarkable man, with his finger on the business and political pulse of Northeastern Ohio. Each newspaper office has its own personality, and this one reflected a more parochial view of news through the lens of its editor, Jim Collins, something of a local character in Lake County. It didn't take long to realize Collins treasured his various friendships, and sometimes stories were shaded or ignored, such as a major burglary ring. Nonetheless, I soldiered on in the best way I could. I eventually won the top prize from the Ohio Newspaper Women's Association for a series on "The Silent American." In my case, the stories were self-generated. From Horvitz I was assigned a story on Sen. Howard Metzenbaum and his past association with the National Lawyers' Guild and his role as a signatory on the incorporation papers of the Communist Party of Ohio with Marie Wing. I also wrote stories on Cleveland's mayor, Carl Stokes, and his stock market dealings, and I co-wrote the story on Stokes that resulted in a libel suit, which was later dismissed.

Dealings with Horvitz were a pleasure, but soon we parted company with Collins on a mutual basis. We never would have seen eye-to-eye with him. Then, out of the blue, I was offered a public relations job with the Republican Cleveland mayor Ralph J. Perk, who had risen from an aggressive Ward 14 councilman to become Cuyahoga County recorder. After the political disarray in Cleveland's City Hall, Perk was well received by Cleveland voters. I had known Perk for years, covering his council activities when he fought pollution from East Side steel mills that blanketed his constituents in the E. 55th Street and Broadway area. Many times I walked the streets with him, pausing in backyards of families whose white sheets, beating in the wind, were covered with soot and chemicals from the mills. He pushed the mills into adding smoke stack scrubbers, which were an environmental novelty at the time. Before, I was the outsider newsperson, looking in at politicians; now, I was an insider looking out at politicians and reporters. Believe me, it was a huge difference.

I had learned about political patronage from my mother and our large political family, so Perk's hiring of rabid political supporters, many from major ethnic organizations, didn't throw me. But there was another element that did. It involved the various unions among workers at City Hall, whose leaders were linked in various ways to organized crime figures. Perk's main man, hired to keep union peace, was, to me, a big question mark, and once I invited two policemen friends from the crime unit to sit in my office, watching the parade of characters that walked into this guy's office. After some checking, my cop friends found that a couple of these characters were on the FBI's Most Wanted list. This gave me pause, but I shut my mouth and figured if the police made a move, it was their business. I was, however, in a strange position when regular beat reporters, covering city hall, stopped daily to ask me: "What's new?" I had decided when asked this question that my answer would simply be a shrug. Had I been asked when I saw a wanted thug in my next-door office on such and such a day, I would have answered truthfully. I learned that technique at University Hospitals' public relations office. One should never answer a vague question. Only answer a direct, specific question.

The job with the mayor reminded me of the Cleveland Zoo where a prominent board member and one of my bosses once slipped off with a bottle of Wild Turkey with a *Plain Dealer* reporter to watch wild animals copulate. I'll never tell the names of these characters! But I was amused at the zoo when Vernon Stouffer, another board member, after a visit to the London Whipsnade Zoo, where monkeys were fed packaged goodies, suggested doing the same thing—except the goodies would be leftovers from his Stouffer restaurants. Needless to say the idea didn't fly.

I toiled for Perk, writing speeches and setting up neighborhood town halls and numerous events for newspaper and television coverage. Our biggest project was organizing virtually one member from every one of Cleveland's vast ethnic neighborhoods to create a Mall Festival with native foods. What a mess that turned out to be. We paid special attention to assure none of the home-made ethnic food poisoned the festival visitors. But Perk won a lot of community support. Whenever we needed music, I simply called the musician's union, who in turn called the Teamsters, and ward parades and music festivals fell into place.

I liked the job and the many key department heads Perk had recruited from private industry. Lunches were spent with clerks and secretaries, who clued me in to a lot of behind-the-scenes stuff. Perk was lucky, coming in after Stokes, because the federal government uncorked funds they had refused Stokes, and Perk had money to spend.

Back at the Beaufait home in Novelty, in rural Geauga County, Howard was offered a job in Pennsylvania through the good graces of two great people—Alan Nicholas, a one-time Pittsburgh news-man and former consultant to Harry Horvitz, and Queenie Otis Hanna, widow of our former and late publisher, Daniel Rhodes Hanna. A guy by the name of Richard Scaife had bought a news-paper in Greensburg, Pennsylvania, and was looking for a few veteran hands to help reorganize it. He sent feelers to old family friends, including Queenie Hanna, as her brother, Bill Otis, had married into the Scaife family. Queenie knew Dick Scaife's late mother, Sarah Mellon Scaife, through their travels to Europe. She called Howard and suggested he call Scaife. She filled us in on Scaife, whose mother was a Mellon, as in Mellon Bank.

Things progressed to the point that Howard drove to Greens-burg, looked over the situation, was impressed, and I later joined him to meet Scaife and his top guy, Michael Jones. A deal was struck, and Howard stayed to find a rental while I returned to work on Perk's election campaign. I resigned, put our house up for sale, packed, and with our big Newfie, Sam, we drove east to a new newspaper and a new career. At this stage in our lives, what did we have to lose?

-30-

-22-

Me and the Mayor

*C*arl Stokes and I had one thing in common: we were both born on June 21, he in 1927, me in 1921. Although a stargazer once said persons born in June "can be likened to straws in the wind which never seem to find a place to rest, but which have the flexibility to twist on into difficult places, right themselves and drift unharmed," that's all we had in common.

The talented Mr. Stokes became mayor of Cleveland in 1969 and died of cancer on April 3, 1996, while on medical leave from his post as U.S. Ambassador to the Seychelles, where he had been posted by President William J. Clinton. In my career as a newspaper reporter, which began in 1944 and lasted until February 20, 1996, I spoke to Stokes twice, once when he was campaigning for mayor in the general election in the fall of 1967, and once again in 1971 in the law offices of a prominent Cleveland firm for depositions in a lawsuit. Stokes had filed a $2 million lawsuit, charging libel in a story I co-wrote with my husband, Howard Beaufait, for the *News-Herald* of Willoughby, Ohio. I saw him a third time, although neither of us spoke to the other, in the lobby of the Justice

Center in Cleveland. He was thin and wan, no longer the dapper, dynamic young politician, lured by the white establishment to city hall to "cool" the racial turmoil of a changing city. I never saw him again before his death in April 1996.

Those fragile years—1965 through 1971—from the Hough riots to the libel suit, marked me by several newspaper and reporter critics as some kind of "hatchet man" on Stokes. But there's another side to the story, which started with a misunderstanding on Stokes's part. Because he rarely gave interviews to newsmen, that miniscule event was never talked about, and I dismissed it as some kind of paranoid attitude of his, not realizing his inbred sensitivity. We, in the newspaper business, believed then and do today that public officials or those seeking public office are fair game for questions. Stokes did not share that view. His attitude was that newsmen bore a vendetta against him, when all we actually did was report, as usual, on a politician. And so he avoided us.

Because Stokes refused interviews, three of us—me, Jim Naughton, and Mike Roberts—were assigned to cover him at a political drop-in at the Perkins Day Care Center near downtown Cleveland. Jim had a political angle, which was often like a knife—he asked only one simple question. Mike Roberts, assigned to do a profile à la the *New Yorker*, was to get the facts from birth to the present, as the general public knew little about the candidate. Mike's mode was like a jackhammer. Me, I was told to ask about whether a divorced man had a more or less chance of election. And I did.

In those days political lives were turned inside out for reporters and a person's marital status was part of the package. (It still is today; it even applies to Charles and Camilla.) When we surrounded him Stokes gave his usual rambling speech about "voting for the man." He looked like a deer in headlights. He stumbled forward, refusing to give us any answers He couldn't leave fast enough. I say in retrospect that he probably couldn't recall which one of us asked which question. The evening was a bummer for us, although Jim was able to write a piece.

The next morning I had an urgent call from Dr. Kenneth Clements, a prominent black physician and Stokes's campaign manager, who asked me to meet him for a hurried lunch at the exclusive

Cleveland Athletic Club. "What the heck did you do to Carl last night? He's berserk." Clements, handsome and superbly tailored, thought we had done something to Carl. I was dumbfounded. I gave Dr. Clements a play-by-play description of the night, telling him about our questions and Carl's abrupt departure. I repeated questions by Jim and Mike and said mine was about his earlier divorce. (He divorced his first wife, Shirley, remarried her, and again divorced then married another Shirley, to whom he was now married. Later, Stokes's second wife Shirley, a librarian, divorced him in 1973, charging adultery. He then married Raija Kostadinov in 1981.) Dr. Clements said, "Carl is nuts about his father. He wants me to take him to the cemetery, here or in the South." Obviously Carl had something that deeply bothered him, but we were clueless. I explained to Dr. Clements that we were doing our normal vacuum-cleaner job on a candidate. We were under the impression he and his brother, Louis, had the same parents. Dr. Clements was satisfied with our integrity and said he'd pass this along to Stokes.

Word of Stokes's tiffs with us got around the African American community, and he complained to our editors. Apparently, with Stokes's *Plain Dealer* endorsement, he concluded he had a free ride with reporters. But that's not how the game is played. Little did he know the newspaper business. Further, unknown to him and to my fellow reporters, an executive editor had asked me to turn up whatever I picked up from the black community about Carl. I didn't go out of my way, because it was easy and natural to chat with city councilmen, lawyers, cops, and others interested in politics. Having lived with a black family, I had pipelines to friends who were activist black women, promoting Stokes's candidacy and only too eager to talk. He also had his enemies—former state liquor inspectors, who were usually black, again only too eager to add a story about shootings, shakedowns, and Gov. Frank J. Lausche's banishment of Stokes out of state, instead of hauling him up on charges. None of this saw the daylight of print. It all went into notes that were filed away. Surely Stokes, with a law degree, a stint in the city prosecutor's office, and a state legislator, should have figured out the newspaper business. Our editorial obligation to readers was an honest profile of the guy who wanted to run the city. He was NOW NEWS, no longer invisible. Papers made him transparent in a city with 35 percent black minority. At the same time, his moneybackers, with a shameless goal of electing a black man to "keep things cool," were happy with a big shield around their man.

For me, life throbbed along as I did the things I wanted more than anything on earth to do—report, write the news, and live on excitement each day with new challenges. I lived for a story, any kind, anywhere, big or small, front page or back page. It made no difference. And it's no secret I liked the game of politics and frequently lunched with city councilmen and lawyers, king-makers in the Democrat and Republican parties. I didn't ignore secretaries and clerks, the little people toiling in the Great Halls of Governance. They knew the little secrets. On the police beat I formed friendships, and during the Hough riots I met a handful of FBI agents who picked my brain about black nationalists I had met at the JFK House, a hotbed for Black Power. Councilman Leo A. Jackson became a high-powered and vocal critic of the Stokes administration, making copy for the papers. I traveled his East Side ward with him many times and quoted him on declining housing and living conditions. Naturally, I got bylines, and it never occurred to me that Stokes could link me with Jackson's stinging outbursts. Councilmen in other East Side wards, active in area council organizations, joined Jackson, demanding more city service and police protection. This rankled the new mayor Stokes, who was under the impression his black councilmen were buddies not critics. I never thought about this at the time.

Glenville's shoot-out raised the level of gripes against Stokes, and during the summer of 1968 the *Plain Dealer* assigned seven of us to a series called "The Cleveland Police; What's on Their Minds." This was on the heels of the deaths of white cops and black nationalists in Glenville. The stories were compiled by me, George J. Barman, William C. Barnard, Donald L. Bean, William D. Evans Jr., Robert G. McGruder, and Robert T. Stock. We branched out, interviewing lawmen all over town. Each of us wrote an individual piece, and my contribution was considerable since I went from police garages to station houses to cops on the beat to men in patrol cars for quotes. The upshot was vocal bitterness over Glenville. The series began with an eight-column banner: "Rumors, not rifles, are the chief element dividing our city and its police department. Rumors are everywhere, whispered insidiously, growing daily, hard to pin down, hard to believe. To get to the bottom of the rumor mill, [we must] find out what is really bothering the Cleveland police."

For Stokes, the you-know-what hit the fan. More complaints came in to editor Tom Vail that charged the series was underhanded, unfair, vicious, you name it. We were doing our job. Was he? Stokes's presumed friendships with editors and CEOs curdled fast as safety forces screamed for leadership. It was pretty sad. But the thing that killed the entente between Stokes and the *Plain Dealer* was when he fired Police Chief Pat Gerity and hired William Ellenburg from Grosse Pointe, Michigan. Within hours, word blasted around, making headlines that Ellenburg, according to a Detroit lawyer, had ties to the Detroit Mafia. Top lawmen from Detroit and Washington expressed concerns over Ellenburg, and within several days it was "Good-bye, Ellenburg." Stokes refused to talk to Bob McGruder, the *Plain Dealer*'s top African American reporter. Stokes flew to Rome to visit the Pope and then on to Israel. His star safety director, Gen. Benjamin O. Davis, a retired, black, high-ranking air force officer, left shortly after, describing conditions as "horrible." General Davis told me Stokes was too close to the hoodlums.

At the time of the Ellenburg fiasco I was no longer at the *Plain Dealer*, having left in the autumn to take my trip to Ireland and then work for the *News-Herald* in Lake County. But I wrote about the Ellenburg fiasco based on first-hand information from Phil Sheridan, an old friend I knew in the U.S. attorney general's Justice Department when Bobby Kennedy was the head honcho. Sheridan was the chief investigator of Teamsters' president Jimmy Hoffa and the Teamsters. Hoffa ultimately was sentenced to a federal prison.

Before quitting the *Plain Dealer* I had written a three-page letter to Tom Vail on August 17, 1969, noting nine instances where stories or pertinent facts were omitted or deleted. Vail responded with, "I have the problem in mind." In September my frustration reached new heights, and I decided to quit. It was tough. Vail wrote me: "Writers and reporters seldom come in one package but with you it is Christmas every day in both these departments." He wished me well. I also left a laundry list with my managing editor, Ted Princiotto, who was a great editor and who had all the right basic instincts—fair and patient. To him I wrote: "All too many of my colleagues enjoy being nice guys and playing it safe for their selfish interests, while others get a reputation for being a hatchet man." I told him things I had held secret, like the federal official who offered to buy me a house and send an airplane for me whenever I wanted transportation. Then there was another state official who offered information on Stokes in exchange for a boat ride on Lake Erie. I can't swim. One city official made obscene proposals. Another federal official offered the whole nine yards—at his convenience and on his conditions!

At the *News-Herald* the publisher, Harry Horvitz, had an insatiable interest in area politics. His firsthand information came from an insider's knowledge of events. He was a student of government on local and state levels, astonishing me with stories behind the news. He directed me to investigate Mayor Stokes's stock market dealing, providing basic information to follow up. Another project involved Sen. Howard Metzenbaum, for which I produced a comprehensive three-part series on the senator. We published Stokes's stock holdings, but Horvitz withheld the Metzenbaum series, thanking me for the job and adding he hoped I wasn't too disappointed. He was the boss; it was his decision. Weeks later, however, my material was broadcast on a Columbus, Ohio, radio station. Publishers work in mysterious ways.

The wrap up on Metzenbaum was a summary of his rapidly rising business career, starting with filing articles of incorporation for the Communist Party of Ohio and activities with the National Lawyers Guild. It was my distinct impression there was a visceral discord between Horvitz and Metzenbaum. Later, I was assigned to follow a tip about the possibility of Stokes's business interests in Freeport, in the Bahamas. It was this trip and resulting story that erupted in the $2 million libel suit. I know we were "in the right church, the wrong pew" on tracking Stokes's interests, since another reporter, tipped to various corporate names, found records in Nassau, also in the Bahamas, that we did now find. Checking realtor offices in Freeport I stood stock-still as I faced one of Stokes's closest associates, Fleet Slaughter. In Cleveland, this sharp businessman owned the popular Slaughter's Steakhouse on Carnegie Avenue, a cosmopolitan meeting place of movers and shakers, black and white. We said at the same time: "What the hell are you doing here?" I told Fleet that I was "looking for Carl's money." He laughed and said Carl had used his apartment when he vacationed in Freeport. Aha! Graciously Fleet drove me around Freeport, pointing out the real estate boom, the seedy casinos, then to the exclusive Xanado Club, where photos were hung of Stokes, Sammy Davis Jr., and Detroit mayor Jerry Cavanagh. Cleveland attorney John Bustamante, an intimate of Stokes, was also plastered on the walls. Jackie Onassis had a wall spot, along with Dick Kleindiest, once in the justice department, and other celebrities. Staffers reported most visitors came by boat. We wrote that Stokes, under stress, impetuously ran off when things got "hot," and Freeport was an escape haven. Actually the lead said Freeport was Stokes's "home away from home."

The lawsuit was a blow. We did not think it was libel. Horvitz hired a private detective from Chicago to bird-dog Stokes's life, the suit opening him up to scrutiny from the day he was born. The suit made me doubt Stokes's legal background, but we learned he was getting all kinds of advice from a cynical former newspaperman to "nail" the papers. I worked with the PI, but Cleveland wasn't Chicago. It would be years for him to know the town. For me, the suit was great. Tips and calls came in from all sorts of people, some good, and some bad. The upshot was when we settled on the first deposition in swanky law offices, our clever lawyers had twelve huge boxes of material on Stokes—virtually all gathered by me. Each box was displayed around the conference room, and they were marked: Stokes No. 1, Stokes No. 2, etc. I sat across from him with my young lawyer, Bill Wickens from Lorain, a counselor to the *Lorain Journal* who was brilliant. Some questions were bland; others pointed about his career as a state liquor inspector, relative to shakedowns of bar owners. He refused to answer on the advice of counsel. Just before noon Wickens spread a fanfold of black and white photos of black women arrested for prostitution. They were police mug shots with identifying numbers around subjects' necks. Stokes recognized them as official Cleveland police photos. He stood up, sweat running down both sides of his face. It was the attorney's speculation that he handled prosecution of a number of hookers while in the city prosecutor's office and that he had strong ties to a number of black law firms representing the women. We'd never know, because he walked out, giving us no explanation, and never returned.

We'd been tipped of questionable connections with Stokes and the girls. Weeks later, his lawyers deposed me, demanding my notebooks, which I happily turned over. My peculiar way of taking notes baffled them. Some were in shorthand. Others were key words I used for mental connections. I had notes on napkins but they didn't ask for them. My lawyer introduced character letters, including ones from my former publisher Tom Vail, who wrote "everyday was Christmas" with me on the staff. Stokes's lawyers knew less about the newspaper business than he did. Our defense was the Sullivan vs. New York City libel suit regarding public officials.

In 1964 the U.S. Supreme Court issued a ruling that revolutionized libel law in the United States. The famous decision in *New York Times* vs. Sullivan once and for all created a national rule that squared more fully with the free press guarantees of the First Amendment. The court decided that public officials no longer could sue successfully for libel unless reporters or editors were guilty of "actual malice" when publishing false statements about them. Our story merely described the Bahamas as Stokes's getaway and described his relationship with Slaughter and the use of his swanky high-rise apartment. Ironically, a new high-rise called "The Clevelander" had been built there recently. Realtors described the owners as British investors, which we stated in our report.

On May 21, 1971, Stokes met with Horvitz to drop the suit. Court journals show Horvitz paid court costs of $84 and a statement: "The suit grew out of a series of articles on the Bahamas written by Doris O'Donnell and Howard Beaufait. The articles did not state nor were they intended to convey the impression that Mayor Stokes had any interest in real estate or business in the Bahamas, nor that he had any connection with any illegal activities. The *News-Herald* regrets if there were any impressions to the contrary." We had been told, in confidence by federal officials later, that a "bag man" from Cleveland was involved in the transfer of funds from Ohio to the Bahamas. Our lawyer said: "I personally think the guy gave in completely." Our lawyer also said Stokes was ill-advised.

Harry Horvitz detailed his personal meeting with Stokes, who demanded a settlement. Harry would pay only for his out-of-pocket expenses for the deposition, nothing else but minor court costs. The case was a dismissal. Stokes told Horvitz: "I realized, looking back, the antagonist was not Doris O'Donnell, but everyone at the *Plain Dealer*, particularly Tom Vail and [managing editor] Ted Princiotto. I felt I had to do something. I couldn't stand the picking on." Stokes blamed the *Plain Dealer* executives for urging on him various actions. He blamed the paper for the income tax failure. Harry said after the meeting ended and Stokes left he was left "feeling sorry for him." Stokes issued a statement that he was satisfied with the statement in the *News-Herald*.

When it was all over I felt sorry for Stokes, too. His ego and personality locked him in. He had it all but he blew it. Stokes's mayoral career ended, and old friends found him a television job in New York City. A former Cleveland television personality in New York said that NBC icon, John Chancellor, and Stokes had near physical blows one night at the famous Costello's Irish Saloon on Third Avenue under the old "L." Stokes climbed high, got close, but slipped down. Back home, he was a labor attorney, municipal court judge, and U.S. ambassador, another shot by politicians to curry favor with the black vote. In his lengthy obituary is buried his theft of a screw driver and a bag of dog food from a pet store. There is a building in downtown Cleveland named for him. Former city council president, James V. Stanton, added this to the Stokes's years: "Stokes seeks the obstacle rather than the right way. Whenever things are going smoothly, he seeks the chuckhole to bust the tire open."

For reporters, Stokes made copy. It was an experience that didn't deter me from digging, and you can bet other politicians took more critical measure of the relationships between the media and public officials. The sad effect of libel suits is on publishers, who are becoming less aggressive in investigative reporting. After all, the newspaper business is a business, and teams of lawyers and private detectives are expensive. As newspaper circulation diminishes it appears a new breed of investigators has arrived on the scene. They are called Bloggers, and their pages are on the Internet. Thank God for them.

-30-

-23-

Newspapering in Pennsylvania and Beyond

*M*y husband and I joked that on weekends half of Ohio drives to Pennsylvania and half of Pennsylvania drives to Ohio. In late 1973 we were the Ohioans driving to Pennsylvania, to our new rental home in the valley of the Laurel Mountains in the miniscule community of Rector, a stone's throw from Rolling Rock Club, one of the commonwealth's most prestigious country clubs. We had so much to learn, so much to see. Our office was at the *Tribune-Review* in Greensburg, the county seat of historic Westmoreland County. I had resigned from Mayor Ralph Perk's office in December of 1973. Making changes since I left the *Plain Dealer* had become easier and easier. Howard and I were excited to be together at another newspaper, facing another challenge. Howard, with vast experience as a writer and city editor, was on the copy desk, editing, rewriting stories; I was again on general assignment.

In our newspaper careers we worked for millionaires—who else could afford to own a paper? The afternoon *News* was once run by Daniel Rhodes Hanna, of the famous Hanna family of iron ore, shipping, and political fame. Later the *News* would be folded into the *Plain Dealer* under the banner of the Forest City Publishing Company, and the money behind that corporation was the wealthy Holden family of which Tom Vail was a descendant. Then the millionaire Newhouse family bought the *Plain Dealer*. At the *News-Herald* the operation was solely owned by Harry Horvitz, heir to both a newspaper fortune and a highly profitable asphalt business.

In Pennsylvania we were introduced to the Mellon-Scaife family wherein the *Tribune-Review* in Greensburg would be solely owned by Richard Mellon Scaife, the great grandson of the founder of T. Mellon and Sons, forerunner of the Mellon Bank. A recent *Financial Times* article on billionaires around the globe lists Scaife as number thirteen of its list of twenty-five. In November 2004, at seventy-two years old, Scaife inherited wealth amounting to $1.2 billion, according to *Financial Times*. Warren Buffett, investor and the world's second richest man, is listed as number sixteen by the same magazine. And at forty-six years old, Microsoft's Bill Gates is the world's richest man, number one on the list.

Scaife's first ancestor on the Scaife side arrived in America in 1802, and the first Mellons came from Northern Ireland in 1818. Our new publisher did not flaunt his money or background, in fact, he seemed quiet and shy. We researched books about the early settlers in Western Pennsylvania and their contributions to the industrial and banking wealth of Greater Pittsburgh. What struck us was Dick Scaife's intense interest in newspapers, local and national, although the *Tribune-Review* was the first one he bought. As a young man in Pittsburgh he'd buy out the complete stock of papers at a Smithfield Road newsstand. "The whole idea of newspapers just excited me." His enthusiasm was infectious. We felt we'd be working for a publisher with a mission. And we had an abundance of local news and a good share of national and international news. Until 1967 his life was involved with foundation grants, buying art for a Pittsburgh museum, and shedding his late father's industrial factory. By a fluke, heirs to the Dave Mack estate, previous owners of the *Tribune-Review* in Greensburg, held an auction to sell the assets. While Scaife had looked at other properties in his newspaper search, he bid just under $4.3 million and got the paper. A publisher from the Pennsylvania Newspaper Publishers Association told him he "paid too damn much for it." And others added that "Richie Rich had bought an expensive toy." They didn't know Dick Scaife. Of course, he was in his own back-yard—he had homes in Pittsburgh and Ligonier, and Greensburg was geographically in between. But his reasons were philosophical and ideological. He had ideas to advance, which were known only to a tight group of close associates. The deal was consummated in 1970, three years before we moved to Pennsylvania.

Now, as a publisher with an office whose glass windows faced a roomful of advertising salesmen and a roomful of editors and reporters, Scaife read the paper line by line, questioning this story or that story and instituting, through editors, investigative journalism. That opened a can of worms, because generally staffers of small-town papers were intimately and socially tied into the town's political power structure; partisanship was showing in news stories. One thing and another led to a staff walkout on October 10, 1973, and Scaife and his paper made news in the *Columbia Journalism Review,* where the magazine tagged Scaife with the moniker "Citizen Scaife" to echo the dramatic film *Citizen Kane.* Scaife dates attacks on him by the political left from that article, and, if anything, the article reinforced his deeply ingrained conservative and patriotic views. The newsroom was run by leftist or mostly leftist young staffers whose views collided with the new boss; some who walked out were fired, some left voluntarily, and a few asked to stay.

We walked into the middle of that uneasy crucible, but Scaife's actions cleared the air; he was the publisher. The editorial page belonged to him, and his editors could either take his orders or find another job. Newspapers are packages—it's a competitive business. Staffers had grown up under old-shoe locals who lacked the sophistication of a guy like Scaife, born into wealth with parents who traveled widely with relatives and close friends in higher echelons of American government. Scaife's father, Alan Scaife, was in England during World War II as acting chief of secret intelligence with the Office of Strategic Services (OSS), the forerunner of the Central Intelligence Agency, and young Scaife grew up in Washington, D.C., where he read bundles of newspapers his father brought home. The scope of Scaife's worldwide background was a new dimension at the paper.

There is little doubt that my husband and I were, reporter-wise, more in tune with Scaife than the young staffers. Howard was educated in London, Detroit, and New York and had worked as a Korean War correspondent, and I had spent years reporting major news and brought a blasé and seasoned perspective. Thinking back, I realize we weren't the most popular people in the newsroom, but we operated on the theory that we should do the job and take the paycheck. Howard handled rewrite and desk duty; I took whatever assignment I was given. We learned early that our new colleagues who had "mutinied," but came back, wanted freedom to run the paper as they had under the Macks. It wasn't long before they learned the guy who bought the shop ran the shop. We had lived under those rules before; it was nothing new to us. At one point Dick Scaife offered me the editorship, but I had taken the measurement of the men and women in the newsroom and turned it down. That headache wasn't for me. I was not a human relations director; I was a street reporter, as I would remain.

But I thanked him.

Our private lives in Pennsylvania centered on our small clapboard house in Rector, the Catholic Church, the library, weekend forays into the beautiful Laurel Mountains to get our bearings, and making friends through the generosity of both Scaife and his wife, Frannie, and his number-two man, William McMichael Jones and his wife, Pat, and their friends. Sunday night suppers were the weekend highlights, where conversations gave insight into the community and the politics of the area. Covering the county courthouse I met the judges, county commissioners and felt very much at home again in that environment. I even covered the federal court in downtown Pittsburgh.

It was pretty normal stuff until one very windy, cold, damp morning in March 1974. Home with a nasty head cold, my brief respite was interrupted by an emergency call from Howard at the paper. "Get over to Duggan's. He's been killed." That was Allegheny

County prosecutor Robert W. Duggan, husband of Dick Scaife's sister, Cordelia Scaife May Duggan. Duggan was a local Ligonier figure and was running for his third term as the Republican DA in Pittsburgh. He and Cordy Scaife had been childhood friends, but any romance was squashed by their families over religious differences. She had married and divorced Herb May while Duggan remained single. Duggan had finally married Cordy shortly before his untimely death on his Route 30 estate. At the time Dick Scaife was the treasurer of Duggan's reelection campaign, although he had grown suspicious of cash donations without benefit of donors' names. Word got to Scaife to contact the Pennsylvania State Police over Duggan's alleged connections to the Pittsburgh-Youngstown Mob.

That morning I threw on winter clothes and drove to Duggan's, a country farmhouse surrounded by fences and a huge lake where his relatives once "raised" blocks of ice for iceboxes. The body, found near a pond, had already been removed, but state police, several of whom I had met at the courthouse, were measuring distances from where the body was found to the fence, driveway, and other key points. A shotgun was found in the grass. "Who shot him?" I asked. "Where's the body?" I got no answer. I guessed he had been taken to Latrobe Hospital, and I knew information was tight, so I raced in, called Cordelia on the phone—she was listed locally—and to my amazement, she was there and responded to my polite questions of where she was, when she had last seen Mr. Duggan, and so forth.

I had my story. Although married, the Duggans lived apart, she several miles south of his home in a small cottagelike house she called "Cold Comfort." Actually, at the time of Duggan's death, it had been only six months since Scaife had learned of his sister's marriage to Duggan. Cordy told me that she and her husband had seen *The Sting* the night before. It had been a simple evening. She couldn't add much, and she never spoke to another reporter.

The coroner ruled that the cause of death was self-inflicted wounds. Few cops or smartasses around the courthouse believed the ruling. One of Duggan's top aides had been convicted earlier of criminal activities, and after hours of long conversations with troopers I believed Duggan was accosted that morning by a mobster with an order of something like, "You do it, or we do it." The bullet entered his chest at an angle and came out under his left armpit. But the key to the death was timing. On March 5, 1974, the federal grand jury in Pittsburgh brought down a six-count indictment of tax fraud against Duggan. Somehow there had been a leak in the federal DA's office the morning Duggan bought his death. To say Duggan was spending money like a drunken sailor was putting it mildly. He had a home in Ligonier and another in Florida, membership in ten swanky clubs—a lifestyle beyond the means of a supposedly honest, hardworking public servant. In Switzerland he was involved in complicated currency manipulations in the millions. The word on the street was that he was on the take from the Mob big time. State police accused Duggan and his staff of tipping off mobsters to major police raids. But the game was over, and Scaife's new brother-in-law got a big Catholic funeral, based on the coroner's ruling.

The stories never ended. The *Pittsburgh Post-Gazette* exhumed the story in 1981 in a six-part series accusing Federal Prosecutor Dick Thornburgh of being in cahoots with Dick Scaife to smother the Duggan investigation. The *Post-Gazette* called me time and time again for comment and even sent me registered letters about the Duggan case. Did they think I was dumb enough to talk to them? At local events in Ligonier, where I did volunteer work under my married name, people were unaware I worked for Scaife, and I heard comments that Scaife had had Duggan killed. The rumors were vicious. The series of events surrounding the case expanded my acquaintance with troopers, public officials, and of course my publisher. I must say now that Scaife never read my copy before it was in the paper. He read it like our subscribers.

Needless to say Scaife and his sister stopped talking to each other after the Duggan tragedy and only resumed a somewhat stilted relationship a few months before her death from cancer in April 2005. Cordy died childless; her estate was in the billions. She previously had donated funds to a small western Pennsylvania Catholic college in memory of Bob Duggan. Intimates claimed she had had been impregnated by Duggan twice but had both pregnancies aborted; the abortions were reportedly arranged by a prominent lawyer who later attempted to blackmail her.

What a sad, sad story. Dick's take on family stories or big local ones was always: If there's a story that checks out print it. We did, and that happened whenever a Mellon made news even though attempts to cover up court filings by slick lawyers were tried now and then. When we found them, we printed them. As a new publisher, especially a millionaire and a Republican, Scaife got a baptism of fire. His private life was nonexistent. Libel suits against scurrilous stories would make it worse, he figured. During his relationship with Duggan and his campaigns, Dick joined Duggan at national Republican conventions, where he developed an addictive interest in politics and was a major supporter of various organizations, notably the Heritage Foundation. Members of Scaife's inner circle at his office kept him up to speed on major political developments, flying regularly to Washington, D.C., for conferences and private meetings with young Republican leaders. I flew there with him to spend a morning with Newt Gingrich when he took over speakership of the House. I loved politics as much as Dick did and subscribed to national magazines and developed pipelines into Washington, D.C., for news contacts when I needed to localize a national story.

At the *Tribune-Review* we had an editorial board that interviewed all political candidates for state and national elections. Candidates never snubbed Westmoreland County, which was, area-wise, the largest in the commonwealth. We grilled candidates and took votes on whether or not to endorse them. We were a very democratic bunch. Scaife sat in on the meetings, too. He had one vote, also, and never intimidated us. We endorsed Democrat Bob Casey for Pennsylvania governor. My task was to interview candidates and write stories on their platforms.

Our chief editorial writer, Molly Brown, had begun investigations into the operators of a local hospital and its relationships with federal programs. I inherited some of these follow-up stories about the Monsour Medical Center in Jeannette, Pennsylvania, and the four doctor-brothers who ran it. There, too, staffers whose family members had been patients of the Monsours resented the

investigations, creating more turmoil in the newsroom. Nonetheless, when legitimate news broke about hospital labor problems
or bankruptcies, I wrote them. When Gene Cerili, the top Democrat and state employee, was charged with macing employees, I
drove into Pittsburgh daily for his trial. Sometimes I left Ligonier
at 5 A.M. to be on time at 9 A.M. for court. Going through traffic
into Pittsburgh, going downhill toward the three rivers level and
threading through tunnels, was a major headache. Westmoreland
County was pretty much landlocked by the Democrats, and major
county and state offices were held by Democrat appointees.

There was no lull in newsgathering, and back in historic Ligonier Howard and I contracted to build a new house on a five-acre
tract on Old Forbes Road, a highway once traversed by pioneers
and soldiers. It was pretty exciting, watching the two-story house
rise on a mountain ridge. Then Howard became ill, and without
reliving the agony of those months—nurses at home, Latrobe Hospital, a nursing home—Howard died of cancer the night Jimmy
Carter was elected president in November 1976.

My job was a godsend after this ordeal, and I felt my reporting feet were set in Westmoreland when I was shifted to Station
Square in Pittsburgh, temporarily, to edit *Pittsburgher Magazine,* a
monthly Scaife had launched with the urging of his close friends.
Every town, they reasoned, needed a good hometown monthly.
Again the staff was intact, the founding editor canned, and my
task was to pull the team together. I loved the challenge, the enthusiasm of the staff, tons of ideas to kick around, and then the
heavy task of producing a slick monthly, with provocative cover
and stories. The magazine was the talk of Pittsburgh. My only
handicap was not knowing the town the way I knew Cleveland,
but here were veteran consultants on standby.

The Scaife millions had revitalized the south bank of the Mon
River. There was a refurbished office building, a top-billed restaurant in the old train station, a sparkling mall with shops like little
jewels on a bracelet. Pittsburgh underwent a makeover and became the envy of other American cities. That temporary job lasted
seven months. With a new editor on fulltime, I returned to the
paper, writing for both the magazine and the paper. Then another

personal tragedy occurred—my eighty-nine-year-old mother, living in Cleveland, died. In less than a year after the death of my mother my only brother, Jack, died at the young age of fifty-eight. The three most important people in my life were gone. It was tough. Then I watched the toddling *Pittsburgher Magazine* wither and die. When auditors weighed the subscription figures against costs, it was decided to jettison the venture. It was too bad, but there are only so many dollars to spend on reading material, as publishers learn sooner or later. Again, I say the job was a godsend, as keeping busy is the best way to handle grief.

In Pennsylvania I was appointed to Gov. Richard Thornburgh's Merit Selection Committee for Judges, an experimental venture. I received awards from the Pennsylvania Women's Press Association, the oldest in the country, for new stories and features. My biggest assignment was a trip to West Germany, France, Belgium, and England on a tour of NATO countries and NATO bases, a project put together by a retired Associated Press foreign correspondent and the Center for Strategic and International Studies in Washington, D.C.

When a knowledgeable friend learned of the NATO trip, he said: "Boy, you'll have a lot to ask about President Reagan's Pershing Two missiles. Those European protestors are having a cow!" He swamped me with files on the current European problems, focusing on nuclear warheads and sensitive military plans. Until we got to West Berlin I did not realize the threats faced by the Germans miles from the poised Soviet missiles. This stuff was now not theory but tactical. We in the heartland of America weren't thinking of Soviet missiles landing in Pittsburgh or Cleveland. This new reality was a wake-up call. Not since 1956 when I was in the old Soviet Union had I felt such apprehension over war and peace. The itinerary indicated our hosts would be Germany's Helmut Schmidt and Helmut Kohl; Britain's Margaret Thatcher; General Rogers, head of NATO; and a roster of other dignitaries.

Boning up on NATO, I discovered that Ligonier's Adolph Schmidt, who married into the Mellon family, was one of the founders of the Northern Atlantic Treaty Organization. He was among those visionaries who were sick of horrors of war who had created this dream. It was designed as a massive path to peace or something to protect oneself from monsters like Hitler and Stalin. Other Americans created the Marshall Plan, which was described by one historian as "galloping to the rescue of Europe." Planning this trip in 1981 I recalled Berlin in 1956 when I was on my way home from weeks in the Soviet Union. At the end of Kurfurstendamm, the main drag, were the skeletal remains of a cathedral, surrounded by new emporia. Raw in my mind was Stalingrad, where the Russians horribly crushed the German army, and where some citizens still lived underground. Our military losses in Europe were great, yet we at home had nests of security. Years later in Northern Scotland, a friend and I stopped for tea. The proprietor asked us if we were "Yanks." We nodded. "See that over there? You Yanks built that and flew out of there. Thanks a lot."

Would we find the Germans of 1981 humble, arrogant, grateful, pompous? When our group met for the first time that was one topic we discussed at length. Nine of my companions were Washington bureau chiefs of major newspapers. There were three women, representing big and small dailies. My background notes focused on the so-called "wise men" of the postwar world—Harry Truman, Dean Acheson, Averell Harriman, George Kennan, John McCoy, Paul Nitzke, Charles Bohlen. I met Harry Truman, his wife, Bess, and daughter, Margaret Truman Daniels, when they were guests in the Cleveland of Cyrus S. Eaton. I was a guest of Chip Bohlen and his wife in their U.S. ambassadorial quarters in Moscow.

At the Bonn Airport in 1981 our reportorial contingent was faced with soldiers cradling AK-47 rifles who whisked us off to our hotel to freshen up for a series of heavy-duty meetings. Helmut Schmidt, the stocky, full-nosed, full-jawed chancellor of the Federal Republic of Germany, was our first host. In good English he boasted of his one-hundred-plus relatives who lived in the Twin Cities and Duluth areas of North America, and he said: "I know what Americans think." Well, that was boastful, but he *was* smiling.

For us NATO neophytes, Schmidt dwelt on his role in the historic 1979 NATO summit, which focused on the modernization of forces in Europe. In his role as chancellor of Germany Schmidt brushed aside leftist demonstrations throughout Europe. He looked instead to the coming November 30 U.S.-USSR talks in Geneva on modernization of NATO forces on the European continent. As we met, European leaders showed they were skittery over the Soviet SS20 mobile missile buildup of strategic rockets targeted at Europe, the Mediterranean, and the Middle East. Schmidt described the Long-Range Theater Nuclear Forces, which had been discussed at the 1979 summit, as nuclear, land-based aircraft, missiles, and artillery. He faced us at a long table, describing the Soviet buildup to two hundred missiles with three reloadable warheads, each facing west. He predicted a Third World War with Germany being the battleground again. He prayed, he said, that President Ronald Reagan would renegotiate the Salt II Treaty with the Soviets to change the imbalance of security in Europe. "All Germans have to undertake anything within their power to prevent the terror, the horror of the immediate past from happening again." And he was depending on us, on Reagan. He gave us sobering facts: In Germany there were six thousand nuclear warheads with additional hundreds of missiles aimed at Soviet targets. And there he sat eating apple pie with us! This was serious stuff. He was in no hurry to break up the meeting, instead answering lots of questions. He wanted more journalists, more Americans, to visit Germany, not to depend on sketchy news reports.

The tall, imposing Helmut Kohl, both federal chairman of the Christian Democratic Union and chairman of the Christian Democratic Union-Christian Social Union in the Bundestag (the German parliament), was our next lecturer, as I viewed him. Dr. Kohl, a former university political science professor at the universities of Frankfurt and Heidelberg, was visibly annoyed when several male members of our group were late and wearing jeans. He adjourned the meeting until these gentlemen returned in formal garb—navy jackets and gray trousers. Talk about protocol! We three gals had worn modest sweaters and business suits.

Dr. Kohl used an interpreter, although he understood English well. His message was clear: Russia must disarm because Europe was facing the most difficult stage in fifty years. He said Soviets played mind games with the Germans, feeding into their anxiety about being a divided country and living with a choice between freedom and reunification with East Germany. The peace movement, he said, was composed of true pacifists but many confused young people, Communists, and "fellow-travelers." The German worker, he said, was not confused; it was the "intelligentsia, media people, and fellow-travelers." He had not forgotten us. "The young German generation must be taught that we wouldn't be a free country at this moment, thirty years later, without the U.S." He said America and Europe must harmonize; do good in the Middle East. He called Camp David "a scandal. The third world is a scandal, and German policy is a scandal in the Third World. We want non-interference in internal affairs from the Soviets, but we want reasonable relations with them."

We got heavy doses of geopolitics and we were exhausted from hand writing notes from these long sessions. Eventually we stole a few hours to walk along the Rhine River with university students—males in suits, females in skirts and sweaters, biking along river paths. Dinners were served with lots of wine, solid food, more speakers. Dressing for dinner—just changing a sweater for a blouse—I was surprised to watch topless ladies on television soap operas. But none of this trip was boring; I ate up the lectures. Not one of my companions checked out on meetings. Each took their reporting job seriously, since this was the first time these German figures had opened up to the American press. My major worry was being able to write about it. Would the paper give me enough space for the thousands of words I felt I needed?

English-speaking Dr. Hans Apel, the Republic's minister of defense, came on like gangbusters, asking, "How can we secure peace and freedom and yet have weapons that will destroy us?" He believed the protesting youths were not as anti-Communist "as I am. The youth have added a new dimension to the peace movement. The invasion of Czechoslovakia does not belong to their personal experience, and to them, the Soviet Union is not an imperialistic state." He added: "The 250,000 demonstrators in Bonn were there because the bus arrived on time, and the soup kitchen was set up." He reiterated that the Germans wanted our missiles and troops, not a "neutralized Germany the Soviets wanted."

In West Berlin we felt more like tourists, especially at the handsome Bellevue Palace as guests of Dr. Karl Carstens, the Yale-educated president of the Federal Republic. How come we never knew about this patrician guy back home? In this elegant building we were served tea and coffee in a royal setting in beautiful china and on real linen. Although fluent in English, this aristocratic president used an interpreter. "A military potential is the best means to assure that no war will happen." These guys all seemed to be echoing Reagan, at least to those who had paid attention to the former movie star. We got the message. The peace movement had legs, but these leaders, with the West, decided military deterrence was the only answer.

On a break, we hired cabs for a quickie tour of West Berlin. We checked areas where Turkish and Polish "guest" workers lived in bombed-out apartments. West Berlin had over one thousand empty houses and nine thousand empty flats of squatters, a major problem for local government trying to clean up these squalid nests. Dr. Richard von Weizacker was Berlin's third mayor that year, trying to handle "hundreds of foreign squatters." Boy we never read about that back home. We also visited a depressing Holocaust museum and a cemetery where markers showed both German and Russians soldiers were buried there. Not everything looked as good as the Bellevue Palace. Our hosts frowned on our visits to the squatters.

Dr. Manfred Womer, vice chairman of the Christian Democratic Union-Christian Socialist group, praised Reagan for ordering the shooting of Libyan planes that attacked a U.S. carrier–based aircraft. We knew these men were playing up to us, praising Reagan for keeping troops and missiles in Germany. Away from them, we pretty much agreed that Germany—within Soviet missile eyes—needed us. But we had little time to debate among ourselves; we were too busy listening and writing.

In Brussels incidentally we traveled only by air and train, learning from W. Tapley Bennett Jr., the permanent ambassadorial representative of the United States at NATO, that Swedes had recorded fifteen instances this past year of Soviet submarines in their waters and dropped a depth charge on one of them. The top guy, Gen. Bernard W. Rogers, supreme allied commander in

Europe, asked: "How can we be even with the Soviets when every month there are five more launch missiles deployed in Russia?" The white-haired former Rhodes Scholar also said the Soviet 5520, a mobile missile with a range to reach Europe, had added fifteen new sites since 1979, with 70 percent of its firepower aimed at Europe and 30 percent aimed at China. Pacifists, he said, "were dupes of the Soviet Union." In answer to questions about American troops' drug addictions, he said, "Reduction of heroin, cocaine and alcohol problems in the military is being addressed." He praised a volunteer army but recommended a two-year draft. This general minced no words, saying France will cooperate with NATO but she won't come into an integrated military structure. He gave us good headlines—if only we could rush out to a phone. But that was a no-no; our stories were to follow, although one guy broke the rule and was severely chastised. He also got the story wrong.

Our brief time in Brussels was again not touristy, although one of my female companions, who spoke fluent Arabic, left me at a pub when she went off with two Arab men. I had to pound on her door the next morning to get her up. Her father, a wealthy Alaskan publisher, was an early investor in Saudi oil, and as a young woman she had traveled extensively in the Middle East. She was quite a gal, and I admired her a lot.

I could barely wait for London and Margaret Thatcher, although that date hadn't been verified; it looked iffy, Sy Slappey, our ex-AP mentor, said. He had booked us into a small hotel on Half-Moon Street that had johns in the hallways. My Alaskan buddy quickly booked herself in the pricey Dorchester Hotel and dragged me along, picking up my tab. It was her elegant style. She boasted to me of several romantic escapades she'd had with a high-ranking U.S. senator at the Dorchester. Wow! I was a babe in the woods, by comparison.

We did finally get to famous Downing Street after a session with British defense people where we were zinged by them for using "selective quotes and inaccurate quotes," as one male reporter put it when he sent the story to his Washington paper. This was the one reporter who couldn't wait to get home to write. John Nott, secretary of state, had actually said "selective quotes" damaged

British prime minister Margaret Thatcher at Downing Street, London, with the author (right) and other reporters, all of whom attended a NATO trip. November 1981; author's collection.

the security of the West and helped the Soviet propaganda machine. We learned that Helmut Schmidt later issued a statement to "clarify" remarks to our group, reported by this one reporter who said Schmidt changed a position on supporting NATO. Wow. Little things with big results. Nott scolded us and then said he would be "doubling on record. We are playing our full part in NATO. We spent more money in terms of collective defense in NATO than any other country than the U.S. We're on target with NATO's dual-track decision to modernize defenses with continuing arms negotiations with the Soviets." To make sure we got his point, he loaded us with five booklets prepared by the Ministry of Defense.

We were happy to leave for the Downing Street Mews, where British prime minister Margaret Thatcher had a spirited press meeting underway, following a full day with Irish prime minister Dr. Garret Fitzgerald, when they had discussed south-north energy-elective connections, gas supplies from Kinsale, pollution in the Irish Sea, television satellite broadcasts, and industrial and economic cooperating in science and technology. It was a full plate for both, and then Thatcher met the raucous British and Irish press; she and they shouted at each other, not like our almost scripted presidential press to-dos. A loud Belfast newsman asked if her cooperative actions with Fitzgerald would be considered "a sell-out by Northern Ireland Protestant leader Ian Paisley." She retorted: "He would find our proposals useful, if accuracy will govern his actions." I had covered Paisley in Pittsburgh, where he brushed aside Irish protesters, calling them "dogs." Someone shouted to Thatcher about terrorists in Northern Ireland, and she said: "I will accept the will of the majority in Northern Ireland." She refused to talk about extradition for terrorists. She didn't skip a beat in answering. It was like watching a tennis match. As she gathered her papers to leave, I feared she wouldn't return and so halted her, asking whether she'd be back. With a great big smile she said, "I'll be back for wine and cheese."

Thatcher was a petite woman with reddish-blonde hair and an unbelievable porcelain complexion. When she returned, wearing a bright suit and spike heels, we surrounded her, each with a glass of wine, as she told us how her Conservative Party was weathering an economic storm. She said the worst was over and the end of the recession was at hand. We didn't need to question her; she plunged ahead, talking about NATO: "All of Europe wants multilateral disarmament because the cost of sophisticated defense systems are so high. And you always want a deterrent at a lower level. There's still a generation in charge of Russian affairs that remembers the last war. Twenty million lives were lost. It must be costing them a packet because they spend on defense twice as much as they spend on health and education." We digested everything from this brainy woman, who impressed me a lot, and when I returned home I wrote a week's series on the experience.

The NATO trip, the tough decisions facing European leaders, made me realize how safe we were—that is until 9/11—and how shallow our understanding of European history is. Back in the newsroom, my colleagues simply wanted to know what I bought overseas. I didn't buy a thing. My absorption in the story was all I cared about. In a Berlin hotel dining room I had been flabbergasted at the display of cheeses and the ridiculous amount and variety of sausages hanging from hooks. In London, on a quickie trip to Harrods department store, I was amazed by the huge department of yards goods on the main floor, where most shoppers were Indian ladies in saris. A trolley cart of tea and cakes was a novelty for me in the lounge of the Dorchester, and I promised myself a return trip to London just for fun and poking around. But the trip had been business, not pleasure.

I loved Pennsylvania but also missed Ohio and my family and friends. I finally made the big decision to sell my mountain house and return to Ohio. It took two years to get my asking price, and while I waited I returned to evening classes at Seton Hill College in Greensburg, where under a learned-experience program my college credits blossomed. My classes were history, Shakespeare, religion, geometry. And I am still shy credits for a Bachelor of Arts degree. In Ligonier, with a handful of friends, we launched the Ligonier Valley Writers, an organization, eighteen years later, still going strong, with annual writers' conferences. I was president for three years. I volunteered at Compass Inn in Laughlintown, a landmark given by Gen. George Washington to a local family. I spun wool, dog hair, cotton, and exotic fibers for weekend visitors.

As a widow with two Newfoundland dogs I kept as busy as I could. Finally it was all over, and in 1991 I drove home, found another country home on a few acres in Summit County, and decided I wanted my job back at the *Plain Dealer*. And I got it.

Back at the *Plain Dealer* I was assigned, at various times, to three suburban satellite bureaus, which was new territory to me. I would have preferred the downtown newsroom, the hub of the paper, but bureau reporting gave the paper hometown news for the expanding suburban circulation areas in Lorain, Summit, and Lake counties. My impression was that suburban reporters were not as close to the public officials as I had been in Cleveland years before. A lot of reporters were down to covering beats by telephone. I thought the bureaus were an expensive operation considering the product, but I wasn't management. When I retired in February 1996, I planned to give more attention to home and housekeeping, volunteer work, and off-campus college classes. But before long Dick Scaife called,

Spinning dog hair at the historic Compass Inn in Laughlintown, Pennsylvania. 1977; author's collection.

asking if I was available for freelance assignments, and like the old fire-eating reporter, I couldn't say no.

Later I learned from the *Tribune-Review* about discs of court depositions that were available in the burgeoning investigations into many facets of the life of President William Jefferson Clinton. I printed out yards of those depositions, by various Arkansas citizens caught up in legal investigations, and I selected depositions by an Arkansas state trooper who had been one of the last policemen assigned to the Clintons when they lived in the Arkansas governor's mansion. I suggested this guy, L. D. Brown, might be worth interviewing about his testimony before we printed it, as we were conscious of libel laws. Brown was one of the state troopers called in on the federal case of Paula Corbin Jones, a former state employee, versus William Jefferson Clinton, a sexual harassment case that occurred while Clinton was governor.

There was a lot of homework required for this assignment due to the eruption of news about the political lives of the Clintons in Little Rock, and I immersed myself up to my eyeballs in background. In my formative journalism life, public records were not as easily available as now, and the Internet became an unending daily treasure of Clinton news from all parts of the country. It was a giant political ping-pong game, and I was clueless about the truth tellers and the liars. We had the depositions from witnesses, assuming none committed perjury before the feds, but the paper wanted face-to-face interviews.

I found in some instances that national magazines were scooping the main-street media facets of the growing Clinton story, so as prepared as I could be I flew to Little Rock to meet with Trooper Larry Douglass Brown. I suggested meeting in the hotel lounge; he insisted on my hotel room. I met a handsome, cocky police officer, already cautious with the press since he was being ardently wooed by national television and magazine reporters for his story about his life as a Clinton bodyguard. We faced each other pretty much as combatants. His attitude toward me was "You've got my deposition, what more do you want?" In his deposition he pointedly told his questioners that he would confine his answers to specific incidents and would not go into the personal lives of the Clintons. So we focused on that major incident involving a conversation he heard between Governor Clinton and a former judge, which related to the raising of money. Brown recounted that incident, which the federal investigations focused on, but this was only a miniscule piece of the big puzzle being gathered by the FBI and investigators.

The ice between us melted when the formal interview ended, and he told me something of his background and I told him about my life on the police beat and covering court, and we established a friendly rapport. Once a close confidant of Clinton's, he talked about the distance between him and the governor and said that Clinton's gal Betsy Wright had asked him whether he planned to reveal anything that would embarrass the Clintons. He said he took that as a threat. His relationship with Clinton had cooled after Clinton refused to transfer Brown to the state crime lab. We were now officially off the record, and I started, tenderly, to probe. Were rumors true about Clinton's sex life? Well, no one was more surprised than me with the answer. After hearing the answer, I said: "Boy, if I worked for a tabloid that story would be all over the paper."

"That story" was Brown's revelation of Clinton's insatiable sex drive, of picking up young ladies on Clinton's constant political campaigning up and down the state of Arkansas. Brown estimated the girl count to be in the hundreds. He should know, he said, because he was the state trooper chauffeuring the governor to political shindigs. Ultimately Brown's comment became public. Later Brown separated from the state police and wrote *Crossfire*, his version of being a witness in the vast Clinton investigation. Brown admitted his personal life had not been snow-white either, leading to the breakup of his own marriage.

In the weeks following my meeting with Brown, I remained in contact with him via telephone, hoping for follow-up stories. But Brown's personal position as a witness before federal prosecutor was precarious, and he sought legal advice, preventing him from public disclosures. We talked off the record from time-to-time as Clinton's private life exploded in the public, and then one day Brown called, reporting that the president had accused him of the murder of Brown's mother. That astounded me. I asked him how his mother had died, as I had heard a version of the events that led to her death and wanted to verify the story. At the time I couldn't fly to Little Rock, so Brown flew to Cleveland and spent several days with me as we unraveled the death of his mother in response to Clinton's charge.

On December 7, 1971, Brown's parents began an argument that escalated into a major altercation. "I tried to intervene when one of them pulled an old shotgun from a gun rack on the wall. As I stepped in-between them the gun fired," he reported. Public police investigations followed, and L. D. was cleared of any complicity. Years later Clinton made a damning accusation even though Brown recalled Clinton commiserating with him over the loss of his own father, saying he understood L. D.'s loss of his mother. In my writing room I called Little Rock officials, including the now retired coroner. He said certain people were desperately trying to get his official records but that he had stashed them, beyond the reach of private investigators. He was dubious about me, but L. D. got on the line, and the coroner promised to get the papers and call back. He did, and I wrote the story. Clinton's attorney, David Kendall, refused comment, and Brown heard no more from Clinton. He talked with independent counsel and congress, "but only after threats, offers of bribes, and intimidation had taken their toll." Several months ago I saw L. D. again when he and his wife and daughter attended a cousin's wedding in suburban Cleveland.

Needless to say, my personal view of Bill and Hillary Clinton was significantly altered by Brown's revelations, and I followed their legal affairs with above-average interest. And my opinion of politicians reached a new low. How could reporters remain objective and neutral in the face of so much derogatory sludge slung at the people we elected as our leaders? It was dispiriting, disillusioning. As reporters and consumers of the news we were now on the 24/7 news cycles, adversarial reporting in all media. I went out of my way to keep personal opinions locked up. When chided by friends about my stories, I kept my peace. I knew more background material than they did, and what was the point in having a personal disagreement? Besides, I never knew when or where a new assignment would pop up, and I wanted to be there, if for no other reason than to be a witness of history.

-30-

Epilogue

Back Where I Started— Cleveland, Ohio

In May of 1991 I paid cash for a new house with yard for two Newfies. When I asked Alex Machaskee, publisher of the *Plain Dealer,* for my job back, he didn't hesitate long, although he must have wondered if he was mad hiring a reporter on the verge of her seventieth birthday. Of course the paper's newsroom operations had changed, but the core was still at E. 18th and Superior. There were also bureaus added in Lorain and Summit and Lake counties, and before I retired permanently in February 1996, I worked in all three.

The paper now had bean counters who added up individual production by the number of stories printed. I was up with the topmost. As always, any assignment was okay with me, but I was nurtured on general assignment. My colleagues were better educated than most of the ones I had known in my early career but with less street smarts. There were computers and digital cameras. I envied my fellow workers the master degrees and the acclimation to technology. But something was missing from them. Many used the telephone more than their legs and were apt to question city room authority more frequently; there were more disagreements over assignments, even resentment. Mostly I came down on the side of the bureau chief; his daily and pressing chore was filling a page on tight deadlines.

Every day we had routine stories to cover from courts, hourly police checks, schools, and so forth. Drama came only with unexpected catastrophes like a huge fire in the Mentor marsh, a major traffic casualty, drownings, or unexpected deaths. I was happy. My weekly paycheck paid the workers for the replacement of all the floors in my house. I also restored a two-car garage, replaced a roof, and enclosed a porch, all done while I was working. It was fun. I had moved a total of fifteen times in my life, and this was the third house I owned.

On the weekends I volunteered as a spinner at the Western Reserve Historical farm in Bath. I hauled my New Zealand spinning wheel to an old farmhouse where we educated and entertained hundreds of visitors with our skills—spinning fiber threads, dyeing yarns in a dye pot, bubbling with colors from home-grown flowers and herbs. Other volunteers wove on antique looms. At home I spun fluffy dog hair, washed in Ivory liquid that I later knit into jackets. My husband had called my hobbies "group therapy at the state hospital." It was a heavenly release from the typewriter and deadlines. Reconnecting with my former newspaper colleagues, most retired, made me realize the years had flown by, leaving great memories and many raucous stories of escapades. For me it was living with one foot in the past and one in the present as my coworkers regaled us with exploits at nightclubs in the flats of downtown Cleveland and stories about seeing Jerry Seinfeld. I had been to the flats joint once and never saw Seinfeld.

About that time I thought of writing about stories I covered for myself and what was left of family. With five chapters under my belt, I met a talented author who prodded me on. I enrolled in off-campus writing classes at Case Western Reserve, and away I went, taking four years to put together a book. It has been hard work, living in the past. Fortunately I am a pack rat with a small backyard barn filled with boxes of newspaper stuff. Recently I gave five boxes of organized crime material to an expert in that field.

As my training had been as an objective observer, I learned that now I would have to inject myself in the weavings of events. This was hard at first, because on stories I was totally absorbed in getting quotes, facts; my personal life was shelved. I wasn't prepared to write about my personal life but was persuaded by my persistent and talented editor, Joanna H. Craig. When I read a book or an interview, however, I searched hungrily for personal tidbits and gossip. I believe readers deserve that extra dimension. That's why tabloids sell—the dating, marriage, divorce merry-go-round.

No one, surely me, ever expected I would marry Howard Beaufait. He was the city editor when I was hired by Hugh Kane, managing editor at the *News* in October 1944. A handful of men, deferred for a number of reasons from service in World War II, ran the newsroom, and young female amateurs did the grunge work, writing about the deaths of area servicemen. At the time there was an engagement ring on my left finger from a young West-Sider who was with the First Marine Air Wing serving in the South Pacific. It was a wartime arrangement, involving family, and frankly I never felt anything would come of it as all I wanted was a newspaper job. When I had had it, the ring was returned with no hard feelings.

I had never dated steadily, mostly attending group gatherings that involved ice-skating or summer cottage–life at Chippewa Lake with classmates. But as anyone could guess, this small newsroom developed a highly limited social life after the paper was put to bed each day with the 3 P.M. Stox edition. Plans for the next day's edition were put in place, and someone always said, "See ya in town." We always ended up at a small, narrow pub, owned and bartended by Al Grisanti, a popular John Carroll graduate. It was the hangout for *Press* and *News* reporters, along with judges, lawyers, and hangers-on from city hall and the police beat. It was where "the elite meet to eat," although it was just beer and pretzels. We young ladies of the press got earfuls of news tips, stories of the town's icons. Storytellers, such as attorney Johnny Butler, kept an audience enthralled with courtroom tales. The scenes in that miniscule barroom were better drama and dialogue than you'd get at the Hanna Theater. These after-hours detours were Friday nighters. If New York had "the 21," we had Al Grisanti.

I was attracted to Howard for several reasons. His clothes were Brooks Brothers. His shoes were London-made. His background, before Cleveland, was New York, Washington, London, New England, where he worked tables at an oceanside hotel and edited a weekly newspaper. Educated in private schools, he also attended Slade School of Art in London, home of his stepfather. Before taking on city-side duties he covered courts and police and then wrote hundreds of creative columns. His coverage of the Cleveland National Air Races made him one of the nation's first airplane and airman reporters. He was a personal friend of Capt. Eddie Rickenbacher. Howard's specialty was rewriting, and reporters liked having him edit their copy because his improvements were so great and the stories won awards. Howard, himself, regularly won awards for his feature stories and especially his coverage of the Korean War, where he climbed mountains with young soldiers and reported from Korean peace talks at Panmunjon. When the editors at the *News* didn't get his regular dispatches, they asked me to put together columns from his personal letters to me. Once one got through the censors with the battle site and events, and we reported it, much to the distress of the military. Unfortunately this was a blooper.

We young gals found Howard a patient teacher, always generous with praise. Again, we were lucky to be around him and the male reporters, who were readers. They loaned us current books on history, politics, and fiction and encouraged us to read the *New Yorker, Harpers,* and the *Atlantic.* We swam in their literary pool. Was I falling in love? I couldn't answer that. I lived my job fully, and to be surrounded by a bunch of writers, poets, reporters, and teachers was beyond my dreams. Our relationship began to change through the reading of poetry—Edna St. Vincent Millay, English and Irish poets, too many to mention. We knew we were on slippery slope because Howard was married with children, and of course, that was his problem and he was in control of that. We talked and we parted, promising to live our lives separately as they were. Sometimes we succeeded; sometimes we didn't.

Then my assignment to the Soviet Union took over my life, and that experience changed me. I loved the overseas life I saw, but my first commitment was to Howard Beaufait and the *News*. They would be paid back for the assignment and then I'd go back to Europe. But, and here's the but, Nat Howard and Johnny Rees, the assistant city editor of the *News*, met me in New York when I deplaned from Paris in June of 1956. With hugs and kisses they both told me Howard was in the process of a divorce. It stunned me. This was too much to digest facing the daunting task of writing my Russian series and speaking engagements that Nat Howard arranged for me. That news was set aside for another day.

When decision time came, Howard and I talked. No way would I marry out of the Catholic Church. Howard was reared Catholic, and he agreed to submit his personal life to the diocesan tribunal, which took its good time in investigating his life in England, Mexico, and the United States. I never thought of pushing the church except for the announcement by once married and later divorced Bill Veeck, owner of the Cleveland Indians, of his engagement to a young, Irish Catholic girl. They were married in St. John's Cathedral. That did it. The cathedral tribunal heard my views, and with the sudden death of Howard's stepfather in Florida, we were quickly married at St. John's Cathedral September 14, 1957.

Were we in love? We were madly in love, the best of friends, and remained so for twenty-two years until his death. We meshed on personal and public views and were active in the Press Club of Cleveland, the American Newspaper Guild, Cleveland chapter, giving hours of volunteer time to both groups. After living in an apartment for some time, we rented a home in Chesterland, where his son, Howard, came to live with us. Later, at a sheriff's sale in Chardon, Geauga County, I bid and won a former Halle estate—a lodge on a ridge with a natural lake below. We loved it and worked like dogs on a Vermont slate floor in the kitchen and the painting of the home's exterior. There's nothing like pure labor to test true love.

I took on freelance writing, but when the paychecks from our full-time jobs bumped up our income, I retired from it, although I typed the Sam Sheppard case Howard wrote with Dr. Samuel R. Gerber. It was rejected, mainly because editors asked Howard "to come up with something new," as if the guilty verdict wasn't enough. Times when we faced emergency medical or job problems, we took trips; once to San Francisco, once to Ireland. Howard's illness started with a blood condition that his doctor and friend thought had its genesis in his trips to Mexico and Korea, where Howard ate unhealthy and toxic diets. This was possible, but eventually it was cancer, which surfaced in late 1975 and 1976.

After Howard's death remarriage never entered my mind. When you have had the best, why take something less? As ill as Howard was, he insisted on remaining at home, painfully climbing stairs to bed, bathing in the tub, and asking me to read the latest nonfiction books. I couldn't have asked for a better life. Tears flow sometimes as I drive along and hear a song we might have sung at one party or another. I am happy to have saved Howard's stories and the hundreds of columns he wrote for his son. For me, he brought Newfoundland dogs into my life, and I now own Rory of Belmullet, Newfie number fourteen for me. His number one Newfie was a gift from a Berea, Ohio, family who brought Newfies to Ohio, rescuing them from the buzz-bombs in London in the Second World War. In gratitude to his column about saving the breed, this nice family gave him the runt of the litter. After we bought our home in Novelty, our first guest was another Newfie.

I wasn't prepared to write of my personal life, yet I will pay tribute to Howard as a teacher, an inspiration, a companion, the best of friends. My poetic talents are far, far below those of Edna St. Vincent Millay, but her words from a book Howard once gave me, with the note that said, "To a girl I know—and an Island we have lost," sum up the love affair:

Time does not bring relief; you all have lied
Who told me time would ease me of my pain!
I miss him in the weeping of the rain;
I want him at the shrinking of the tide;
The old snows melt from every mountain-side,
And last year's leaves are smoke in every lane;
But last year's bitter loving must remain
Heaped on my heart, and my old thoughts abide!

There are a hundred places where I fear
To go,—so with his memory they brim!
And entering with relief some quiet place
Where never fell his foot or shone his face
I say, "There is no memory of him here!"
And so stand stricken, so remembering him.

[*Collected Sonnets of Edna St. Vincent Millay.* New York: Harper
and Brothers, 1941.]

-30-